Destructive and Formidable

Destructive and Formidable

British Infantry Firepower 1642–1765

David Blackmore

FRONTLINE BOOKS, LONDON

Destructive and Formidable: British Infantry Firepower 1642–1765

First published in 2014 and reprinted in this format in 2022 by
Frontline Books
an imprint of Pen & Sword Books Ltd,
47 Church Street, Barnsley, S. Yorkshire, S70 2AS
www.frontline-books.com

CIP data records for this title are available from the British Library

For more information on our books, please visit
www.frontline-books.com, email info@frontline-books.com
or write to us at the above address.

Printed and bound by 4edge Limited, UK

Typeset in 12/14.4 point Jenson Pro by JCS Publishing Services Ltd

Contents

Chapter 1

Introduction

The year 1759 has been described as 'The Year Britain became Master of the World'.[1] A true *annus mirabilis*, it saw the Royal Navy and the British Army establish supremacy over Britain's great rival, France. Of greatest importance were the victories that year at Minden in Germany, and Quebec, in modern-day Canada. At Minden, on 4 August, the French Army under Marshal de Contades opposed an Allied army under the Duke of Brunswick that included just six British infantry battalions. Due to a misunderstanding at the beginning of the battle, these six battalions, accompanied by three Hanoverian battalions, set off towards the centre of the entire French Army. The British Army today still celebrates what followed. They were first attacked by three successive lines of French cavalry, a total of some seven thousand sabres. These they drove off. 'A series of crashing volleys from the superbly disciplined British regiments tore the heart out of the French cavalry.'[2] As Brunswick hurried to bring up more infantry to support these battalions they were attacked by French infantry, who were also driven off. Eventually Brunswick reinforced the British and Hanoverians and the French Army broke.

Just weeks later, on 13 September, on the Plains of Abraham, outside Quebec, a small British army under the command of James Wolfe met the French army under Montcalm that defended the city. In a scene that foreshadowed later battles in the Spanish Peninsula and at Waterloo the British infantry stood in line as the French advanced on them in three great columns. What followed was described by Fortescue as the British infantry delivering 'the most perfect volley ever fired on a battlefield'.[3] The ferocity of the British infantry fire halted and then broke the French columns. As a consequence of the battle the French were ejected from Canada, which subsequently became a British colony.

By 1763 and the end of the Seven Years War, British infantry had established a considerable reputation and become recognisable as the troops who would fight well, but in vain, in the American War of Independence, and most effectively against the forces of Napoleon. The period covered by this book, from the English Civil War to just after the end of the Seven Years War, is thus the formative period in the history of the British Army.

Modern writers of military history hold the opinion that the infantry of Britain's armies of the seventeenth and eighteenth centuries repeatedly achieved a high level of effectiveness and superiority over their enemies in firepower and relied on that firepower to win battles. That assessment is justified, but a sufficiently searching investigation to explain how that superiority was achieved and then maintained over such a long period has been lacking

In fact identifying the tactical doctrine and battlefield combat techniques of British infantry and analysing their effectiveness, starting with the English Civil Wars and continuing up to 1765, in the immediate aftermath of the Seven Years War, is quite possible. The results identify previously unrecognised aspects of doctrine and technique and pinpoint times when key changes were brought about, such as the organisation of platoons into firings. This in turn exposes long-held misconceptions, such as that concerning the form that platoon firing first took.

There are some related tactical issues that had a bearing on the successes of British forces that have not been considered here, such as the actions of the other sections of the army. On occasion artillery played its part, particularly during the period when battalions had pairs of guns attached to them to bolster their firepower. For instance, at Culloden there was a pair of three-pounder cannon in every gap between the battalions in the front line. One of those between Barrell's and Monro's fired its last round of grapeshot at a range of only six feet. While it is usually stated that the rate of fire of artillery was two rounds a minute, evidence suggests that far higher rates of fire were achievable – sometimes in excess of ten rounds a minute – with clear implications for battlefield effectiveness. At Fontenoy and Minden, however, the infantry were deprived of this support, although the Royal Artillery did give some protection to the right flank of the infantry at Minden. At Quebec the Royal Artillery got just a single cannon to the battlefield, but it caused significant casualties. However, the artillery of the period covered is outside the scope of this work and it is worth pointing out that the contemporary correspondence of infantry is largely silent on the matter, suggesting that it had little direct bearing on the outcome of combat between battalions of infantry.

The influence of the other part of the army, cavalry, has also been omitted. Its actions, such as at Warburg, and inactions, as at Minden, were often vitally important to the success or otherwise of British forces.[4] The charge of the allied cavalry at Laffeldt enabled the infantry to make their retreat successfully.[5] But the way the cavalry fought did not influence the methods of the infantry and the two arms frequently fought their own separate battles.

The nature of the enemy, almost invariably the French, was also important. Given the repeated success of British infantry against them, it is perhaps surprising that the French did not adopt any of their combat techniques. However, while the British were always fighting the French, the reverse is not true. France had many enemies during the period under consideration and Britain was a relatively minor military power, so far as its army was concerned, and thus was of limited influence on the international art of warfare. On a global scale the Royal Navy was far more important. In addition the French consistently held to the belief that their forte was the attack and that in the attack firepower was less important than élan and the bayonet.

Both the doctrine and the techniques of British infantry through the period from 1642 to 1765 have been analysed to ascertain their effect on the actual combat performance of the infantry. Making that analysis required an approach that started with understanding the workings of the infantry at the most basic level. Until the founding of the Royal Military College by the Duke of York in 1801 there was no formalised training for officers. A new young officer learnt his trade 'on the job' with his regiment. As Houlding puts it:

> With the assistance of brother subalterns or of a senior NCO he learned how to perform the manual and platoon exercises of the firelock or carbine, and the great variety of movements, commands, and posts it

was the subaltern's duty to learn, to perform, or to occupy when the unit was carrying on its basic training.[6]

Wolfe considered Bland's *Treatise of Military Discipline* 'indispensable to the military education of young officers'.[7] This was the knowledge that a junior officer in the British Army required in order to carry out his duties, but many historians endeavour to understand and explain the functioning of the army without a similar level of knowledge. This does not prevent the production of accurate narrative accounts of battles and campaigns, particularly as these tend to be based on the accounts of officers and men who did have the professional knowledge to understand events. Similarly other aspects of military history – such as training, finance, uniforms, equipment, strategy and social history – can be effectively addressed without this knowledge. Yet it is essential to understand the drill manuals used to train soldiers in order to understand their doctrine and techniques. Military historians risk misunderstanding or even completely misinterpreting those accounts written by professionals because they do not share the same practical knowledge of how things were done and managed. In turn this gives rise to the danger of drawing incorrect conclusions about tactics and doctrine.

This book employs an approach that starts by considering the procedures and practices of soldiers in a given period and analyses those in order to understand how things were done and, in turn, why events unfolded as they did. This is not an entirely new approach; it has been successfully employed by others to address some aspects of military history.[8] It is, however, worth some further explanation and giving it a name: practical military history. In effect it requires the researcher to acquire a similar level of knowledge to that of, at least, a junior officer of the army under consideration. This approach provides the understanding of warfare that is required to be sure of correctly interpreting descriptions of events, of understanding not just what happened in a simple narrative way, but why particular actions were executed and why they were, or were not, successful. It allows the historian to judge what courses of action were open but not followed and thus to analyse decision making.

Important sources include drill manuals and similar guides to the conduct of war relevant to each period. Some of these were published and are readily accessible to military historians, although little used or understood. Others exist only in manuscript form. Developments in drill have been identified by a close analysis of the differences between successive manuals, but the manuals do not explain why the changes were made or what their effect was. That was achieved by understanding how the changes in the manuals changed the actions of an individual soldier or of a unit. Once that was achieved it became possible to analyse the eyewitness descriptions of combat that are to be found in the diaries and letters, published and unpublished, of combatants and others. This, in turn, allows an assessment of the effectiveness of the doctrine and combat techniques of the infantry, leading to an explanation of how British infantry gained and maintained their battlefield superiority over their enemies.

Between 1642 and 1765 British troops were engaged in six major wars, but it must be remembered that until the Act of Union of 1707 there was no British Army, rather there were two separate organisations: the English Army and the Scottish Army. However, after the English Civil Wars, and particularly following the Glorious Revolution of 1688, this separation was more of a political and financial one than an operational one. As each of the six wars saw its own particular developments and challenges, each is dealt with in turn. In addition, one chapter addresses one specific, very important development for British infantry, but one that took place largely elsewhere in Europe: the introduction of platoon firing.

The English Civil Wars is the first period of warfare dealt with and it is during that series of wars that a distinctly British tactical doctrine for infantry can first be identified: a single volley at point-blank range combined with immediately closing to hand-to-hand combat.[9] This was a departure from the usual European practice and its impact on the battlefield is described. Following the Glorious Revolution of 1688 platoon firing was introduced to the British Army by the Dutch and effectively combined with the new doctrine. It is now possible to describe the earliest form that platoon firing took. During the War of the Spanish Succession further important developments in platoon firing occurred that have not been previously recognised. They are now described and their contribution to the success of the Duke of Marlborough is analysed.

The long period of peace from 1714 to the outbreak of the War of the Austrian Succession, 1740–8, had a detrimental effect on the infantry's firepower and the consequences of that are clear in the actions of the battle of Dettingen, 1743. Analysis of subsequent battles, Fontenoy, 1745, and Laffeldt, 1747, shows how the infantry recovered from that early difficulty and establishes the effectiveness of the tactical doctrine of the infantry and its application. Analysis of the actions of the Jacobite Rebellion of 1745–6 and the battle of Culloden, 1746, demonstrates the ability of the infantry to adapt to challenge while continuing to adhere to the same underlying doctrine.

The Seven Years War in Europe and the French and Indian War in North America, although both part of the same global conflict, had very different characteristics. In Europe formal, linear battles in open countryside were the norm, with the British infantry continuing to seek, and finding, ways to further improve the effectiveness of their firepower, concentrating on the practical while in the rest of Europe there was considerable theoretical debate on the best way to fight. By contrast, the North American theatre presented very different challenges, which were met with different techniques. It is clearly demonstrated, however, that despite those differences, British infantry in both theatres continued to hold to the same tactical doctrine that had been developed in the seventeenth century.

Throughout this book the term British infantry is used to describe the subject of the work. This is, of necessity, something of a catch-all phrase. As has already been pointed out, until 1707 there were two separate army establishments in Britain. To further complicate matters, during the eighteenth century many regiments were posted to Ireland, on the Irish Establishment, a political and financial expediency.[10] With regard to the regiments themselves, they contained men of all the four home nations and others. The terms used to describe the soldiers also varied throughout the period under consideration. Regiments of the English Civil Wars consisted of 'pike' and 'shot', that is pikemen and musketeers. During the second half of the seventeenth century the pikeman gradually disappeared and the grenadier appeared. This was a soldier trained and equipped to use hand grenades and who quickly became the elite element of any regiment or army. They were distinguished by their tall mitre caps, not unlike a bishop's cope, and within a regiment they were formed into a single grenadier company. The men of the other companies wore broad-brimmed hats, later cocked hats, and became known as hatmen and their companies as hat companies.

I should like to take this opportunity to express my thanks for the contribution to this book of a number of people. In the first place I must express my gratitude to the late Professor Richard Holmes, who encouraged me to undertake this work.

The extracts from the Cumberland Papers are quoted with the permission of Her Majesty Queen Elizabeth II. The staff of many archives and other institutions are due my thanks, not least: the British Library Reading Rooms at St Pancras and Boston Spa; The National Archives; the National Army Museum; Stuart Ivinson at the Royal Armouries; Micol Barengo at the Huguenot Library; the Swedish Army Museum, in particular the director, Eva-Sofi Ernstell and her colleague Martin Markelius; the Military Archives of Sweden; the Dutch National Archive; and Mary Robertson at the Huntington Library, California.

Individuals who have helped along the way, sometimes with relevant material, sometimes with simple, but sound advice, include: Jan Piet Puype, formerly of the Dutch Army Museum; Dave Ryan of Caliver Books; Dr Christopher Scott; Dr Eric Gruber von Arni; Dr Lesley Prince; Dr Hannah Hunt; Dr John Houlding; Dr Olaf van Nimwegen; Dr John M. Stapleton, Jr.

Of course, a great deal of thanks goes to my supervisory team at Nottingham Trent University: Professor Martyn Bennett, who rescued the whole thing from a premature end, Dr Kevin Gould and Dr Nicholas Morton.

The greatest thanks go to Janet McKay, with whom this all started over a bottle of wine and who never, ever wants to hear about platoon firing again.

Chapter 2

The Age of the Matchlock, 1642 to 1688

From 1618 to 1648 most of Europe was embroiled in the Thirty Years War, a war notable for its brutality. Whilst a significant number of individuals from the British Isles took part in this war as volunteers – particularly from Scotland – England and Scotland themselves were not overly involved. The last English military foray into Europe before the Civil Wars, the expedition to the Île de Rhé in 1627, was a complete fiasco. Nor were things any better in the Bishops' Wars of 1639–40 between England and Scotland when Charles I's English army suffered a humiliating defeat at Newburn in 1640. At the outbreak of civil war in Britain in 1642 there was no standing army north or south of the border. Neither England nor Scotland could be said to be countries with any sort of military standing. However, by the end of the Civil War Britain had produced an army that, in a few campaigns in the 1650s, won a considerable reputation amongst European neighbours, who had been at war almost continuously since 1618. Fighting with the French against the Spanish in 1658 the English infantry were described as having 'such a reputation in this army that nothing can be more'.[1]

The most common firearm of the infantry during the English Civil Wars, and throughout Europe in the mid-seventeenth century was the matchlock musket. In England in 1630 the dimensions of a musket barrel had been set at a length of forty-eight inches and of 12 bore.[2] Despite moves in 1639 to introduce a musket with a barrel length of forty-two inches, forty-eight inches was to remain the standard size of a musket barrel throughout the Civil Wars.[3] The procedure for loading and firing a matchlock musket and how to organise and manage formed bodies of musketeers was described in a number of drill books. One of the most popular, running to a total of six editions between 1635 and 1661, was William Barriffe's *Military Discipline*.[4] The drill contained in Barriffe was based on that developed at the end of the sixteenth century in the Netherlands by Maurice of Nassau and which was to become the universal drill of the Thirty Years War. The full matchlock-musket drill as detailed by Barriffe consisted of sixty different movements, each with its own command, of which thirty dealt with the process of loading and firing. The gunpowder was carried in small, cylindrical wooden or tin boxes on a bandoleer, usually twelve in number, with each box containing powder for one shot. Part of the complexity of the drill was due to the need to keep separate the powder and the means of igniting it, a length of burning slowmatch. The musketeer in Barriffe's drill was also hampered by a musket rest, used to take the weight of the musket and steady it when firing.

The drawbacks of the matchlock were itemised by the Earl of Orrery when he compared it to the fire-lock or flintlock musket that was in limited use at the time:

> For with the Fire-lock musket you have only to Cock, and you are prepared to Shoot; but with your Match-lock, you have several motions [to fire it], the least of which is as long a performing, as but that one of the other, and oftentimes more hazardous; besides, if you Fire not the Match-lock Musket as soon as you have blown your Match, (which often, especially in Hedge Fights, and in Sieges, you cannot do) you must a second time blow your Match, or the Ashes it gathers, hinders it from Firing.[5]

Orrery was describing how the flintlock only required the cock, holding a flint, to be pulled back to full cock for it to be ready to fire. The matchlock, in comparison, required that the end of the burning slowmatch was blown to red hot and free of ash, it was then placed in the serpent or cock of the gun, the priming pan cover was opened by hand and only then could the trigger be pulled to fire the musket. He went on to enumerate the risks posed by the burning match, which could ignite the powder in the soldiers' bandoleers or even in barrels of powder when they were refilling their bandoleers. Added to this the wooden boxes on the bandoleers clattered together noisily, giving away the presence of musketeers at night, and both the match and powder in an open pan were susceptible to the weather. Rain could dampen both causing a misfire and the wind could produce dangerous sparks from the match. With the flintlock, pulling the trigger caused the flint to strike sparks and opened the pan instantaneously. With the matchlock, there was an inevitable time delay while the priming pan was opened by hand and the trigger pulled to lower the burning end of the match into it. The match itself was a problem as considerable quantities were needed; it attracted moisture, thus reducing its viability, and it was difficult for soldiers to keep dry.[6]

The resultant rate of fire was slow as the musketeer juggled musket, rest, priming flask, match, powder and ball. Some measures were taken to speed things up from the very beginning. On the battlefield soldiers carried musket balls in their mouths and just spat them down the barrel to avoid fumbling for them in the small ball bag on the bandoleer, and in action the orders given for firing were reduced to just three: 'make ready', 'present' (that is, they levelled their muskets at the enemy) and 'fire'.[7] After firing, reloading was carried out without any further orders. However, in order for a body of musketeers to maintain a reasonable rate of fire as a unit it was necessary to organise them in a series of ranks that took turns to fire and then reload while the other ranks were firing; the number of ranks depended on the length of time taken to reload. According to Turner the requisite depth was initially ten ranks, Barriffe required eight and for most of the Civil Wars the usual number was six.[8]

In firing, the movements of the musketeers were carefully choreo-graphed and fell into two main types, firing by files and firing by ranks. Barriffe described these and their numerous variations using a single infantry company for illustrative purposes. He showed two small blocks of musketeers in ranks of four with eight men in each file, separated by a central block of eight files of pikemen, each of eight men.[9] Barriffe's infantry company was equally divided into musketeers and pikemen, although during the Civil Wars the usual ratio was two musketeers to one pikeman.[10]

At the outbreak of the Civil War a large number of troops had to be raised and trained quickly by both sides and as a result a number of abbreviated drill manuals were produced that reduced drill down to

Figure 2.1: An infantry company drawn up for drill according to Barriffe.

Front

C

E

Sr m m m m D p p p p p p p p p D m m m m Sr

m m m m   p p p p p p p p   m m m m

m m m m   p p p p p p p p   m m m m

m m m m   p p p p p p p p   m m m m

m m m m   p p p p p p p p   m m m m

m m m m   p p p p p p p p   m m m m

m m m m   p p p p p p p p   m m m m

Sr m m m m D p p p p p p p p p D m m m m Sr

L

Rear

Key: C=Captain, E=Ensign, L=Lieutenant, Sr=Sergeant, D=Drummer, m=musketeer, p=pikeman

Source: Barriffe, Military Discipline (1635), p. 184.

a practical minimum. From these it is possible to identify which of the many firings detailed by Barriffe and others, such as Ward, were actually considered useful and practical.[11] In Scotland, General Lesley produced a drill that was subsequently published in London in 1642.[12] Like Barriffe he specified files eight deep. Another drill manual claimed to be *A True Description of the Discipline of War* used by the Earl of Newcastle and Prince Rupert.[13] The drill described in this manual made use of files that were only five deep. Of all the various ways of firing, Lesley's manual only contained one, firing by two ranks advanced, which Newcastle's manual also contained, along with firing by files.

Firing by two ranks advanced was probably the commonest method of firing found in drill books generally and its selection for these two manuals further supports a case for it being the preferred way of firing at the start of the Civil Wars. In this manoeuvre the front two ranks of a body of musketeers marched forward ten or twenty paces under the command of a sergeant. The front rank then presented and fired, faced to the left or right and marched in single file to the rear of the body, each man falling in at the rear of his file and reloading. As soon as the first rank was out of the way the second rank fired and then marched to the rear to reload. Once the second rank had fired the third and fourth ranks began to march forward to where the first two had halted to fire, and then fired in their turn. This firing was also carried out without the musketeers advancing, in which case each rank in turn simply stepped forward to the front of the body before firing and filing off to the rear: this was known as firing maintaining ground. If the body advanced slowly while the musketeers fired then each pair of ranks advanced further than the previous pair.[14]

A second method of firing was that of forlorn files, which is found in Newcastle's manual. In this case individual files marched forward as far as required, wheeled to march across the face of the unit and then, by halting and facing the enemy, the file became a rank. After firing each file marched back to its original place to reload. As a variation on this the file could stay as a file and each man in turn fired and marched to the back of the file to reload. Because of the time spent marching forwards and backwards both of these, particularly the latter, produced relatively low volumes of fire.[15]

When firing either by ranks or by files there was a three-foot gap between both the ranks and the files, which was judged to be the space required by a musketeer to be able to reload safely.[16] A third method, firing by introduction, required the gap between files to be increased to six feet. The front rank fired and began to reload where it stood. Then the rear rank men marched up through the gaps between the files and placed themselves in front of the front rank to fire. They in turn were followed by the fifth rank and so on until the front rank was at the back and had reloaded. As an alternative the front rank fired and the whole body moved forward, the second rank placing themselves at the front, then the third and so on. As the amount of movement required of each musketeer was less than in the other two methods, this method may have produced a higher rate of fire, but the fire produced was spread over a wider front. Barriffe, however, was critical of it: 'I will not dispute how useful it is; but sure I am, it is over-balanced with danger.'[17] Although he did not say why he considered it dangerous it is possible that he was concerned about accidents as musketeers with lit match moved between others reloading. The less dense formation was also more vulnerable to attack.

What was noticeably absent from the pre-war and early war drill manuals was almost any mention of firing in three ranks. This had been developed by Gustavus Adolphus of Sweden and famously and effectively employed at the battle of Breitenfeld in 1631. It was, however, just one of the ways of firing that the Swedes used.[18] The other methods, by files, ranks and divisions, were the same as described by Barriffe. There was no lack of opportunity to know about it as a number of English and Scottish soldiers served in the Swedish army and details of the battle were widely available through such publications as *The Swedish Intelligencer* and *The Swedish Discipline*.[19] These also contained information on Swedish tactical formations that found its way into the 1639 edition of Barriffe. Barriffe wrote that the Swedes fired by 'salves, powring on showers of Lead, by firing two or three Ranks together', but that is all he says.[20] There was no explanation or any instructions on how to carry it out. It was, however, something that would become a trademark of British infantry.

An infantry regiment of the English Civil Wars usually consisted of ten companies, each of pikemen and musketeers, although these two different types of soldier did not fight together in their companies. When a regiment was drawn up for battle it was, depending on its strength, formed into one or two battalia. This was a linear formation first developed by Maurice of Nassau at the turn of the century in Holland. A battalia consisted of three divisions of approximately equal size, two of musketeers flanking a central division of pikemen. The divisions of musketeers were in turn organised into subdivisions of between four to six files, which was the same size as a subdivision of a company's musketeers when drilling as a company. Between each subdivision a gap of six feet was kept for musketeers to march down to the rear of their subdivision.

The first major engagement of the English Civil Wars was Edgehill, fought on 23 October 1642. The Parliamentarian army formed in what would become the conventional manner, based on the Dutch linear form. The Royalist army formed up according to the far more complex Swedish form, further evidence of knowledge in England of Swedish tactics.[21] However, there is no suggestion in any of the contemporary accounts that the Royalist musketeers employed the Swedish method of firing in three ranks, or *salvee*. This is not surprising as the decision to adopt Swedish tactics was taken on the morning of the battle, leaving no time for instruction and training in the Swedish *salvee*.

A number of eyewitness accounts provide evidence of the performance and effectiveness of musketeers in this battle. One was written by the future James II.[22] He described how both sides opened fire as soon as they were in range, with the Royalists advancing firing while the Parliamentarians held their ground. Eventually they were so close that hand-to-hand fighting broke out; however, neither side was able to overcome and defeat the other and a stalemate ensued with both sides firing away at each other until night fell. James II commented that this was:

> a thing so very extraordinary, that nothing less then so many witnesses as were there present, could make it credible; nor can any other reason be given for it, but the naturall courage of English men, which prompted them to maintain their ground, tho the rawness and unexperience of both partys had not furnished them with skill to make the best use of their advantages.[23]

Neither side had the skill or experience to overcome the resistance of the other, the firing was sustained, but not sufficiently effective as to bring about a conclusion to the combat.

Elsewhere at Edgehill the insufficiency of firepower left infantry vulnerable when cavalry acted in unison with infantry. A Parliamentarian account described the effect of a cavalry and infantry attack on Royalist infantry.

> But their foot . . . came up all in Front . . . that part of it which was on their Left, and towards our Right Wing, came on very gallantly to the Charge, and were as gallantly received, and Charged by Sir Philip Stapleton and Sir William Balford's Regiment of Horse, assisted with the Lord Robert's, and Sir William Constable's Regiments of Foot, who did it so home thrice together, that they forced all the Musqueteers, of two of their left Regiments, to run in and shrowd themselves within their Pikes, not daring to shoot a shot.[24]

The account of James II also recorded these events, claiming that the Royalist regiments 'were not broken by this charge, yet they were put into some disorder'.[25] However, it is further evidence that infantry alone were not able to overcome other infantry.

Both James II's and the Parliamentarian accounts, written by a number of senior officers, described the battle petering out as night fell and ammunition ran out. 'After this neither party press'd the other, but contented themselves to keep their ground, and continued fireing, till night put an end to the dispute.'[26] 'By this time it grew so late and dark, and to say the truth, our ammunition at this present was all spent.'[27] The accounts of the battle make it clear that both sides had suffered problems with ammunition running out. Barriffe made no mention of any arrangements for the resupply of ammunition, or how it was to be managed except in his description of Swedish formations. Here he simply wrote that the musketeers to the rear of the formations were there 'either to guard the Baggage or Cannon, to be Convoyes to bring ammunition or victuals to the rest; or to continue a reserve to waite upon all occasions'.[28] Elton simply echoed Barriffe when he wrote that regiments should have 'always in the Reer a sufficient number of Muskettiers for the guard of the Baggage, Cannon, or to be Convoys for to convey Ammunition and Victual to the rest of their fellows'.[29] It is clear that there were attempts at Edgehill at resupply, a Royalist soldier 'in fetching Powder (where a Magazin was) clapt his Hand carelessly into a Barrel of Powder, with his Match lighted betwixt his Fingers, whereby much Powder was blown up, and many kill'd'.[30] The inability of either side effectively to resupply their infantry with ammunition during a battle further hampered attempts to achieve a decision through the use of firepower.

Whilst the precise details of the sequence of events at Edgehill continue to be debated there is no doubt that the outcome was inconclusive. This is due in no small part to the inability of the infantry of either side to achieve outright success on their own. The accounts of the battle suggest not only that there were prolonged firefights, to the extent that ammunition ran low or ran out on both sides, but also that these were conducted in such a manner that they failed to achieve a decision. There is little doubt that the Parliamentarian infantry attained a degree of superiority over the Royalists, but not sufficient to break them.[31]

The fire-delivery methods used at the beginning of the Civil Wars and at Edgehill – firing by ranks advancing and firing by forlorn files – were not capable of generating sufficient firepower to force a conclusion in a firefight or cause sufficient disruption to ensure success in hand-to-hand combat. In addition the ability to generate sufficient firepower to achieve victory was hampered by the amount of ammunition available, usually twelve rounds a man. In the aftermath of Edgehill there is an absence of any discussion of the methodology of delivering infantry firepower, or of any orders or instructions to change, by either side. It is in the accounts of the actions that followed Edgehill that evidence of change and increased effectiveness is found.

Just over two weeks after Edgehill, Charles I made an abortive advance on London that ended with the stand-off at Turnham Green, the closest he got to recovering the capital. During his advance there was a small but bloody skirmish at Brentford. The Royalist John Gwynne describes how the assault on the Parliamentarian forces in Brentford drove them 'to the open field, with a resolute and expeditious fighting, that after once firing suddenly to advance up to push of pikes and the butt end of muskets, which proved so fatal to Holles and his butchers and dyers that day'.[32] The key words here are 'resolute and expeditious', suggesting that the tactics used were intended to force a conclusion. Gwynne also recorded that at the second battle of Newbury in 1644 one Royalist regiment received orders 'not to give fire upon the enemy until they came within a pikes length of him'.[33] Whereas at Edgehill the infantry had begun to fire once within musket range, they now began to reserve their fire until the range was minimal, both on the offensive, as at Brentford, and on the defensive as at Newbury. At the battle of Cheriton in 1644 Slingsby recorded how Royalist infantry fought off a cavalry attack, 'the foote keeping theire ground in a close body, not firing till within two pikes length, and then three rankes att a time, after turning up the butt end of theire muskets, charging theire pikes, and standing close, preserv'd themselves and slew many of the enemy.'[34] This event not only demonstrates fire being held to a minimal range, but that musketeers were able see off cavalry, in contrast to events at Edgehill.

Precisely how this change in combat technique came about is uncertain. Using a Swedish formation for the Royalist army at Edgehill was a suggestion that had originated with Patrick Ruthven, Earl of Forth, who had fought under Gustavus Adolphus. It is possible that the impetus for the change came from Scottish officers in Charles's army who had served in the Swedish army. The descriptions of subsequent combat are similar to the description of Swedish infantry attacking other infantry at Breitenfeld in 1631. A Scottish officer there described how he reserved his fire until within pistol shot, fired just two volleys, each of three ranks, and then immediately attacked with musket butt and sword, defeating the enemy.[35]

These developments can also be seen amongst Parliamentarian infantry. At the successful storming of Arundel in December 1643, by Sir William Waller's Parliamentarian army, Colonel Birch, having crossed the Royalist's first line of fortifications, received a counter-attack. The account of what happened was written by Birch's secretary and addressed directly to him:

> At this instant, the enemy spending their shot at too great a distance, your order was to horse and foote instantly to assault the enemy; your selfe with cheerfull speech assureing they would not stand, which proved accordinglie. For the enemy, feeling the force of shott poured on them with three ranks at a time, after short time gave ground, and your selfe entered the towne with them.[36]

It is also interesting to note that the enemy was considered to have fired at too great a range.

At the first battle of Newbury, 1643, the Blew Regiment of the London Trained Bands was attacked by two regiments of Royalist cavalry. What happened was described by a Sergeant Foster in the Red Regiment. 'Two regiments of the Kings Horse which stood upon their right flanke a far off, came fiercely upon them, and charged them two or three times, but were beat back with their Muskettiers, who gave them a most desperate charge, and made them flie.'[37] Foster's own regiment was similarly attacked:

> Then two regiments of the enemies horse, which stood upon our right Flank, came fiercely upon us, and so surrounded us, that we were forced to charge upon them in the front and reere, and both Flanks, which was performed by us with a great deal of courage and undauntedness

— 17 —

of spirit, insomuch that wee made a great slaughter among them, and forced them to retreat.[38]

These accounts make it clear that after Edgehill there was a fairly immediate and dramatic change in the way that first the Royalist infantry and then the Parliamentarian infantry delivered their fire. Fire was reserved to a range of the length of a pike or two, which is five to ten yards, and then delivered by three ranks firing together. In the case of infantry on the offensive this was followed by an immediate assault. This change proved effective not only in the case of attacking other infantry, but also defensively against cavalry.

In Yorkshire the Parliamentarian forces were commanded by Lord Fairfax, and the infantry, in contrast to other Civil War armies, seem to have mainly consisted of musketeers.[39] Why Lord Fairfax's infantry was mainly made up of musketeers is not known, however many of the battles and skirmishes fought in the north of England were characterised by the presence of enclosures and hedges. It might simply be that these would hamper attempts by pikemen to close to hand-to-hand combat and consequently more reliance was laid on musketry. Whatever the explanation, the experiences of this army can demonstrate both the strengths and weaknesses of firepower during the Civil War. At the battle of Adwalton Moor in June, 1643, Fairfax's infantry seems to have totalled some four thousand musketeers. In contrast the Royalist army commanded by the Earl of Newcastle had about the same number of infantry, but only half were musketeers, the rest being pikemen.[40] The Royalists had a considerable advantage in cavalry.[41] Initially the Parliamentarian musketeers, fighting from hedge to hedge and through enclosures, gradually gained the upper hand. Newcastle started to give orders to retreat, but at this point the Royalists launched a counter-attack with a large body of pikemen that turned the tide of the battle. The reason for the success of this body of pikemen in amongst hedges and enclosures and against musketeers is not clear. The most likely explanation comes from Joseph Lister:

But there was one major Jefferies keeper of the ammunition, who proving treacherous, and withholding it from the parliament men; who calling for it and being able to get none, were forced to slacken their firing, which the enemy perceiving, and very likely having private intelligence of, presently faced about, and fell upon Fairfax's men with that fury that they soon regained their guns, and put them to the rout, slaying many of them.[42]

How the musketeers delivered their fire in this battle is not clear from the accounts. However, what is clear is that the Parliamentarian musketeers were able to achieve superiority over their opponents and to neutralise any threat from the Royalist pikemen while they had an adequate supply of ammunition. It also suggests that a system for resupplying ammunition in battle was in place, but on this occasion broke down. A similar event happened at the battle of Tadcaster in December of 1642 when, after successfully holding off Newcastle's forces, Fairfax was forced to withdraw under cover of night for want of ammunition.[43] Whether or not there was treachery at Adwalton, these incidents do emphasise the importance of the supply of ammunition and the difficulty of resupply on the battlefield.

As with Adwalton, other accounts of the fighting in the north of England provide little evidence of how the musketeers from this region fought. They are commonly described as fighting from hedge to hedge, which may indicate that firepower alone was frequently relied on, with little hand-to-hand combat. Although there is no indication of how that fire was delivered, without the option of hand-to-hand combat to finish off an opponent already shaken in a firefight, the firepower element alone had to have been effective enough to decide the outcome. The Parliamentarian musketeers at least were capable of holding their fire in defence in order to produce decisive firepower. At Tadcaster Sir Thomas Fairfax recorded how 'Our Men reserv'd their shot, till they came near, which they did then dispose of to so good purpose, that the Enemy was forced to retire, and shelter themselves behind the Hedges.'[44] They were, however, also involved in the storming of a number of towns, where hand-to-hand combat is implicit in the accounts. At the storming of Leeds, 'The business was hotly disputed for almost two Hours; but the Enemy being beaten from their Works, and the Barricado's into the Streets forced open, the Horse and Foot resolutely entered, and the Soldiers cast down their Arms, and rendered themselves Prisoners.'[45] At the storming of Wakefield Sir Thomas Fairfax recalled that 'after an Hour's dispute, the Foot forced open a Barricado, where I entered with my own Troop.'[46] From this it would appear that while the nature of the terrain in the north of England affected the way battles were fought there was an understanding of the need for musket fire to be delivered at close range in order to produce effective firepower and that this had to be combined with a readiness to engage in hand-to-hand combat to achieve a decision when necessary.

Unfortunately there is little evidence concerning the performance of Lord Fairfax's infantry at the battle of Marston Moor in 1644; after an initial success they mostly ran away. Five armies were engaged in that battle, which followed the raising of the siege of York. There were two Royalist armies: the Earl of Newcastle's, which had been defending York, and Prince Rupert's, which had raised the siege. Opposed to them were the two Parliamentarian armies of Lord Fairfax and the Earl of Manchester, and, allied with the Parliamentarians, a Scots army; that had all been besieging York.[47] What is evident about Marston Moor is that it was a particularly bloody affair. It lasted only an hour and a half, perhaps two, but well over four thousand were killed, mostly Royalist infantry. The language of the accounts reflects this ferocity and violence. One of Cromwell's officers described 'thinking the victory wholly ours and nothing to be done but to kill and take prisoners'.[48] Another eyewitness of many battles wrote: 'This victory was one of the greatest and most bloody since the warre begane.'[49] These comments, the high casualties and the brevity of the battle when compared to Edgehill could be a reflection of the change in infantry fire tactics since the start of the war.

At one point in the battle, part of the Scots infantry came under considerable pressure. The cavalry of the Royalist left wing

assaulted the Scottish Foot upon their Flancks, so that they had the Foot upon their front and the whole Cavalry of the enemies left wing to fight with, whom they encountered with so much courage and resolution, that having enterlined their Musquetiers with Pikemen they made the enemies Horse, notwithstanding for all the assistance they had of their foot, at two severall assaults to give ground.[50]

The significance of this description is that this appears to be one of only two instances of infantry interlining pikemen and musketeers to defend against cavalry, the other being at Edgehill. The general response to a cavalry attack seems to have been to deliver close-range volley fire sufficient to drive off or at least halt the cavalry's attack. Once cavalry have stopped moving they are, as individuals, vulnerable to the infantry who will almost always have greater numbers.

In Scotland evidence of similar fire tactics to those developed in England can be found. At the battle of Tippermuir in 1644, Montrose, the Royalist commander, was facing a larger enemy and was in danger of being outflanked. He instructed his infantry accordingly.

> He caused his Army to be drawne out to as open an order as could be possible, and makes his Files onely three deep. He commands the Ranks all to discharge at once, those in the first Ranke kneeling, in the second stooping, and in the hindmost, where he placed the tallest men, upright; he chargeth them also to have a care of mis-spending their powder, of which they had so small store, and that they should not so much as make a shot till they came to the very teeth of their enemies; & as soone as they had discharged their muskets once a piece, immediately to breake in upon the enemy with their swords & musket ends; which if they did, he was very confident the enemy would never endure the charge.[51]

Whilst six ranks were necessary for sustained fire, three ranks were the maximum that could be fired together in a single volley. Montrose has here made a virtue of necessity, the three-deep line firing in a single volley at close range maximising the fire of his infantry while also extending his line to avoid being outflanked and conserving powder by avoiding a prolonged musketry engagement. The delivery of the fire was then to be followed by an immediate assault. The result was a victory for Montrose.

At the battle of Inverlochy, 1645, the Royalist left wing of Montrose's army was commanded by Colonel Occaen. He ordered his musketeers to hold their fire to close range, which they did, ignoring the enemy's fire until 'they fyred there beardes', which made 'a cruell havoke'. They then promptly attacked with their swords and targes, disordering and dispersing the enemy.[52] Here again the fire was maximised by firing at very close range, followed by an immediate assault. Once again, these tactics resulted in a Royalist victory. It would appear that the adoption of developing maximum firepower at close range followed by a rapid assault was a nationwide development.

The battle of Naseby, fought in 1645, provided clear evidence of the use of both brief, short-range volleys in the assault and the use of lower-intensity firing when the situation required it. The Royalist army, led by Charles I in person, took the offensive although outnumbered, and marched towards the Parliamentarian army, the newly raised New Model Army commanded by Sir Thomas Fairfax. In the centre the position of the Parliamentarian infantry, drawn back from the edge of a slight ridge, meant that the infantry regiments lost sight of each other as they closed. The Royalist Sir Edward Walker wrote: 'The Foot on either side hardly saw each other until they were within Carabine Shot, and so only made one Volley; ours falling in with Sword and butt end of the Musquet did notable Execution.'[53] According to the Parliamentarian John Rushworth, 'the Foot charged not each other till they were within twelve paces one of another, and could not charge above twice, but were at push of Pike.'[54] If the Royalists fired a single volley before closing to hand to hand it seems likely that they had reduced their musketeers from six ranks to three. To stay in six ranks would have meant the rear three ranks could not have fired, a considerable waste of firepower. Additionally, going into three ranks would have lengthened the frontage of the Royalist units, thus better matching the frontage of the numerically superior front line of the New Model Army. The New Model Army was formed on a constricted front and with little space between the front-line regiments would not have been able to copy the Royalist formation.[55] It is possible that the New Model fired by three ranks twice, thus producing the two 'charges' or volleys recorded by Rushworth. Clearly both armies were capable of and prepared to use firing in three ranks at close range to maximise their firepower immediately before hand-to-hand combat.

During the battle the New Model Army's infantry commander, Major General Skippon, was shot at close range, apparently 'by one of his own Souldiers in wheeling off'.[56] This seems to have occurred at a point after the initial contact and when Skippon was bringing forward reserves to counter the Royalist's initial success, most likely during the period of an extended exchange of fire suggested by archaeological evidence.[57] If that was the case it would appear that firing by ranks was in use at this point, presumably because the Royalists had run out of momentum and the New Model Army was recovering from its initial setback. Neither side was in a position to try to force the issue and so both resorted to low-intensity, but sustainable firing. Ultimately the New Model was victorious and Naseby was followed by a series of successes as it campaigned from Northamptonshire to Cornwall, finally bringing the First Civil War to an end at Oxford in 1646.

The tactics used by the New Model Army and their capability with them are summed up in a letter written by Cromwell about the battle of Preston during the Second Civil War fought in 1648. 'There came no band of your foot to fight that day but did it with incredible valour and resolution . . . they often coming to push of pike and close firing, and always making the enemy to recoil.'[58]

There are few descriptions of English Civil War engagements that are sufficiently detailed to allow an analysis of how firepower was delivered and how that delivery developed. Many speak of hedge fights and driving the enemy from hedge to hedge, but without any explanation of the techniques involved. Many engagements were protracted affairs, which raises questions about the supply and conservation of ammunition in battle. However, some further evidence of changes in the way fire was delivered can be found by comparing the military manuals of William Barriffe and Richard Elton, Barriffe being pre-war and Elton post-war. Elton described much the same firing manoeuvres as Barriffe, but based his descriptions on a company with a 2:1 ratio of musketeers to pikemen and files six men deep, rather than Barriffe's 1:1 in files eight deep, which indicates that there had been both an increased reliance on firepower and an increased rate of fire. He prefaced his descriptions with a comment on the variety of firings suggesting that not all of them were considered to be practical for the battlefield.

I shall therefore for the good of my Country, and for the benefit of all such as are herein concerned, collect forth some firings, which shall be every one differing from the other in one kind or other, either in the execution or reducing, whereby the ingenious Souldier may cull forth such as he best likes to make use of, what he shall think to be most fit and pertinent to his intended purpose, be it either for delight or service.

Figure 2.2: An infantry company drawn up according to Elton.

Front

```
                         C
S                        E                        S
m m m m m m m m D D p p p p p p p p p D D m m m m m m m m
m m m m m m m m     p p p p p p p p       m m m m m m m m
m m m m m m m m     p p p p p p p p       m m m m m m m m
m m m m m m m m     p p p p p p p p       m m m m m m m m
m m m m m m m m     p p p p p p p p       m m m m m m m m
m m m m m m m m     p p p p p p p p       m m m m m m m m
S                        L                        S
```

Rear

Key: C=captain, L=Lieutenant, E=Ensign, S=Sergeant, D=Drummer,
m=Musketeer, p=Pikeman

Source: Elton, Compleat Body, *p. 16.*

He then went on to describe forty-five different ways of firing that do not differ from Barriffe except in the number of ranks.[59]

However, while the main body of his text remained unaltered, Elton made an important addition to the second edition of his book in 1659. This amounts to four unnumbered pages added to the very end. First he gives the drill movements for the matchlock musket without the musket rest. In doing so he was reflecting a change that came about during the wars, which was the rest's abandonment. It is difficult to be sure when this happened, it was probably a gradual, piecemeal process, but when the New Model Army was being fitted out in the winter of 1644–5 no musket rests were supplied to it. This change undoubtedly speeded up the process of loading a musket as the musketeer had one less piece of equipment to juggle. It may also indicate that muskets had become lighter, although there is no evidence to suggest that the design of muskets changed during the wars.

Elton also wrote in this section: 'I have thought good to set down the plain way of exercising a company, as usually it is practised in the Army', that is during the 1650s.[60] He went on:

> We usually fire in the Front sometimes two Rancks standing, the rest passing by turns, then standing after they have gained the ground before their Leaders do fire, till all have fiered twice; other times three Rancks fire together the first kneels down, the second stoops; the third stands upright, then falling down, the three last Rancks pass through; and do the like.

Whether firing one, two or three ranks the idea of ranks filing off down the side of their unit to the rear to reload seems to have been abandoned. Instead all the firing appears to have been by introduction with musketeers moving in the gaps between files. Furthermore the musketeers reloaded where they fired while the musketeers who were loaded moved past them, further reducing the loading time. These then stood and fired immediately in front of those who had just fired, there was no advancing ten or twenty paces to fire, which reduced the time between volleys. Elton also seems to be saying that the distance between the files of musketeers was 'order', half that stated by Barriffe as necessary for firing by introduction. This would have had the effect of concentrating the fire over a narrower frontage.[61] What is just as important is what is not there. Firing by two ranks advanced and by forlorn files have disappeared. Instead the firing by ranks was carried out in a much brisker manner and the aggressive firing by three ranks had become normal practice.

While the developments in firing methods enumerated by Elton in his 1659 edition appear to have increased the rate of fire of a body of musketeers, he did not approve of all attempts to do so. He was insistent 'that the Souldiers present and give fire upon their Rests, not using that slovenly posture of popping their Matches into the Pan, their Muskets being on their left sides, which is not only hurtful unto themselves, but much endangers their fellow-Souldiers, and by so doing they scarce or ever do any execution against an Enemy'.[62] Elton did not mean that the soldiers had the muskets on the left side of their bodies, but rather that the muskets were held with the left side of the musket downwards. The advantage of this was that it ensured the powder in the priming pan was over the touchhole and thus made ignition of the main charge more certain. That Elton was railing against a widespread practice is supported by an account from the far west of Wales. Here the Parliamentarian commander, Major General Laugherne had been reinforced by some troops from Ireland. The actions of these troops were described in a skirmish near Carmarthen in 1645. In the account they are described as 'English, Irish foot as had somewhat before fled out of Ireland' and then simply as 'Irish'. This is to distinguish them from other Parliamentarian infantry and does not mean that they were of Irish nationality. 'The Enemy very Souldier-like, had a forehand lined the hedges on the high-wayes, and approaches to the Towne, with store of Musketeers, which the Irish foot, with other seconds, beate from hedge to hedge, firing in a new dexterity, with their matches lighted in their hands, charging the enemy twice for once, which they performed with much agillity.'[63] Elton, however, seems to be making the case that rapid fire did not necessarily equate with effective fire.

From the information that can be gleaned from the myriad accounts of battles and skirmishes and from the few drill manuals some conclusions may be drawn about the application of firepower during the English Civil Wars and how it changed during that period. After Edgehill there was a rapid move away from relatively slow and low-intensity fire sustained over long periods of time to delivering fire in sharp, close-range bursts followed by an immediate assault. Not only was this more decisive, frequently in favour of the aggressor, but it also conserved ammunition while maximising effectiveness. At the same time the ability to maintain low-intensity, sustained fire was retained. Although not a battle winner it still had a role to play. That there were measures employed to resupply musketeers during a battle is evidenced by comments concerning the use of reserve musketeers to bring up ammunition and the numerous occasions when careless musketeers blew themselves up when replenishing their powder.

The test of these developments came during the 1650s and 1660s when English infantry were pitted against foreign infantry who had the benefit of experience gained during the European-wide Thirty Years War. At the battle of the Dunes in 1658 they found themselves allied to the French and fighting the Spanish. The English were posted on the left flank of the French Army and were opposite a large force of Spanish infantry posted on the top of a large sandhill. Lieutenant Colonel Hughes described how the English infantry 'on hands and knees crept up the hill, and gave the enimies foote two good volleys, and with our pikes forced them to retreat'.[64] Morgan, commanding the infantry, described the result of the attack: 'Immediately the enemy were clear shocked off their ground, and the English colours flying over their heads, the strongest officers and soldiers clubbing them down.'[65] The battle was a complete victory for the Anglo-French army. From Hughes's account it would appear that the infantry fired two three-rank volleys, just as described by Elton.

Another view of the hand-to-hand combat at the Dunes comes from the future James II, who was commanding an exiled English Royalist army fighting for the Spanish. He led a frontal cavalry charge against Lockhart's regiment, but was repulsed with considerable losses.[66] Shortly after this he led another desperate cavalry charge against Lockhart's. This time he attacked them in the flank and broke into the regiment.

> Tis very observable that when wee had broken into this Battalion, and were got amongst them, not so much as one single man of them ask'd quarter, or threw down his armes; but every one defended himself to the last: so that wee ran as great danger by the butt end of their muskets, as by the volley which they had given us. And one of them had infallibly knock'd me off from my horse, if I had not prevented him when he was just ready to have discharg'd his blow, by a stroke I gave him with my sword over the face, which layd him along upon the ground.[67]

James's attacks against Lockhart's were ultimately futile, and did nothing to prevent a French victory, but they did demonstrate the ability of English infantry to defend themselves in line against cavalry attacking them frontally. An attack from the flank, however, was something that would continue to be a threat to infantry in line.

Following the restoration of the monarchy Charles II sent a small force, many of whom were New Model Army veterans, to Portugal to help in the struggle for independence from Spain.[68] Colonel James Apsley gave an account of the actions of the English infantry at the battle of Ameixial in 1663.

The English marched on shouting as if victorious, but discharged no shot till they came within push of pike of the enemy, and then they poured in their shot so thick upon them that made them quit their ground and fly towards the left wing, leaving their cannon behind them, which were afterwards turned upon them, much to their prejudice. Notwithstanding the rich baggages and coaches and wealthy plunder which were on top of the hill – the English seeing the field not cleared – there was not one man of them stirred out of his rank, but kept close serried together to prevent any second onset, which immediately followed, for they were assaulted front, flank and rear by divers of the enemy's troops of horse, but having their fire ready at all hands, they quickly quitted themselves of those troops.[69]

This account offers nothing new in terms of combat doctrine for English infantry: the infantry fire is delivered at a typically close range and a counter-attack by cavalry is driven off in typical fashion. The interest lies in the reaction of other Europeans to this action. The King of Portugal

acknowledged that in this year's great defeat 1663 he gave Don John of Austria neer Ebora, that Brigade of English who servd there, though not much considerable in number, did perform the toughest part of the service, and first shewd them the way of using the Rests of the Musquet to knock down the Enemy; which made the French-men cry out, *Faisont comme les anglois*, Let's do as the English.[70]

The King's generals 'having not been accustomed to see so close an approach before firing, did give up the English for lost and did believe they all had intended to joined with the Castillians, but when they saw their thick firing and the good success the English obtained thereupon, they called us comrades and good Christians'.[71]

The implication of these comments, particularly from Portugal, was that the English were doing something new that European enemies could not cope with and which very quickly gained them a considerable reputation. That was, firstly, their particularly effective and aggressive use of firepower that required the soldiers to ignore enemy fire and hold their own fire until they had closed to a range of five to ten yards when they would deliver one or two devastating volleys, depending on whether they were in three ranks or six. The effect on the enemy of the realisation that they had fired but that the English had not and were still advancing must have been considerable. Conversely, the English infantry were encouraged if the enemy fired too soon or inaccurately, as with Birch's men at Arundel. At the battle of Preston John Hodgson recorded how 'the enemy let fly at us (a company of Langdale's men that was newly raised). They shot at the skies, which did so encourage our men, that they were willing to venture upon any attempt.'[72]

Secondly, this aggressive firepower was combined with a willingness, if not eagerness, to close to hand-to-hand combat immediately after firing and to club down their opponents with their muskets. This eagerness was evident at the battle of the Dunes when the English infantry cheered at the sight of the enemy and the prospect of the fight, something that seems to have surprised Marshal Turenne, the French commander.[73] However, that did not mean that they were incapable of less intense, sustained firing when necessary. Again at the Dunes, when the English infantry first advanced they halted within musket range of the Spanish, who fired two volleys at them that caused a few casualties. Instead of allowing themselves to be drawn into a long-range firefight they prepared for the assault, covered by commanded, or detached, musketeers who kept up a continual fire on the Spanish. Once the main body of infantry was ready to attack, the commanded musketeers opened to let it through.[74] Again the attacking infantry ignored the enemy fire in order to get close to deliver their own fire.

By contrast, there is nothing to suggest that the infantry of other European nations were doing anything other than continuing to use methods of firing similar to those developed at the start of the century and described by Barriffe. The two nations most closely connected to Britain as, variously, friend and foe, were the Netherlands and France. The French continued firing by ranks rotating to the front until they devised a new form of firing by ranks in the 1670s.[75] The Dutch also continued with the drill first devised by Maurice of Nassau until the 1670s.[76] The Swedes, so influential on tactics in the 1630s, also seem not to have changed until the end of the century when they devised a technique for the offensive known as 'ga-pa'. This required the infantry, in four ranks, to ignore enemy fire and close rapidly, pausing for the two rear ranks to fire at about fifty paces and the two front ranks firing immediately before contact.[77] This could be said to have similarities with the British method of firing three ranks at a time at very close range before closing to hand-to-hand combat, but by the time it was in use British infantry fire techniques had developed further.

Another feature of what English infantry was doing was their ability to defend themselves against cavalry in line, without the musketeers having to fall back on the pikemen. Although this was done by the Royalist musketeers at Edgehill and the Scots at Marston Moor these are rare occurrences and the preferred response to cavalry of short-range fire and then using clubbed muskets showed a high degree of confidence in firepower.

Despite the numerous manuals available, such as Barriffe and Elton, it was only in 1676 that the first official drill book for the English army was published. It was titled *An Abridgement of the English Military Discipline* and was published 'By His Majesties permission'.[78] A later edition, diplomatically titled *An Abridgement of the Military Discipline*, was published in Edinburgh in 1680 for the use of the Scots army.[79] The drill for the musket was still for the matchlock and was unchanged from Elton except for the order it was given in and some of the phrasing. The result was a simpler and briefer set of instructions.

In describing the various ways of delivering fire the first given was firing by two ranks advancing. This was just the same as described by Barriffe forty-one years earlier, down to the marching to the rear around the outside of the unit, except it did allow for the two advanced ranks to fire together. The manual went on to describe firing to the flanks and rear, which were variations of firing advancing. These were followed by a description of street firing. In this the pikes blocked the street, or any narrow passage, while the musketeers loaded behind them and then, rank by rank, filed up one side of the pikes, formed a rank in front of them, fired and then filed to the rear down the other side of the pikes. This was followed by a method called the 'Swedes Way', which is discussed in detail in the next chapter.[80] This is similar to the three ranks firing described by Elton and used by the English troops in Holland and Portugal. For the first time there were instructions on how to form a square, in this edition both a hollow and a solid square. In this formation the square of pikemen was surrounded by the musketeers three deep.

When attacked by cavalry all three ranks fired together, the front rank of musketeers kneeling, the second stooping and the third standing upright. A section of the manual headed 'Orders for Battel' included the direction: 'As soon as the Battalion comes to thirty Paces distance from the Enemy, let the Musqueteers Fire, the manner of which Firing shall be ordered them before.'[81] There were also sections dealing with cavalry drill and camps.

There were a further seven editions of the *Abridgement*, the first five with mostly minor alterations and additions.[82] In the 1685 editions published in Dublin and London there were major changes, which also appeared in the next and last edition of 1686. Many sections were enlarged with more detailed instructions. Drill for the firelock musket made its first appearance and there were also separate sections for battalions with firelocks and with matchlocks and others dealing with horse grenadiers, garrisons and mounting guards. The most significant changes, however, were in the methods of firing. When firing in square the front rank was to kneel while the other two fired and then stand and fire in its turn.[83] Firing by two ranks and the 'Swedes Way' disappeared. Instead, when firing to the front, the first five ranks of musketeers were to kneel while the sixth, rear rank fired over their heads. The fifth rank was then to stand and fire, followed by the fourth and so on. After firing, each rank was to reload, the obvious problem being that the sixth rank would be reloaded and ready to fire before the first rank was reloaded. The 1685 *Abridgement* also claimed that this method of firing could be carried out by two ranks or even three ranks at a time, one kneeling, one stooping and one standing, or the first two stooping, presumably if there were other ranks kneeling in front of them.[84] Clearly this method of firing was only possible if the battalion was stationary. When advancing, a battalion was to halt briefly to allow the front rank to fire. After firing, this rank was to file to the rear and the battalion was to march on until its commander halted it again for firing.[85] However, the 'Orders for Battel' no longer specified any range for opening fire. Another, quite separate, section gave an alternative way of firing. This required the musketeers to be reduced from six ranks to three, but not to fire in three ranks. Instead the first rank was to kneel while the other two ranks fired and then to stand and fire in its turn. After firing, the musketeers were to club muskets and fall on.[86] This method retained something of the doctrine of delivering maximum fire, albeit by two ranks rather than three, immediately followed by closing to hand-to-hand combat. Generally, however, these changes appear to have reduced the firepower of the infantry.

This change in approach to the delivery of fire seems to be down to the adoption of French ideas. A British brigade served in the French army from 1672 to 1678 and a copy of the French drill manual *Le Major Parfait* was inscribed 'this book did belong to King James' and dated 1686.[87] Writing in 1670–1 Sir James Turner referred to the French General Martinet describing a way of firing in six ranks: 'Of six ranks of Musqueteers he would have the first five to kneel; the sixth to stand and fire first, then the fifth to rise and fire next, and consecutively the rest, till the first rank have fired, after which he will have the foremost five ranks to kneel again, till the sixth discharge, if the service last so long.' Turner expressed severe reservations about firing in this manner, suggesting that it put the men in the front ranks in danger from their own side.[88] However, the French writer Demoriet wrote in 1686:

The best way of firing is by ranks when it is desired to fire in line, parallel to the foe. To do this, and to fire without embarrassment, it is best to fire at the halt without making any move except that needed to make the first five ranks kneel on the ground; and the sixth is that which makes its first fire, the fifth than doing the same and the rest consecutively.[89]

The introduction of drill for the firelock musket in the 1685 edition of the *Abridgement* reflected the increasing use of firelocks by the infantry. This was a process that had been under way from the time of the English Civil Wars. At Cropedy Bridge some of Waller's Parliamentarian infantry had firelocks and during the night after the battle Richard Coe recorded that 'our Fire-locks were placed under a hedge, and light matches hung alone on pallisadoes a Musket shot off.'[90] At the battle of the Dunes, Morgan had four hundred men armed with firelocks.[91] In January 1683 the Coldstream Guards were ordered to replace their matchlocks with firelocks, while in March it was ordered that two companies in each infantry regiment should be armed with firelocks.[92] On 21 February

1687 a regulation was issued giving specifications for infantry firearms. The musketeers of the Guards regiments were to have snaphance muskets with a barrel length of forty-four inches, other musketeers were to have matchlock or snaphance muskets with forty-two-inch barrels.[93] Fusiliers, a new type of infantry originally formed to guard the artillery, were to have snaphance muskets with forty-four-inch barrels while the grenadiers of infantry regiments were to have carbines with thirty-eight-inch barrels.[94] The carbine was traditionally a cavalry weapon with a relatively short barrel. The description of the grenadiers' muskets as carbines was a reference to the bore size, a carbine having a smaller bore than a musket. Undoubtedly the reduction in barrel length and weight from the musket of the 1640s and 1650s made these muskets easier to handle and thus quicker to load. However, only the fusiliers and grenadiers were to use cartridges, the rest continued using bandoleers.

The adoption of the firelock, or flintlock, musket and the cartridge by some units in the army would make a difference to the speed of loading of individual soldiers in those units, but in the 1680s the majority of the infantry was still using the matchlock. What was as important as the weapons in use was how the infantry was organised to produce its firepower. In this regard the adoption of French firing methods and the apparent abandonment of the aggressive tactics developed in the 1640s and 1650s would appear to be retrograde changes, but these changes were not to be tested in battle.

An account of the siege of Tangiers contains some interesting information concerning the supply of ammunition on the battlefield. From 1661 to 1684 England was in possession of Tangiers, part of the dowry of Charles II's Portuguese bride, Catherine of Braganza.[95] During this occupation the garrison was in frequent conflict with the Moors and was besieged in 1680. John Ross described how on one occasion the fighting continued 'for the space of Seven or Eight hours desperately, and continually firing on both sides from right to left, that it was nothing for a Musketeer to empty three or four Bandeleers notwithstanding of their reliefs every two hours.'[96] This represents the expenditure of between thirty-six and forty-eight rounds a man, a considerable amount of ammunition. However, Ross also gave some clues as to how this was managed. On another occasion he recorded that:

The Scots Granadeers once forgot their Pouder and Ball in the Enemies Trench: Their Lieut. called Mackrackan, endeavoured to recover and regain it, but in vain, which perceiving; he threw three or four Granades with his own hand to set it a fire before it should fall in the Enemies hands, to the great danger of his life.[97]

He also made a reference to 'Gentlemen of the Pouch': 'This is a most useful Officer in an Army, and 'tis requisite he be stout also, otherwise they may want Powder, and Ball when they have most to do.' He also referred to 'Powder-monckies'.[98]

From this evidence it is possible to make some tentative proposals about how the resupplying of ammunition was being managed on the battlefield. As also suggested by instances from the English Civil Wars of musketeers accidently blowing up powder barrels, it would seem that it was normal practice for units to carry into battle a supply of loose powder and musket balls. It would have to be loose powder in order to be able to refill the individual charges on a bandoleer. How this was done was suggested in the Earl of Newcastle's drill manual of 1642 when it said: 'A measured charge shall be given to every Musketier that holds just so much powder as halfe the bullet weighes at ten bullets in the pound, to fill their Bandaliers withal.'[99] This ammunition may have been carried in small barrels or leather pouches, hence the 'Gentlemen of the Pouch' at Tangiers. Monck wrote in 1646 that, in addition to a bandoleer with powder and musket balls, 'each musqueteer ought to have twelve Bullets a-piece in their pockets; and each company must carry with them a Powder-Bag full of Powder.'[100] It seems that this supply was set down on the ground during combat, either to facilitate distribution or so that the carriers could fight. One thing is certain: the weight of powder and ball for a single bandoleer amounts to one and a half pounds. To supply, for example, a company of sixty musketeers with refills for their bandoleers just once required thirty pounds of powder and sixty pounds of musket balls. This was a not-inconsiderable weight to man-handle around a battle field. It is not possible, on this limited evidence, to say exactly how ammunition resupply was being managed or that this reflects anything other than the practice in Tangiers in the 1680s. However, it does begin to offer a possible answer to the question of ammunition resupply to musketeers using bandoleers rather than cartridges, which were already beginning to come in to use. The cavalry had used them for their firearms since the 1630s and Orrery was a champion of their use.[101]

During the English Civil War a particularly aggressive way of fighting based upon the close-range delivery of overwhelming firepower followed by an immediate advance to hand-to-hand combat was developed in England and Scotland and used by all protagonists. This was not something found in the drill books and although it was similar to the Swedish *salvee* developed by Gustavus Adolphus there were important differences, primarily in the manner of its application. The Swedes used this as a part of their fire tactics and with limited application.[102] In contrast English and Scots infantry would frequently, even habitually, fight in this manner. Given the widespread availability of information about Swedish tactics it is possible that this represents a uniquely British development of the use of the Swedish *salvee*, but the manner of that development and its adoption right across the British Isles is unknown. This development occurred in isolation and was not matched by any similar development in Europe where the application of this way of fighting achieved dramatic results. In 1685 the adoption of a French firing system resulted in the loss of the ability to concentrate the firepower of a whole battalion into a single volley, thereby making it impossible to continue to rely upon the aggressive application of firepower as a key element of battlefield doctrine. This retrograde position was, however, short lived. In 1688 the Glorious Revolution placed the English and Scottish armies firmly under the influence of Holland when the French ways were swept aside and replaced by the latest Dutch practice, and in particular the recently developed platoon firing.

Chapter 3

The Origins of Platoon Firing and its Introduction into the English and Scots Armies

From the late seventeenth century and into the middle of the eighteenth century the method employed by British infantry to deliver its firepower was platoon firing, which was a major factor in British success on the battlefield. Its introduction from the Dutch Army to the British Army certainly followed the Glorious Revolution of 1688 when William III and Queen Mary succeeded the deposed James II.[1] It has, however, been far from clear until now what the origins were of platoon firing, just when and how the English and Scottish armies adopted it (for they were still two separate establishments), and precisely what form it first took.

It is generally accepted that the introduction of platoon firing to British troops took place in Flanders in 1689 when Marlborough took a contingent of the army there to join William's Dutch Army.[2] But there has been no explanation of how platoon firing came to be in use throughout the English and Scottish armies and not just that part in Flanders. Furthermore, no historian has yet identified just how platoon firing was first carried out by the English and Scots armies. The most commonly given description of platoon firing is based on Kane's instructions in his *Discipline for a Regiment of Foot*.[3] This formed part of Kane's book *Campaigns of King William and Queen Anne; From 1689 to 1712*, which was not published until 1745, after Kane's death, and his version of platoon firing is clearly of a later date than 1689. Most obviously it contains no reference to pikemen, then still an integral part of infantry regiments. Furthermore the full title for this section of Kane's book is *A New System of Military Discipline for a Battalion of Foot on Action* and the introduction states that Kane wrote it because he considered other military manuals available to be inadequate. He was writing what he considered to be contemporary best practice for the period after 1712 and before 1736, when he died, and not describing the practice of some twenty-five years or more earlier.

The questions about the origins and first form of platoon firing have remained unanswered for some time. In seeking to establish the origins of platoon firing the French writer Le Blond wrote in 1758: 'Platoon fire, introduced in France as part of the 6 May 1755 Ordinance, was a well established practice by the Dutch; there is some evidence that they can be credited with the original idea and that it was they who introduced the practice to the other European nationswho adopted the practice.'[4]

More recently Chandler wrote: 'It is almost impossible to trace the real origins of the platoon firing system with any certainty.'[5] However, as well as crediting the Dutch as the originators of platoon firing Chandler also records the suggestion made by some that platoon firing actually originated with the Swedes under their king, Gustavus Adolphus, in the 1630s.[6] It is now possible to give an account of the introduction of platoon firing into the English and Scottish armies, and identify and describe its original form as practiced in 1689.

There are three elements that when combined give platoon firing its unique character and distinguish it from any other fire-delivery system. First, the infantry were organised into platoons, a tactical sub-unit of a larger battalion or regiment that did not necessarily correspond to any other sub-unit, such as the company. Second, the soldiers were drawn up in three ranks, later reduced to two ranks, and all the ranks fired together. Third, the platoons were drawn up in a line and fired in turn along the line according to a preordained pattern, which ensured that a part of the line was always loaded and ready to fire.

Two of these elements – the platoon as a sub-unit of infantry formations and putting musketeers into three ranks rather than the more usual six – were well known before the start of the English Civil War in 1642. Both practices originated in the Swedish Army under Gustavus Adolphus and were described in some detail by the professional Scottish soldier Robert Monro, who served in the Swedish Army from 1630 to 1634.[7] He described

Figure 3.1: Diagram of a Swedish Brigade from an illustration in Barriffe based on Monro's description.

Front

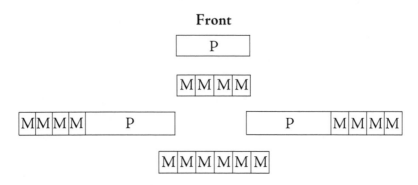

Blocks marked M contain eight rots or files of musketeers
Blocks marked P contain thirty-six rots or files of pikemen

Source: William Barriffe, Militarie Discipline or The Young Artilery-Man (*London, 1661, 6th edition*), pp. 172–3; Brockington, Monro, pp. 316–17. William Barriffe's Militarie Discipline *was first published in 1635, but without the information about Swedish formations, which first appears in the second edition of 1639.*

the organisation of the infantry into brigades with the musketeers in platoons or, as he writes, 'Plottons', of forty-eight men in eight 'rots' or files, each of six men, that is with each plotton having six ranks, see figure 3.1.

Monro then described the process for firing three ranks together in what he called a 'salve' and later became known as a *salvee* or volley.

> When you would command the body of your musketiers to give fire in a salve, as is ordinarie in Battell, before an enemy joyne, or against Horsemen; then you command the bringers up or Reare to double the Front to the right hand, and to make readie, having the match cocked and their pannes well guarded, having closed the three Rancks, though not the Files, the Officers standing in equall Front with the foremost Rancke, betwixt two Divisions, he commands to give fire, one Salve, two or three, and having charged againe, and shouldered their Armes, they retire to the left hand againe, every man falling behind his owne Leader.[8]

In this manoeuvre the rear three men in each file marched forward and placed themselves alongside the front three, either to their left or, as described by Monro, to their right. This three-deep formation was shallow enough for all three ranks to fire together, with the front rank kneeling, the second stooping and the third standing upright.[9] After firing as many *salvees* as required the men from the rear could march back to their original positions, bringing the plotton back to six ranks.

The Swedish Intelligencer, published in London, described the effect of this form of firing at the battle of Breitenfeld in 1631:

> The Scots ordering themselves in sevrall small battagliaes, about 6 or 700 in a body, presently now double their rankes, making their files then but 3 deepe (the discipline of the King of Sweden being, never to march above 6 deepe) this done, the foremost rancke falling on their knees; the second stooping forward; and the third rancke standing up; and all giving fire together, they powred so much lead at one instant in amongst the enemies horse, that their ranckes were much broken with it.[10]

Its use against infantry at Breitenfeld has already been described.[11]

This practice was deliberately spread to other armies allied to Sweden. On 9 May 1632 at Munich Gustavus Adolphus:

> Held a generall Muster before the City: himself (to shew some content to the Bavarians) drilling and exercising his souldiers: teaching them especially how to give a Charge or Salvee; some upon their knees, other behind them stooping forward; and the hindmost ranke standing upright, and all to give fire at once, the hinder man over his foremans shoulder.[12]

Monro's service with the Swedish Army ended in 1634 when his regiment was destroyed at the battle of Nordlingen while he was in Scotland recruiting.[13] Two years earlier, in 1632, Sir James Turner had joined the Swedish Army and served briefly under Gustavus Adolphus who was killed that year at the battle of Lützen.[14]

In *Pallas Armata* (written in 1670–1) Turner gave a slightly different account of the Swedish use of musketeers. He also gave a description of the 'Swedish Brigade' and, referring to the gaps between the three blocks of pikemen as being like sally ports, described how the musketeers would sally out from behind the central pike block.

> There were two passage like sally ports between the reer of the advanced Body of Pikes, and the two Batallions that staid behind, out of one whereof on the right hand issued constantly one or two more hundreds of Musqueteers, who before all the three Bodies of Pikes gave incessantly fire upon the Enemy, and when the word or sign for a Retreat was given, they retir'd by the other passage on the left hand, back to the great Body of Musqueteers, where so many of them as came back unwounded, were presently put into rank and file, the fire continuing without intermission by Musqueteers, who still sallied through the passage on the right hand; and it is to be observed that the firemen fought thus in small Bodies, each of them not above five files of Musqueteers, and these for the most part but three deep.[15]

There is, however, no suggestion of any pattern to this fire. Turner's description also varies from Monro and others in that he has all the musketeers formed behind the blocks of pikemen and none flanking the pikes as in figure 3.1.

While two of the requirements for platoon firing, the use of platoons and firing in three ranks, can be attributed to the Swedish Army under Gustavus Adolphus, the third element, a line of platoons firing in a set pattern, is absent. Furthermore, after the death of Gustavus Adolphus the Swedish Brigade disappeared from use.[16] Despite its success under Gustavus Adolphus it was complex and demanded a high degree of training and discipline. During the first half of the seventeenth century, the rest of Europe had gradually adopted the simpler linear deployment of infantry developed by Maurice of Nassau at the end of the sixteenth century and which, by the middle of the century, had become the norm.

The depth of infantry units had gradually decreased from the beginning of the century, when the tactics developed by Maurice of Nassau employed ten ranks, to the middle of the century when six ranks was the rule. The number of ranks was dictated by the length of time it took to reload a musket. As Turner discusses, initially ten ranks were required to keep up a sustained fire from a unit because it took as long for one rank to reload as it did for the other nine to come successively to the front and fire in their turn.[17] As muskets were lightened and improved and loading was speeded up it became possible to reduce the depth to five or six ranks, but not to have less than that, let alone as few as three ranks. Turner states specifically that firing one rank at a time in three ranks does not give the first rank time to reload before the third has fired.[18] As for firing in three ranks all together, the military writers of the first half of the seventeenth century are consistent in their reservations about this, which is that it leaves a unit open to attack before it can reload. Consequently they considered that it was only to be used *in extremis*, such as against a cavalry attack when firepower must be maximised to stop it or immediately before charging home against an enemy. Monro wrote that its use was 'ordinarie in Battell, before an enemy joyne, or against Horsemen'.[19] For all other occasions he says that firing by ranks is 'the forme that I esteeme to be the best'.[20] Thus, while the devastating effect of a three-rank volley was well known, the circumstances under which it could be employed were considered to be severely limited. For example, the description given above from the *Swedish Intelligencer* is of the effect of firing in three ranks against a cavalry attack at Breitenfeld.

Monro and Elton, although writing some twenty years apart, both described units of musketeers, six ranks deep, firing two ranks at a time – that is, in three volleys.[21] This would seem to be at odds with Turner's statement that three ranks could not reload fast enough to keep up a sustained fire. However, sustained fire was not always the objective. When Monro describes each pair of ranks advancing ten paces in front of the unit before firing, he is describing attacking an enemy, 'ever advancing to an enemie, never turning backe without deathe or victorie'.[22] Under those circumstances it would seem that a brief period of a high rate of fire was preferable to slower sustained fire. Elton also described firing the six ranks in two lots of three, which also would not allow enough time to reload in order to keep up a constant fire, but he also described firing one rank at a time, which would.[23]

Orrery, in his *Treatise of the Art of War* published in 1677, also discussed the number of ranks and the rate of fire.[24] Based on his own experience, he recommended fighting in four ranks, whilst acknowledging that the idea would not be readily accepted.

The chief objection that I know of, is, as to the Musketeers, who being but four deep, and advancing firing, the first Rank cannot have loaded their Muskets again, by that time the fourth Rank has done firing; so that there will be an intermission of shooting. To that I answer, Let the Musketeers Charge their Muskets with such Cartridges as I have mentioned, and the first Rank will be as soone ready if you are but four deep, as the first Rank will be if you are six deep, loading with Bandeleers, especially if I use the Fire-lock, and the Enemy the Match-lock.

What Orrery was saying was that musketeers with cartridges and firelocks could reload in two-thirds of the time that it took musketeers with matchlocks and bandoleers. Thus, a unit in four ranks could deliver fire from a rank just as often as one in six ranks. Given two units of the same size, the unit in four ranks would also have half as many men again in each rank as the unit in six ranks, thus firing half as many shots again from each rank. What four ranks could not do, however, was all fire at once, which was only possible with three ranks.

The cartridge had the advantage over the bandoleer that the powder for loading the musket and the ball were both contained in a roll of paper, the cartridge. The musketeer simply bit open the cartridge at the end opposite the ball and poured the powder down the barrel, followed by the paper and ball. Initially the musket was still primed from a separate flask. The advantages were spelt out by Orrery who was 'a great approver of Boxes of Cartridges; for then, but by biting off the bottom of the Cartridge, you charge your Musket for service with one Ramming'.[25] As for the firelock he gave a whole list of reasons for its superiority over the matchlock.[26]

The use of the cartridge and the firelock, or flintlock, musket had the effect of speeding up the reloading process. If Orrery is correct and four ranks could keep up the same rate of fire as six with matchlock musket and bandoleer, that is a reduction in the loading time of one-third. This, in theory, made it possible to reduce the number of ranks needed to keep up a continual fire. However, the introduction of both into the British Army was slow and while the matchlock and bandoleer remained in service six ranks remained the norm. It was not until 1685 that James II ordered the army to be completely equipped with flintlocks: a process accelerated by William III and only completed in the early years of the eighteenth century.[27]

There are two key points to understanding the ways in which infantry firepower was delivered during the period predating the introduction of platoon firing. The first is that for defensive firing it was important to maintain a steady and continuous fire. The great fear was of being attacked when a unit was unloaded, particularly by cavalry. To avoid this danger a sufficient depth of ranks was required to allow time for reloading. By the 1640s this was generally taken to be six ranks. The second point is that when attacking it was advantageous to maximise the rate of fire to deliver as much firepower as possible in as short a time as possible before closing to hand-to-hand combat, at which stage there was no point in being loaded, particularly with a matchlock. This required breadth rather than depth so that all the musketeers could fire at once. As Turner put it:

> Next, firing by three ranks at a time, should not be practised, but when either the business seems to be desperate, or that the Bodies are so near, that the Pikemen are almost come to push of Pike, and then no other use can be made of the Musquet but of the Butt-end of it. I say then that this manner of six ranks to fire at two several times is not at all to be used; for if it come to extremity, it will be more proper to make them all fire at once, for thereby you pour as much lead in your enemies bosom at one time as you do the other way at two several times, and thereby you do them more mischief, you quail, daunt, and astonish them three times more, for one long and continuated crack of Thunder is more terrible and dreadful to mortals than ten interrupted and several ones, though all and every one of the ten be as loud as the long one.[28]

Thus the reason for the various ways of delivering fire was the necessity to be able to meet the differing tactical demands of attack and defence, something that no single fire-delivery system could do prior to the development of platoon firing. The use of the short-range volley given in three ranks in both attack and defence that was developed in Britain during the Civil Wars is overlooked by Turner. Similarly it has no place in the writings of Orrery and Monck. These were all soldiers with experience in the Civil Wars, as well as on the continent, who were writing after those wars and the restoration of the monarchy, but all three make very little mention of anything from that time. It is as if diplomatic considerations had rendered invalid any practical lessons. Regardless of the efficacy of the close-range, three-rank volley, however, the fact remained that it did not solve the question of how to combine heavy, effective fire with sustainable fire.

A new way of firing made its appearance in 1676 with the publication, 'by His Majesties Permission', of *An Abridgement of the English Discipline*.[29] In addition to the usual and well-established firing by ranks, either singly or in pairs, this official publication also included a description of what it called the 'Swedes Way'.[30] This involved reducing the ranks of musketeers from six to three by doubling their front. Each block of musketeers, one on each side of a central block of pikes, was then subdivided.

Figure 3.2 shows how the subdivisions were arranged, slightly in advance of the pike division and alternating one forward and one back. The advanced subdivisions fired first, either all three ranks – kneeling, stooping and standing – or the first rank kneeling and reserving its fire while the second and third ranks fired. These subdivisions would

Figure 3.2: A diagram showing The Swedes Way, based on the 1684 edition of An Abridgement of the English Discipline.

```
                              PPPPPPPP
                              PPPPPPPP
                              PPPPPPPP
                              PPPPPPPP
                              PPPPPPPP
        mmmm         mmmm PPPPPPPP mmmm              mmmm
        mmmm         mmmm              mmmm          mmmm
mmmm mmmm mmmm mmmm                    mmmm mmmm mmmm mmmm
mmmm         mmmm                      mmmm          mmmm
mmmm         mmmm                      mmmm          mmmm
```

Front

Key: M represents a musketeer, P represents a pikeman

Source: An Abridgement of the English Military Discipline (*London, 1684*), *p. 35.*

then reload where they stood while the rear subdivisions advanced to fire in their turn. As the subdivisions were split into two lines that fired alternately, it was still considered necessary to have the option of reserving the fire of one rank in order to avoid the danger of having all the musketeers reloading at the same time.

The illustration appears to be purely indicative of how the formation should appear; it contains 144 men in the ratio of two musketeers to one pikeman. The *Abridgement* did not state how many subdivisions there should be for a battalion formed up for battle. However, it did say that a battalion normally comprised six companies, which was half a regiment.[31] One possibility was that the musketeers of the six companies were divided into eight subdivisions as in the illustration. This would result in each subdivision of musketeers being between twenty and thirty men.[32] This was a similar size to the subdivision of four, five or six files in six ranks as described by Elton, which gave a strength of from twenty-four to thirty-six men.[33]

At this time the company was a purely administrative unit consisting of both pike and musket that was broken up to form battlefield formations. It would appear, instead, that there was a preference for tactical subdivisions of musketeers to be about twenty-four to thirty men. The reason for this would appear to be connected to command and control. Monro observes:

> To exercise a squadron of Musketiers, how strong soever they be, the number of Rancks being no deeper than six, the files being even may be so many as your voice can extend to, ever observing that your Command be given in the Front, otherwise may breede disorder . . . and above all things you are to command them to keepe silence, not babbling one to another . . .[34]

In other words, a platoon is limited in size by the reach of the commander's voice.

When firing in ranks Monro wrote that the officer commanding the musketeers must stand 'even in Front with them, the Cannon or mouth of their Muskets of both Rancks being past his bodie'.[35] Similarly when firing in *salvee* he described 'the Officers standing in equall Front with the foremost Ranck, betwixt two Divisions'.[36] The difficulties of command in battle were also touched on by Elton who wrote of 'Commanders, whose voices are drown'd by the loud thundering of the Cannon or Mukettiers; as also by the neighing of Horses, or the lamentable cries of the maim'd and wounded Souldiers'.[37]

This form of firing, the 'Swedes Way', disappeared with the publication of the 1685 edition of *An Abridgement*, but it did represent an attempt at producing linear fire using small subdivisions of three ranks that all fired together rather than depending on ranks coming to the front of a unit in turn to fire. The subdivisions fired in a simple alternating sequence along the line and it thus qualifies as an early form of platoon firing. The problem that had not been solved was how to fire in a linear formation without too long an interval between discharges of fire.

The name for this way of firing, the Swedes Way, leads to considering the possibility that platoon firing was first developed in Sweden. There is no doubt that that the Swedes under Gustavus Adolphus were the first to use platoons of musketeers and to fight and fire in just three ranks. If they had taken the next step towards platoon firing proper, as opposed to simply firing in platoons, then one might expect to find evidence of that before 1676 when the 'Swedes Way' first appears in an English drill book. The last Swedish drill book produced before then appears to be *Een Militarisch Exercitiae Book*, published in Stockholm in 1669.[38] However, it contains nothing that bears any similarity to the Swedes Way. The most likely explanation for the name is that it is simply a reference to the use of platoons and three ranks. When, the Swedes Way disappeared from *An Abridgement* it was replaced by a French system of firing by ranks with a six-deep formation.

The earliest evidence for platoon firing by the Dutch is in a military manual of 1684 by Louis Paan.[39] In the introduction to the second volume of his work Paan wrote that it contained descriptions of the organisation of battalions 'as they have been brought to practice in the last war'. By this he is referring to the war of 1672–8 between France and the Dutch Republic. It describes something not dissimilar to the Swedes Way, but with each wing of musketeers divided into three platoons. As such it would appear to have suffered from the same drawback, which was that it did not allow for continuous firing. Paan also gave a reason for the development of platoon firing. Referring to battalions that fired by ranks he wrote:

Such Battalions as mentioned before have been esteemed for a certain period by most military, however it has been found that the Musketeers, after having fired in ranks, in retreating back made too wide a circle in order to get restored to readiness. This caused great disorder which is why this method has been rejected by several military men; that is to say, as far as giving fire in ranks is concerned it is considered to be better to do such with platoons instead of ranks. This is the reason why such changes have been made in the forming of Battalions as described before.[40]

The Dutch rejected the rotation of ranks by marching them down the sides of platoons to reload at the rear as it caused too much disorder. Clearly keeping the men in their ranks and firing and reloading in platoons was more efficient and less complicated or prone to confusion. They also chose not to emulate the French, who had developed their method for firing by ranks sometime before Turner described it in 1670–1.[41]

Following the accession of William and Mary in 1688 the English and Scots armies found themselves allied to the Dutch and involved in a war with France. One of the first consequences of this was the dispatch to Flanders of an English force under the command of the, then, Earl of Marlborough. In May 1689 Marlborough wrote to William's Secretary at War, William Blaythwayt: 'I desire that you will know the King's pleasure whether he will have the Regiments of Foot to learn the Duch exercise, or else to continue the English, for if he will I must have itt translated into English.'[42]

There is no record of a reply or of any translation of Dutch drill being issued to English regiments, but this letter has been taken to demonstrate the introduction of Dutch drill to the English and Scots army.[43] Much clearer evidence, however, is available that makes it clear that platoon firing was introduced to both the English and Scots armies in 1689. At the same time as Marlborough was in Flanders another combined Dutch and English army under the command of the Duke of Schomberg was fighting the forces of the deposed James II in Ireland. In September 1689 James II offered battle to Schomberg, who refused, keeping his army in its fortified camp at Dundalk. Subsequently James and his army withdrew to Ardee and went into winter quarters. No sooner had the Jacobite army retreated from Dundalk than Schomberg ordered that 'the Brigades that did not mount the Guards, should be exercised at firing at a Mark when it was Fair weather (as t'was very seldom) for the Duke knew most of his men had never been in service, and therefore he would have them taught as much as could be.'[44] Just how poorly trained the infantry was is apparent.

> The Weather for two or three days proved pretty fair, and the Soldiers were exercised with firing at Marks; but it was observable, that a great many of the new men who had Match-Locks, had so little skill in placing of their Matches true, that scarce one of them in four could fire their Pieces off; and those that did, thought they had done a feat if the Gun fired, never minding what they shot at.[45]

Then, on 29 September 1689, 'Lieutenant-General Douglas exercised the Regiments of the first Line, teaching them how to fire by platoons.'[46] Whilst this provides clear evidence of the introduction of platoon firing, there are, unfortunately, no details given of how it was conducted.

At the same time as Marlborough was campaigning in Flanders and Douglas in Ireland, William had sent Major General Hugh Mackay, a Scot in Dutch service, to take command of the forces in Scotland. In his diary he described how, before the battle of Killiekrankie in 1689, he had 'commanded the officers, commanding battalions, to begin their firing at the distance of 100 paces by platoons, to discourage the approaching Highlanders meeting with continual fire', thus demonstrating that platoon firing had also been introduced to the Scottish Army.[47] On this occasion platoon firing was no match for the onslaught of the highland charge and Mackay lost the battle. In 1692 he was killed at the battle of Steenkirk. Then in 1693 a drill book was published in Edinburgh with a title page that stated it included *the Rules of War in the day of Battel, when Encountering with the Enemy.*[48]

This was, in part, a reprint of a drill book of 1690, the first issued under William and Mary, but which was limited to the infantry drill and did not include the *Rules of War*.[49] According to the introduction to the 1693 Edinburgh edition Sir Thomas Livingstone, who had succeeded Mackay to the command in Scotland, had revised and corrected the earlier edition as well as adding the exercise of dragoons and also adding 'Lieutenant General Mackay's *Rules of War for the Infantry*, to be observed when they are to Encounter with the Enemie in the day of Battel'.[50] Given the official nature of this publication, and its recommendation to the Scots and English armies, there would seem to be no reason not to accept Mackay's rules as representing the then current practice in the Dutch Army that was adopted by the English and Scots armies and that it was an approved description of battlefield doctrine for all three allied armies, from 1689 onwards. In these *Rules* the Dutch had solved the problem of keeping up sustainable fire using platoons. It also seems that they were published even before 1693 as the title page for the *Rules* describes them as reprinted, further strengthening the case for them being the practice introduced under William in 1689.

Included in Mackay's *Rules* were detailed instruction on how platoon firing was to be organised and conducted. The *Rules* were organised in twenty-three articles and from the start it is clear that they represented a significant departure from previous doctrine. Whilst Mackay acknowledged six ranks as the norm for forming a battalion and marching he had it in three ranks on the battlefield. There was no place for the older, deeper six-rank formations.

Mackay described the formation of a regiment, or battalion, of thirteen companies, including a grenadier company: see figure 3.3. All the pikemen were formed in a central division, except for eighteen who formed on each outer flank of the two divisions of musketeers. The musketeers of the twelve ordinary companies were formed into twelve platoons, six on each side of the pikemen. The grenadiers were divided into two platoons positioned on the extreme flanks. In the case of battalions that were under

Figure 3.3: A Battalion drawn up according to Mackay's Rules.

g	p	m	m	m	m	m	m	p	m	m	m	m	m	m	p	g

Key: g=grenadier, p=pikemen, m=musketeer

This drawing is schematic only. The central division of pikemen was the same size as each wing of musketeers.

strength it would appear that it was considered more important to keep up the size of platoons rather than the number of platoons.

> If the regiment be compleat, every company may make a plotton, which makes six Plottons upon each Wing; but if considerably weakened, a Wing may be divided into four Plottons, which ought to be the least number, to give time to charge again, and be ready by that time the Fire is round, that the Battalion, if there be occasion, may entertain a continual Fire.[51]

In this context the phrase 'to charge again' refers to reloading and this tells us that a platoon should be able to reload and be ready to fire again by the time the other three platoons have fired. It is also clear that sustained fire was to be achieved by each platoon firing in turn along the line of each division of musketeers rather than by the rotation of ranks to the front or by ranks kneeling so those behind could fire over them. Instead of using, as Orrery suggested, a minimum of four ranks, this method used a minimum of four platoons.[52] Further, a platoon did not necessarily conform to a company and all the ranks in a platoon fired together. Thus all the three elements required for platoon firing were brought together.

The musketeer still required room for reloading the matchlock musket and, even if not hampered by a rest, the process was still a complex one and on the battlefield the use of just three orders was retained. On the command 'make ready' the front rank of musketeers knelt and the second and third ranks closed forwards and all prepared to fire, on 'present' they took aim and on 'fire' they fired. After firing and with no further orders the front rank stood, the second and third ranks stepped back to a distance of two paces between ranks and they all reloaded.[53]

As Mackay made clear, four platoons could keep up a continual fire, one after the other with the first platoon ready to fire again after the fourth fired. From this it is possible to speculate on a firing sequence with six platoons: see figure 3.4. This could have been first platoons one and five, then two and six, next three and finally four before starting all over again. The benefit of this sequence would be that fire came from both flanks of a wing of musketeers at the same time, covering the central platoons of the division, and then from the central platoons, which in turn covered the

Figure 3.4: A possible firing sequence with six platoons on each flank.

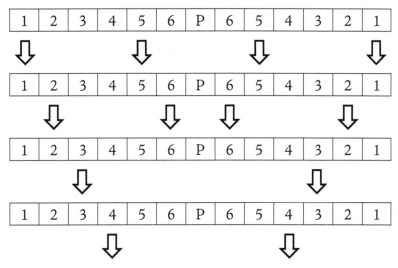

flank platoons. Thus not only was a part of the formation always loaded and ready to fire, but each platoon that was loading was protected by the fire of those platoons. However, it could be that all six simply fired in turn along the line with the first to fire having reloaded by the time the sixth fired.

In terms of weight of fire delivered this system is clearly superior to the other two methods already mentioned. A unit firing by platoons in two wings of six platoons each can deliver all its fire, in four volleys, while a unit in six ranks firing by ranks will, in four volleys, have only fired four ranks. Moreover it can maintain a sustained fire, whilst a unit firing by ranks from the rear, as the French did, has a problem once the front rank has fired – the rear rank cannot fire again until the ranks in front of it have reloaded, which has to be done standing up. A unit firing by ranks rotating to the front to fire and then retiring to reload would be at a disadvantage because of the time lost through the movement of the men, whilst the men firing by platoon reloaded on the spot. A unit using platoon firing could, all other things being equal, generate 50 per cent more fire than a unit in six ranks firing in ranks. Furthermore, being in three ranks a unit using platoon firing would be longer than a unit of the same size in six ranks and would be able to fire into its flanks. This represented a considerable improvement on the French method introduced under James II.

In describing how to fire in three ranks Mackay also gave the earliest known description of what was to become known as 'locking up'. This is the manner in which the three ranks closed and inter-locked so that they could all fire together safely. Houlding suggests that this was not introduced until the 1720s.[54] In this he contradicts Chandler who claims it was introduced under Marlborough, though without giving any evidence.[55] Curiously, after Mackay, subsequent military writings make no further mention of it until the 1720s, when it reappears in a drill book written by Humphrey Bland.[56] Prior to the introduction of locking up each man in a file had stood directly behind the man in front and, in the case of the second and third ranks, fired over the head of the man in front. Whilst the man in the front rank knelt, the man in the second rank had to stoop so that his head was below the level of the musket of the man behind him. In Mackay's *Rules* the second-rank man placed his left foot between the feet of the kneeling man and the third-rank man placed his left foot between the feet of the second-rank man. This had the effect of moving each man slightly to the right of the man in front so that the third-rank man could level his musket past the shoulder of the second-rank man, who no longer had to stoop.[57]

When a battalion was to fire the whole line was to halt and the platoons were to fire from their position in the line. Mackay advised against advancing the platoons that were to fire ahead of the line. His argument was that doing so could result in confusion that an enemy might take advantage of.[58] The importance of maintaining the line was again emphasised in Mackay's instructions on what to do when an opposing enemy battalion was beaten:

> If by a resolute continuance and close fire, the Battalion happen to break the opposite enemy, the Officers must take special care their men do not break after them, but content themselves to make the Granadeers fire amongst them to augment their Terrour and Confusion, that they may receive in good order, such of the enemy as shall come up to sustain those

which you ought to have routed, This Article the more carefully to be observed that in the advancing of the Line you are subject to be flanked by the enemies Horse posted betwixt the Lines for that purpose.[59]

Mackay is drawing attention to the need to maintain formation and the threat to infantry in a linear formation from cavalry, not attacking frontally, but attacking a flank.

Another new departure for any English or Scots drill book was the advice on managing fire control. Mackay stressed the need for the men not to present or fire without order from their platoon commander. The reason for this being:

> because if the battalion be attacked by horse, and the Commander, to avoid confusion, chosing rather to keep his fire whole, till they be very close, and then to fire by Plottons, upon a mint of the enemies squadrons, as break in upon his Battalion [he] think fit to cause it present without design of firing at that distance, sometimes makes the first rank of the squadron not only stoop short, but fall in confusion upon those that follow, but to bring the Souldiers to a custom of this last they must in Exercise be often accustomed, & commanded to present & recover their Arms without firing, telling them at the same time the reason for it, particularly at the same time of Action, and against Horse. The Commander judging it safest to manage his first fire, least their quick motion might prevent the second.[60]

Mackay's rules left something to be desired in terms of sentence structure and clarity, but what he was saying was that when attacked by cavalry a battalion commander may wish to make the enemy cavalry think he was about to fire by ordering his men to present, but not fire. In these circumstances the cavalry might baulk at advancing further and cause confusion in their own ranks. This would allow the commander to reserve his first and usually most effective fire for when the cavalry came closer. There was always a danger that fire at too great a range would not be sufficiently effective to stop cavalry, who could then close with the infantry before they could reload. Mackay reinforced the importance of keeping a firm control on management of the fire with the following advice.

If the commanding Officer of a plotton, be not altogether perswaded of his Souldiers Patience and exact Obedience, as to the order of firing, to prevent a confused fire he shall march softly, according to the motions of the line, with shouldered Musquets permitting none to make ready, but such Plottons as he intends immediately shall fire.[61]

This advice also reinforced the suggestion that there was a very specific sequence in which the platoons were to fire. Clearly there were still concerns about the threat posed to infantry by cavalry, but there is also a confidence that, handled properly, infantry in line could defeat cavalry by firepower alone.

During the Nine Years War that followed the accession of William and Mary there were a number of instances when English or Scots infantry are recorded as making use of platoon firing, several by Edward D'Auvergne who was chaplain to the Earl of Bath's regiment. He wrote that in August 1693, in an action near Halle, 'Sir Bevil Granville, who commanded the Earl of Bath's Regiment, marched up to the relief if this Lunenburg Regiment, bearing the enemies fire before he suffered any Platton of his Battalion to discharge once.'[62] He also recorded the effectiveness of platoon firing. Writing about the same action he said the French 'infantry was so harras'd by our Fire, that they seem'd unwilling at last to come to the Charge'.[63] Clearly the doctrine of getting in close before firing was not just theoretical and was also found to be effective.

Platoon firing as defined at the start of this chapter and described by Mackay would seem to have been developed in Holland between 1678 and 1688 before being introduced to Britain in 1689. Thus, by the early 1690s the infantry of both England and Scotland had adopted the principles of the platoon fire delivery system and were making effective use of it. This meant that British infantry, with its penchant for the aggressive application of firepower at close range, would no longer be hampered by the need to choose between depth in formations to ensure continuous, but low-intensity fire, or a three-deep line to maximise fire but with the risk of being caught unloaded. Platoon firing in a three-deep line would mean that a British infantry battalion could manage and control the rate and intensity of its fire without changing formation.

Chapter 4

William III and the Nine Years War

At the time of the Glorious Revolution of 1688 there was little difference between the drill and tactical doctrine of the French Army and the armies of England and Scotland, as shown by the 1685 edition of *An Abridgement of the English Military Discipline*.[1] Yet the reign of William III and the war that followed was a period of considerable improvement for the English and Scots armies where the foundations were laid for the development of the fighting capabilities that Marlborough would later employ so effectively. Furthermore, for most of the Nine Years War this was done without the assistance of Marlborough who, despite playing a major role in the revolution in support of William, was out of favour with William from 1691 and did not hold a military command again until the outbreak of the War of the Spanish Succession in 1702.

Through the course of the Nine Years War platoon firing developed from the form introduced in 1689, adapting and changing in response to the significant changes in the weapons used by British infantry during this period. These developments, however, are not readily identifiable. Following the publication in 1690 of *The Exercise of the Foot with the Evolutions*, and its 1693 Scottish edition with Mackay's *Rules*, there was no official, printed drill produced until 1728.[2] There was also a scarcity of eyewitness accounts to allow a comparison of theory with practice and few of these writers concerned themselves more than occasionally with the detail of drill and tactics. Some provided nothing, such as Captain Blackader, whose work was little more than an account of his own piety.[3] Despite this it is possible to produce a broad description of the developments of the last decade of the eighteenth century and to analyse their implications and impact.

The period of the Nine Years War was one of considerable change for the British army as, in common with other European armies, it exchanged the matchlock musket and the pike for the flintlock musket and the bayonet. During the same period bandoleers were phased out and replaced by cartridges, although priming from the cartridge was not yet introduced. The disadvantages of the matchlock musket when compared to the firelock have already been discussed, but the firelock's advantages can be summarised as being more-certain ignition and quicker to load. When combined with the use of cartridges the firelock could achieve a rate of fire half as fast again as with the matchlock.[4] Despite these advantages the French were particularly slow to change and it has been suggested that this was because they were preoccupied with the attack, in which they considered firepower to be less important than in defence.[5] The gradual disappearance of the pike as a weapon of British infantry also meant that, eventually, half has many men again would be armed with muskets. Put simply, this increase in the number of muskets and the rate of fire meant that, when compared to a unit of the same size from the English Civil War, an infantry unit at the end of the seventeenth century had the potential to generate in excess of double the firepower.

The narrative of these changes in equipment is far from clear, consisting of piecemeal changes carried out during the last decade of the seventeenth century and the first few years of the eighteenth century and as finance allowed. Chandler, however, does give an account that is sufficient to grasp the outline and further, more technical, details are to be found in Blackmore's *British Military Firearms*.[6] What neither writer does and it is really outside the scope of Blackmore's book, is to analyse what these changes meant for the firepower generated by British infantry. The departure of the pikeman also meant that a reorganisation of the battalion was necessary and, consequently, changes in the organisation of platoon firing. The pike, however, was slow to disappear as there were difficulties with its replacement, the bayonet, which quickly became apparent.

Platoon firing was a relatively new development for the Dutch as well as the English and Scots and the battle of Killiekrankie in July 1689 was the first opportunity for its use, against a Jacobite army of Highlanders. The infantry of a small government army under the command of Lieutenant General Hugh Mackay was a combination of three English regiments and three regiments from the Scots Brigade in Dutch Service. In accordance with his own *Rules of War*, Mackay's infantry were drawn up three deep and the battalion commanders were ordered to 'begin their firing at the distance of 100 paces by platoons to discourage the approaching Highlanders meeting with continual fire'.[7] This was an unusually long range at which to open fire and the reason for this was a combination of the nature of the early bayonet and Mackay's understanding of the way Highlanders fought, advancing at speed to get to hand-to-hand combat. As Mackay himself observed, 'if a battalion keep up [reserve] his fire till they [the Highlanders] be near to make sure of them, they are upon it before our men can come to their second defence, which is the bayonet in the musle of the musket.'[8] By opening fire at a longer range than usual, and then keeping up a 'continual fire' by platoon firing, Mackay hoped to give his infantry time to inflict casualties by fire and to fix their bayonets before the enemy closed to hand-to-hand combat. Mackay's own account described the fire of some of his infantry: 'Hastings, the General, and Levin's regiments, which made the best fire and all the execution; particularly the General's battalion made a great fire being well exercised thereto by his brother, who, being his lieutenant colonel, commanded the battalion.'[9] However, the fire of the infantry, even in platoons, was insufficient to stop the charge of the Highlanders and Mackay's infantry was broken and overrun.

The bayonet was to have a considerable impact on firepower as it replaced the pike, allowing pikemen to become musketeers, but initially its use was fraught with difficulties. It had made its appearance early in the second half of the seventeenth century and in its early form was of the type known as a plug bayonet, which was simply a dagger with a grip of a small enough diameter to be pushed into the muzzle of a musket. There were a number of drawbacks to this type of bayonet – the main one was that, once in place, the musket could not be fired, as experienced by Lieutenant General Mackay at Killiekrankie in 1689. In defence of Mackay and his unfortunate infantry it must be said the Highland charge continued to be a problem for British infantry up to the battle of Culloden in 1746. Mackay claimed that he subsequently developed a bayonet that attached to the barrel with a pair of rings that slid over the muzzle.[10] He mentioned in his *Rules of War* a bayonet that 'fixt without the muzzles of their Pieces', which would suggest that he wrote the *Rules* between Killiekrankie and his death in 1692.[11]

Brigadier General James Douglass, in his manuscript military manual *Schola Martis or the Arte of War . . . as Practised in Flanders, in the Wars, from Anno 1688 to An: 1714,* also wrote of the problems of using the plug bayonet: 'we could never make use of them till all our shot was spent and then we fixed the wooden hafts within ye caliber of our muskets which was of so little consequence that ye least strok upon ye barall would make them presently fly out whereof I have been often witness.'[12] Subsequently the plug bayonet was replaced by the socket bayonet, something for which Douglass claimed credit. As a captain at the battle of Landen in 1693 he claimed to have captured a French socket bayonet and had it copied for the use of his own grenadier company.[13] Instead of a wooden handle the socket bayonet had a tubular sleeve that fitted over the outside of the musket barrel. A zigzag slot in the socket engaged on a lug on the barrel, securing it in place and giving rise to the 'bayonet fitting'. This allowed the musket to be loaded and fired with the bayonet fitted and meant that it was also more firmly attached.

At the same time as the bayonet was developing and being introduced it was also being discovered that infantry did not necessarily require pikemen to defend themselves against cavalry attacks. The vulnerability of infantry to cavalry was a major consideration for as long as cavalry rode horses. The response in the seventeenth century was twofold. Firstly there was the pike, usually some five metres long, that could present a steel-tipped hedge to attacking cavalry, holding them off beyond the reach of the horseman's sword or lance. Secondly there were complex formations, in which the pikemen formed an all-round defence with the musketeers sheltering under the pikes or between or behind the pikemen. However, as already shown, musketeers in the English Civil Wars were quite capable of defending themselves against cavalry without resorting to such formations. Despite this the various editions of the *Abridgement of Military Discipline* all contained directions for forming hollow squares of pikemen surrounded by musketeers and gave detailed instructions on how to organise the firing of a square. What was missing from the instructions, however, was any actual mention of cavalry and how to deal with an attack by them.

Mackay's *Rules*, in contrast, contained a considerable amount of advice on how to deal with cavalry, and without resort to defensive formations based on pikemen. The key element of Mackay's advice was that the infantry should reserve their fire until the attacking cavalry 'be very close and then to fire by Plottons'.[14] In contrast to earlier drill books Mackay's *Rules* make no mention of forming any sort of battalion square to defend against cavalry, nor were there any accounts of this happening during the Nine Years War. Mackay's *Rules* represented the common tactical doctrine of the three armies under William's control – English, Scottish and Dutch – and just how effective platoon fire could be against cavalry was demonstrated at the battle of the Boyne in 1690 when Jacobite cavalry attacked William's Dutch Guards who were leading the attack across the Boyne and had no pikes. The Guards were isolated on the enemy side of the river and had no protection from any natural obstacle such as a hedge or ditch. William was, according to an eyewitness, extremely concerned: 'But when he saw them stand their ground and fire by platoons, so that the horse were forced to run away in great disorder, he breathed out . . ., and said he had seen his Guards do that which he had never seen foot do in his life.'[15] William's comment that he had never seen such an action before is further evidence of the novelty of platoon firing.

The battle of the Boyne, a victory for William over the Jacobite army of James II, was one of the first occasions on which platoon firing was successfully tested in battle. Only days before, another trial of platoon firing had occurred in Flanders at the battle of Fleurus where Dutch infantry under Field Marshal von Waldeck defeated a French force. Here the Dutch infantry demonstrated the ability of platoon firing to deal effectively with both infantry and cavalry.

For after they [the Dutch infantry] were abandoned by the horse, they also sustained the charge of French cavalry and infantry, and being attacked in front, flank, and rear, all at once, yet remained firm, unbroken and impenetrable: they let the enemy's horse approach within pistol shot of them, and then discharged with such an unconcerned and steady aim, that the whole squadron seemed to sink to the ground, scarce thirty of the whole squadron number escaping: and this course they so accustomed themselves to observe, that at length they laughed at the enemy. The French, on the other side were so confounded with the execution done upon them, that they fled as soon as the Dutch began to present their muskets.[16]

Two important points are apparent in this account. First, the Dutch infantry let the French cavalry come very close before firing, and second, it became sufficient for the infantry to threaten to fire for the French cavalry to retreat, such was the effectiveness of their close-range fire.

Another account tells the same story and adds that the French infantry were just as intimidated by the Dutch firepower as the cavalry: 'So that the enemy, by their [Dutch] close and punctual Fire were so often Galled and Shattered they knew not what to do; the French Infantry could not so much as dare look them in the face.'[17] In all three of the preceding examples the infantry concerned behaved in complete accordance with Mackay's *Rules*.

Chandler comments that 'at the battle of Fleurus, it was widely noted that several German battalions using firearms alone had proved capable of repulsing French cavalry more effectively than others armed with the conventional number of pikes.'[18] William III's army contained troops of many nationalities in addition to English, Scots and Dutch. There were troops from many German states, Spain, Sweden, Switzerland, Austria, Denmark and Brandenburg Prussia. The Prussian infantry were taught platoon firing in the autumn of 1688.[19] It would seem reasonable to suggest that the troops from other nations were at least aware of platoon firing even if they did not adopt it or stick with it. For example, according to Nosworthy the Swedish army under Charles XII employed a tactic from 1701 called 'ga-pa', literally 'go on'. In this they advanced in four ranks and at fifty paces the rear two ranks fired a volley. The advance then resumed with the front two ranks firing at point-blank range before charging home.[20]

Although the examples of the Boyne and Fleurus gave ample evidence of the effectiveness of platoon firing on these occasions the main protagonists were Dutch infantry. English and Scots regiments also made their presence felt in the war and clearly took to platoon firing, which they combined with their previous propensity for getting close to the enemy before firing. In 1689, the same year as Killiekrankie, at the battle of Walcourt one English battalion in particular distinguished itself. The French launched an attack that surprised the allied army under the command of Field Marshal von Waldeck while a large portion of it was foraging in the surrounding countryside. They were protected by the single English battalion of Colonel Hodges. The French attack was led by cavalry and began at about nine o'clock in the morning. The *London Gazette* carried the following graphic account:

> Col. Hodges lined some convenient Hedges, and kept Firing upon them [the French cavalry] till between 10 and 11, in which time most of the Foragers were gone home. The French brought Dragoons and Foot to force Hodges from his Post, who thereupon retired to a Mill, which he maintained till he received Orders to retreat, which he did with extraordinary Bravery, still firing upon the Enemy, till he came about twelve a clock near to a little Town called Walcourt, a Mile from our Camp, and the Pass to it; where we had a Regiment of Lunenburgers, who fired very thick upon the French: so with the loss of Lieutenant Colonel Graham, Captain Davison mortally wounded, and about 30 Men killed, Col. Hodges returned to the Camp.[21]

This action and the actions of British troops in the ensuing battle earned nothing but praise, von Waldeck expressing surprise: 'Mons. The Colonel Hotzes [Hodges] and the English, who are with him, have accomplished miracles, and I would never have believed so many of the English would show such a joie de combattre.'[22] Although it is not explicitly stated that Hodges' battalion was using platoon fire it is unlikely they were using anything else, given its official status.

At the battle of Steenkirk in 1692 it was William's infantry who were on the offensive and the French who had the benefit of hedges. The battle was something of a disaster as William was unable to properly support the English infantry who led the attack on the French; the result was that despite their success the battle was a bloody defeat. The English infantry, however, further enhanced its reputation and demonstrated that they were still perfectly capable of closing with the enemy to make their musket fire tell. D'Auvergne described how:

> Sir Robert Douglass, with his first Battalion, charg'd several of the Enemies, and beat them from three several Hedges, and had made himself Master of the fourth, where going through a Gap to get on the other side, he was unfortunately kill'd upon the spot; all the other

Regiments performing equal wonder, and behaving with the same Bravery, and beating the Enemies from their Hedges so far, that in this Hedge-fighting their fire was generally Muzzle to Muzzle, we on the one side, and the Enemy on the other.[23]

Close-range fire was again being employed, this time offensively. The British infantry were closing with the French, who were protected by hedges, successfully engaging them at extremely close range and forcing them to retreat. The example of the Earl of Bath's regiment has already been given, but includes the detail that the French fire was deliberately ignored in order to get close.[24]

The infantry also demonstrated a considerable amount of discipline and fire control in the subsequent withdrawal.

The night drawing on, the King order'd the Army to retreat, which was done with admirable Order; for tho' the French did follow us for some time, yet they did not fire a shot, such was the order of our Retreat that they did not dare venture upon it; the English Grenadiers brought up the Rear, and whenever the French mov'd towards us, they fac'd to the Right about, and presented themselves to the Enemy; then the Enemy would halt, and so our Rear-Guard then march'd on; this halting and facing, and then marching, continu'd for some time.[25]

Again, this passage shows a close adherence to Mackay's *Rules*, presenting muskets as if intending to fire, and that although the British were retreating the French were sufficiently wary of their fire capabilities that they kept their distance.

The increased firepower generated by platoon firing combined with the introduction of the socket bayonet meant that there was no longer a need for pikemen and over the course of the Nine Years War they were gradually reduced in numbers. Childs has suggested that the ratio of muskets to pikes increased from 2:1 in 1689 to 3:1 by 1697.[26] Certainly by 1702 it would seem that the intention was that infantry regiments should have given up their pikes. Six regiments of infantry going to Ireland in June 1702 all received the same instruction: 'Her Majesty's pleasure is that all pikes already issued to the Regiment of Foot under your command be returned to the Stores of Ordnance, in lieu of a sufficient number of muskets which you are to receive out of the said stores.'[27]

The way that infantry fought and carried out platoon firing at the start of this period was clear from Mackay's *Rules*. The disappearance of pikes, however, gives rise to the question of how regimental organisation and the management of platoon firing were consequently affected. Brigadier-General Douglass' manuscript military manual, *Schola Martis*, contained very detailed directions on drill and platoon firing by battalions without pikes.[28] The difficulty is that the manual was obviously written at some time after 1714 and there was no date given for when the drill described was in use during the twenty-six-year period covered by the title.

Douglass's drill is certainly later in date than Mackay's. When Mackay's *Rules of War* appeared it was published as part of *The Exercise of the Foot with the Evolutions*.[29] In this the drill for musketeers, individually and as part of a battalion, was using the matchlock musket. The drill for the firelock musket was given as a separate section. There was also pike drill. In Douglass's manuscript battalions were completely armed with firelock muskets and socket bayonets. There was no mention of matchlocks and he used the phrase 'since the pikes were out of use', which indicates a date for the drill after the end of the Nine Years War.[30] He also had each company making a platoon, which echoed Mackay.[31] As will be shown, by 1708 it had become the practice in the British Army to divide battalions into fifteen platoons, regardless of the company organisation, which places Douglass's drill before that date. That is if it was a British drill and not a Dutch one. Prior to 1701 Douglass had been serving in Holland with the Scots Guards, but was then appointed lieutenant colonel of Aeneas Mackay's regiment of the Scottish Brigade in Dutch service.[32] As will be shown, the Dutch method of platoon firing remained much as Douglass described it up to the end of the War of the Spanish Succession in 1714. He also included in his manuscript various 'evolutions' or drill manoeuvres that were abandoned in 1708 by the British Army. If he was writing a Dutch manual it could have been reflecting their practice for anytime from 1700 up to 1714, but it would not be unreasonable to expect a Dutch manual to have been written in Dutch. Perhaps most tellingly, however, he described how to salute the king. This must be a reference to William III, who died in March 1702 and was succeeded by

Queen Anne. This evidence points to the turn of the century as the date for when the drill described by Douglass was in use.

As William III was head of both the Dutch Army and the English and Scots Army it is reasonable to assume that the same drill, as described by Douglass, was in use in both armies at that time. This assumption is supported by sections of the manual where Douglass described differences between the Dutch and British organisation of grenadiers and how to allow for that in the drill, so it could be used by either army.[33]

Douglass's instruction on firing included details on the order of firing of the platoons:

> Let the firing begin from yᵉ two extream plotouns upon ye rigᵗ and left of ye Battallion and so continue sucesivly firing till you end in ye centre . . . But if a continuall fire must be keept as in Battell reqd after ye plotouns have fired they must immediately loadd againe & shoulder till ordered by ye Capt to make ready etc and this is done in addvancing and retearing as well as standing.[34]

The firing order of the platoons was specified and simple: it was from the flanks to the centre; gone was Mackay's suggestion of a more complex order of firing.[35] In the other respects of reloading immediately and his comment about advancing, retiring and standing he echoed Mackay. Mackay's suggestions that the best shots be held in reserve and that the grenadier platoons could be hidden behind the flanks of a battalion had also gone, further simplifying the drill.[36]

Douglass also instructed that the men in each rank were to stand with the files at close order, that was 'shoulder to shoulder, but so as they can be master of ther Arms'.[37] This was closer than specified in the *Exercise of the Foot* that also contained Mackay's *Rules of War*: there the distance between files when firing was given as half a pace.[38] This closing up was undoubtedly a result of exchanging the matchlock for the flintlock and had the effect of concentrating a battalion's fire over a narrower front. Both the *Exercise of the Foot* and Douglass said the distance between ranks 'either standing or marching is 4 paces'.[39] Although the number of movements required to load and fire a firelock musket was fewer than for a matchlock, the use of just the commands 'make ready', 'present' and 'fire' continued in action. On the order 'make ready' the ranks closed, the front knelt, the middle stooped and the rear stood, all cocking their muskets. On 'present' they levelled their muskets; then came 'fire'. After firing, the ranks were to open 'backwards to 2 paces distance that they may have roum to charge or load ther arms againe without expecting any word of command for ye same'.[40]

Douglass also included a revised version of Mackay's *Rules* that gave an indication of how combat practices had changed over the course of the Nine Years War. In many places Douglass's *Rules* used the same wording as Mackay, although elsewhere he improved on their intelligibility and simplified some of them. In general the content of both sets of rules was the same, but there were a few differences. For instance, Douglass made no mention of locking up, instead he reverted to the older method of the second rank stooping to fire over the heads of the kneeling front rank with the third rank standing to fire over the heads of the second rank.[41]

Douglass also discussed dealing with cavalry in a much simpler, clearer way, while retaining the need for close-range fire and being able to present without firing.

> If the battallyon be charged with a body of Cavallry, the commanding officer shall keep up his fire until the horse be very close and then to fire either by rank or plotouns as he thinks proper.[42]

> The Enemy in this case will now and then come briskly up as if they designed to fall in with you, although they doe not designe itt, but only to try what countenance you mak, and in such occurancys the Commanding officers must cause the whole Battallion present without any designe of firing wher with beforehand he is to advertise ye officers, and that will redaly make ye first Rank of ye Squadrons not only stoup but fall in confusion upon those that follow.

> And to bring his souldiers to some expertness in this they must be often commanded to present ther Arms and againe recover without firing telling them ye reason for it.[43]

That this theory was put into practice was seen during the retreat of William's allied army following its defeat at Landen in 1693.

Lieutenant-General Talmash had the care to bring off the English Foot of the main Body by Dormal, which he did with as much Prudence as he had before fought with Bravery . . . As the Enemy offer'd to trouble his Retreat, he made the Battalions face, and Present to them, and then they halted, unwilling to feel any more the fire of our Foot.[44]

Clearly the ability to not fire at close range was as important as actually firing.

During the course of the Nine Years War large numbers of new troops were raised, either for new units or to replace casualties, who all needed to be trained quickly.[45] Not all units would have had the training and experience of regiments such as the Dutch Blue Guards. As well as demonstrating how the disappearance of pikemen was dealt with, it is also possible that Douglass's manual represented a simplified version of drill and tactics pared down to the necessary basics in order to avoid confusing newly raised troops. However, it was with this drill and method of platoon firing that the British Army under Marlborough started the War of the Spanish Succession.

A significant difference between the tactical methods of the Nine Years War and those of the English Civil War and the campaigns following the Restoration of 1660 is the apparent abandoning of the infantry assault following close-range fire. Mackay states, and Douglass copies almost word for word: 'If by a resolute continuance and close fire, the Battalion happen to break the opposite enemy, the Officers must take special care their men do not break after them, but content themselves to make the Granadeers fire amongst them to augment their Terrour and Confusion.'[46] This emphasis on beating the enemy by firepower has been seen as indicating an abandonment of the infantry assault. As Chandler writes:

In the 1690s it became rare for infantry to fight hand-to-hand with their opponents, although there were of course notable exceptions such as Steenkirk (1692) where the English and Dutch battalions were divided from the French only by hedgerows. Generally speaking, however, commanders deemed their foot to be a source of more or less static fire-power once they had moved ponderously up into musket range, relying on the wheeling horsemen to decide the ultimate issue.[47]

Some explanation for the abandonment of the previously highly successful tactic of following a close-range volley with a charge to hand-to-hand combat can be found in Mackay and Douglass. They both drew attention to the importance of not breaking the line to pursue a broken enemy unit in case, as Douglass wrote, 'you come to be flanked in yt irregular action by troups ye Enemie may have posted betwixt yr lines for that purpose.'[48] Mackay used much the same words.[49] To close with the enemy to hand-to-hand combat would inevitably leave a battalion in some confusion, making it extremely vulnerable to counter-attack. Thus the infantry chose to rely upon firepower to break an enemy. That they were able to do so was a result of the changes that had taken place since the English Civil War. During the Civil War infantry regiments were not able to generate long-range, sustained fire that was also effective and decisive. On the other hand an infantry regiment that advanced to point-blank range and maximised its fire had little choice but to close to hand to hand immediately after firing. With all its fire delivered in one go and with reloading taking so long, to do otherwise would leave it vulnerable. By contrast a battalion at the end of the century could not only deliver more fire more rapidly at any range, but because of platoon firing it was sustainable fire: there was always some part of it that was firing and thus protecting those parts that were reloading. Furthermore, as suggested by Mackay, the fire of the front rank could be reserved and the battalion would still be able to generate a considerable amount of continuous platoon fire and be protected by the front rank with bayonets fixed.[50] As Douglass wrote, and at the same time summed up the different roles of the infantry and the cavalry:

For now, in our modern way of fighting viz: by platouns alternativly firing, it is not aloud ye Infantry to fall in pell mell amongst any troups in confusion, least therby they bring themselves in to ane equall disadvantage an so change the smyles of fortune in to frouns and threats of loss, therfor whatever confusion ye Enemy may be in the Infantry ar not to brake ther Ranks to persheu but ar still to march softly on in full body closing ther files and making up ther Ranks as the men drops, and so re never out of condition of Battalling or Sustaining wher its requied leaving the accomplishment of the victory to ye Cavalry giving no quarters till ye victory is determined.[51]

Mackay, however, did write about the use of the bayonet:

That such Regiments as are provided of good Bayonets, fixt without the muzzles of their Pieces, may in approaching to the due distance of firing, cause the first rank of the whole Battalion to fix their Bayonets and continuing their march till they be close upon the Enemy, make the first rank kneel with the points of their Bayonets upon the Ground, and the other two Ranks closed up, fire over their heads upon the Enemy, who supposing readily all the fire spent, if he happen to stand it, will come up the bolder to your Battalion, who receiving him with the [fire of the] first Rank, second with the push of pike and Bayonet, will readily break him whether horse or Foot.[52]

Mackay included the need to 'be close upon the enemy' before firing, but rather than maximising the infantry's firepower, held the front-rank fire in reserve in case of a counter-attack, in which case the front rank was to fire and then charge, or present, their bayonets at the same time as the pikemen charged their pikes. It was a description of the bayonet used defensively, just as the pike was, and suggests that the bayonet was seen as an alternative to the defensive qualities of the pike and that its offensive qualities had not yet been recognised.

Douglass omitted any such advice on the use of the bayonet from his version of the *Rules*, although he did record his role in copying the socket bayonet from the French and comment on its superior qualities as a weapon compared to the plug bayonet.[53] Writing of the battles of Fleurus, Steenkirk and Landen, he described how the French socket bayonet was a 'great advantage' as it meant the French 'both push'd and fired at once' and was 'a much better defence than our pikes wer'.[54] Again the bayonet was clearly seen as a defensive weapon.

Chandler wrote, in a comment later echoed by Nosworthy, 'many contemporaries spoke with awe of the fury of the initial French fire in action, although its continuity and effectiveness tended to fall off rapidly after the initial discharge.'[55] As already discussed, the French fired by ranks, and during the Nine Years War, when they habitually formed five ranks, they could deliver all their fire in two volleys of three and two ranks. Whilst this did result in a very heavy fire it also resulted in reloading problems once all the ranks had fired.[56] From contemporary accounts it would also appear that French infantry opened fire at a greater distance than British infantry, allowing the British to get closer to the French, who were presumably busy reloading, before delivering their own, heavy and sustainable platoon firing.

A number of examples of this are available. Although it occurred against Jacobite Irish infantry, Story recorded one instance; 'As our men advanced up the hill, the Irish fired a whole Volley upon them, and then set up the Huzzah, but scarce killed a Man, (for they shot over them) our Men however went on till they were got within Pistol-shot of them, and then fired, by which they galled the Irish, that they immediately run.'[57] It is notable that the Irish are recorded as firing a 'whole volley' and no more. Presumably they were trying to reload as the English infantry advanced and then fired within pistol range. The example of the Earl of Bath's regiment under Sir Bevil Granville has already been given as it 'marched up to the relief of this Lunenburg Regiment, bearing the enemies fire before he suffered any Platton of his Battalion to discharge once'.[58]

There is no doubt that the English and Scots continued to deliver their fire at close range. This was clear from the account of the fighting at Steenkirk already quoted and the actions of the English regiments in the victory over the Jacobites at Aughrim in 1691. 'The Irish at their near approach to the Ditches, fired upon them, but our Men contemning all Disadvantages, advanced immediately to the lowest Hedges, and beat the Irish from thence.'[59]

Platoon firing was extremely effective in a firefight where both sides sought to overwhelm the other by fire alone and one side, as the French did, chose to fire by ranks in a deep formation. It did not, however, always win the day. At Killiekrankie the Highlanders' tactic of firing a single volley and then rushing in, sword in hand, allowed them to overwhelm Mackay's infantry in hand-to-hand combat even though they suffered heavy casualties from the fire of his infantry.[60] Similarly at the battle of Fleurus not all the fighting had gone in favour of the Dutch infantry. No less an authority than Maurice de Saxe in his *Reveries* described how platoon firing could be defeated in a manner not very different from that of the Highlanders at Killiekrankie.

It was an established maxim of M. de Greder, a man of reputation, and who has for a long time, commanded my regiment of foot in France, to make his men carry their firelocks shouldered in an engagement; and in order to be still more master of their fire, he did not even suffer them to make ready their matches: thus he marched against the enemy, and the moment they gave their fire, he threw himself, sword in hand, at the head of the colours, and crying out *Follow me!* rushed at once upon them. By this method he defeated the Frise guards at the battle of Fleurus, and was also successful on all other occasions.[61]

In 1693 French infantry under Marshal Catinat in Italy stormed Austrian positions with the bayonet. The effect of these events is summarised by Chandler: 'Such success, however, encouraged French generals of several generations in the belief that the true métier of the French foot was cold steel – and this assumption led them to disregard the refinements of infantry fire tactics, with what proved to be near-fatal results in the following war.'[62]

Amongst the French generals who subsequently sustained this belief in cold steel was the Marechal de Saxe, whilst the influential writer Folard also adhered to it.[63] 'French 'offensive tactics attached little importance to firefights conducted at a distance, every effort being made to approach the enemy and overthrow them with the threat of the bayonet or drawn sword.'[64] The French remained content to rely on the bayonet and, despite its drawbacks, their version of firing by ranks. In contrast the British adopted an approach that emphasised firepower.

Although often overshadowed by the War of the Spanish Succession, the Nine Years War represents a pivotal period in the development of the firepower capability of British infantry. During this period the pike disappeared and was replaced by the bayonet, which increased the number of soldiers with muskets by half as many again. The matchlock was replaced by the flintlock, which was more reliable and quicker to load and fire. The speed of loading was further increased by the introduction of the cartridge in place of the bandoleer. The resultant increase in firepower was, at the same time, delivered by means of platoon firing, which allowed the full potential of the increase in available firepower to be realised by giving a battalion commander a range of options on how to deliver his battalion's fire.

A battalion could now fire one of its twelve platoons every few seconds and still have the first platoon to fire reloaded and ready to fire again by the time all twelve had fired. Depending upon circumstances this rate of fire could be slowed down if sustainable fire was required over a long period of time. The option also existed for a battalion commander to fire only a given number of his platoons or to fire all his platoons together in a battalion volley. A further option was to fire only the second and rear ranks, in any of the ways mentioned, keeping the entire front rank as a reserve. Furthermore, British infantry retained its ability to sustain the enemy's fire and get close before delivering its own fire, although the bayonet was, in the drill books at least, seen as a defensive rather than offensive weapon.

Despite these advantages platoon firing was not an inevitable battle winner. It was vulnerable to a rapid assault, as at Killiekrankie and Fleurus, and to being overwhelmed by sheer weight of numbers, as at Landen in 1693. Outnumbered approximately three to two, the Confederate Army of William finally collapsed when it could no longer keep the French at bay with musketry.

> The elector upon the Right, order'd two Battalions to Charge the Enemy in Front, whilst three others should Charge them upon their Left Flank . . . The two Battalions, one Dutch and t'other of Scots Gurds, which the Elector had commanded to Charge the Enemy in the Front, had spent all their Ammunitions by their continual Fire for so many hours: The Elector order'd to have Ammunition brought them, but it could not time enough to do business.[65]

This failure was attributed to a lack of ammunition rather than any failing in the men or tactics. However, its ability with this new fire system was usually enough to allow British infantry to overcome its usual enemy of the time, the French. It was also sufficient to deal with frontal cavalry attacks.

Platoon firing as described by Lieutenant General Mackay had been developed at a time when a third of a battalion was made up of pikemen and the musketeers were armed with matchlocks and loaded from bandoleers. Although the disappearance of the pike and the introduction of the flintlock musket and the cartridge led to minor adaptations in the way that platoon fire was delivered, it remained basically unchanged and was the fire-delivery system that the British infantry took into Flanders at the outbreak of the War of the Spanish Succession in May 1702. A battalion in line formed its dozen line or hat companies into a dozen platoons in two wings of six. The platoons fired in turn from the flanks to the centre, starting with the right-hand platoon of the right wing, followed by the left-hand platoon of the left wing and alternating platoons on the right and left until the two platoons in the centre fired. The grenadier company was divided into two and formed a platoon on each flank. They appear to have operated almost independently of the main body. By the end of that war, however, platoon firing had undergone a major change that took advantage of the improvements in weapons and the resultant increase in potential firepower.

Chapter 5

The Age of Marlborough, 1702 to 1714

It is the view of David Chandler, writing about the Duke of Marlborough, that 'England has never produced a greater soldier.'[1] Field Marshal Montgomery of Alamein's assessment is that, 'Of all the military personalities who pass across the stage during his times . . . Marlborough was the greatest . . . I have always considered that it was he who was responsible for the rise of the British army to become one of the foremost armies in Europe.'[2]

Marlborough's praises have been sung by military historians such as Richard Holmes, John Keegan, Andrew Wheatcroft and J. W. Fortescue.[3] But in studying the man and his campaigns historians have tended to ignore the detail of how Marlborough's battles were fought and concentrate instead on the narrative of events, analysing his strategies and manoeuvres. Yet, regardless of Marlborough's brilliance, the battles were ultimately decided by the outcome of the combat between battalions and squadrons, in which technique was critical. As John Houlding put it: 'We are too easily dazzled by the brilliance of Marlborough's grand-tactical dispositions, the more so when these are contrasted with those of William; Marlborough's victories were the fruit of the military genius of the commander, and not of any radical departure in the drill and tactics (save for platoon-fire) of the individual corps under his command.'[4]

Marlborough's greatness is not in dispute and there was little change after the Glorious Revolution of 1688 in the way the British army operated tactically, except, vitally, for the introduction of platoon fire.[5] However, using this new combat technique, British infantry, and their allies the Dutch, repeatedly punched above their weight on the battlefield in the face of frequently numerically superior French forces. In order to explain the success of British infantry it is necessary to look past the brilliance of Marlborough and understand what was happening in the ranks and files of his battalions.

The importance of platoon firing is clear in the views expressed by Houlding. 'By the time of Blenheim a new fire-tactics – the famous platoon-fire system – had established itself as the forte of the British foot.'[6] Houlding also states 'that a sound appreciation of the supremacy of firepower over all other forms of combat had been a lesson well learned by the end of Marlborough's campaigns, and had been taken to heart in the army.'[7] Furthermore, although platoon firing was learnt from the Dutch, the British Army first made it its own and then, after William's death in 1702, further developed it whilst the Dutch platoon fire changed hardly at all. It was thus at the very heart of the success of the British Army under Marlborough. However, despite this fundamental importance, the way platoon firing was organised and carried out and how it continued to develop under Marlborough has not been accurately described nor its application analysed.

Military historians invariably draw upon the description of platoon firing found in Richard Kane's manual as representing British practice during the War of the Spanish Succession and then support this claim with an account of one particular firefight, at Malplaquet in 1709, that appears to match Kane's description.[8] This view of the nature of platoon firing during the War of the Spanish Succession is wrong.

Furthermore, the way platoon firing was conducted at the start of the war is also quite different from what was described at the battle of Malplaquet in 1709.[9] There were a number of key changes to the organisation of platoon firing, something not recorded in any publication at the time and which has eluded historians. Not only was there was a very significant change in the conduct of platoon firing by 1709, but there were also major differences between the conduct of platoon firing in that 1709 firefight and what Kane later advocated.

In 1708 the Duke of Marlborough's *New Exercise of Firelocks & Bayonets* was published, but this was not an official publication and only dealt with drill and not how firing was to be conducted.[10] Fortunately a number of manuscripts and letters survive that record the steps in the development of platoon firing through this period. There was also a scarcity of eyewitness accounts to allow a comparison of theory with practice and few of these writers concerned themselves more than occasionally with the detail of drill and tactics. However, there are sufficient first-hand descriptions to allow an analysis of platoon firing in practice.

Despite his fall from favour with William III in 1692, Marlborough was politically and militarily rehabilitated by the eve of the War of the Spanish Succession, 1701–14. The two men worked together to prepare for the conflict, but, following a riding accident, William died in March 1702, to be succeeded by Queen Anne. The most obvious effect of this was to elevate Marlborough to the position of commander-in-chief of the English and Scots armies. Less obviously it broke the link that had existed between the English, Scots and Dutch armies when William was head of state and commander-in-chief of all three.

The first major engagement of the war for the British Army was the storming of the Schellenburg Heights on 2 July 1704. As part of Marlborough's campaign, which culminated in the battle of Blenheim, it was necessary to acquire a suitable base for supplies. Accordingly a plan was laid to capture Donauworth on the Danube. The town and defences of Donauworth were dominated by the Schellenburg Heights and capturing those was the key to the town. The fight for the Schellenburg subsequently became synonymous with vicious hand-to-hand fighting where there was little opportunity for the disciplined and controlled application of platoon fire. Perhaps the most vivid description came from one of the French defenders, whose account left no doubt that the British infantry had not lost any of their stomach for hand-to-hand fighting.

> It would be impossible to describe in words strong enough the details of the carnage that took place during this first attack, which lasted a good hour or more. We were all fighting hand to hand, hurling them back as they clutched at the parapet; men were slaying, or tearing at the muzzles of guns and the bayonets which pierced their entrails; crushing under their feet their own wounded comrades, and even gouging out their opponents' eyes with their nails, when the grip was so close that neither could make use of their weapons. I verily believe that it would have been quite impossible to find a more terrible representation of Hell itself than was shown in the savagery of both sides on this occasion.[11]

Eventually the defences of the Schellenberg were penetrated and the heights were captured. The garrison of Donauworth itself abandoned the town without a fight.

At the subsequent battle of Blenheim the British infantry were able to demonstrate their courage, discipline and platoon firing to their full effect.[12] The right flank of the French army rested on the banks of the Danube and the village of Blenheim. The village was held by sixteen battalions with another eleven in reserve supported by twelve squadrons of dragoons, many dismounted. The first attack on the village was made by the five British battalions of Rowe's brigade who were at the head of Lord Cutts's column. A vivid account of this attack was written by a chaplain, Josiah Sandby. It began with Brigadier Rowe leading his brigade against Blenheim.

And he had proceeded closely and slowly within 30 paces of the Pales about Blenheim before the enemy gave their first fire, and when this was given there fell a great many brave officers & soldiers on our side, but yet that did not discourage that Excellent officer Brigadier Rowe from marching directly to the very Pales, in which he stuck his sword, before he suffered a man to fire a piece & then our men gave the first volley in the teeth of the enemy. His orders were to enter sword in hand, but the superiority of the enemy & this advantage of the post made y^t impossible. And therefore this first line was forced to retire, but without the Brigadier who was left by the side of the Pales by a shot he had received in his thigh. This was a great disadvantage to the service at the first beginning & his own Lt Col and Maj who but knew his worth endeavouring to fetch him off were both killed upon the spot.[13]

The loss of the three most senior officers of a single British battalion in this attack is an indication of the ferocity of the fire that the French were able to generate. Despite this the account shows a determined adherence to the principle of getting in close to maximise the effectiveness of musketry. The French fired at thirty paces, the British even closer, possibly at as little as five metres. This was followed immediately by an attempt to storm the defences of the village, which failed.

Unfortunately for Rowe's brigade they were attacked by French cavalry as they retreated.

The Hessian Brigade, pursuant to orders, made ready to renew the attack: But while this was doing some Squadrons of the Gens d'Armes fell in upon the Right of Rowe's Brigade, put two Regiments in disorder, & took the Collonels Collours of Rowe's Regiment, upon which the Hessians in the second line, facing to the right, charged those Squadrons so warmly that they repulsed them & retook the Colours.[14]

This incident demonstrates exactly the danger of infantry having a flank exposed to a cavalry attack, but that cavalry could be equally vulnerable to formed infantry facing them frontally.

The fight for Blenheim village continued throughout the battle, with the British infantry and their allies unable to capture it. Neither, however, could the French mount a counter-attack to drive off the British and allied infantry.

The attack then increased in vigour and the enemy were driven into the village, where they were too numerous to act, being wedged up into a dense mass so that our well directed fire produced a murderous effect. We retired about 80 or 90 yards and plied them so warmly with our platoons that they were cut off as fast as they attempted to leave the village to put themselves in order to attack us.[15]

The account of Robert Parker confirms the effectiveness of the platoon firing.

The enemy also made several attempts to come out upon us: But as they were necessarily thrown into confusion in getting over their trenches, so before they could form into any order for attacking us, we mowed them down with our platoons in such numbers, that they were always obliged to retire with great loss; and it was not possible for them to rush upon us in a disorderly manner, without running upon the very points of our Bayonets.[16]

By standing at eighty or ninety yards from the French defences the British infantry put themselves outside truly effective range, so that when the French tried to counter-attack and came out of Blenheim they had to leave the protection of their defences and move closer to the British in order to form up. This placed them within effective range of the British platoons. The alternative was to just attack in a rush, which was also not a practical option.

Having given up trying to capture the village of Blenheim, Cutts kept the French, who had twenty-seven battalions to Cutts's sixteen, bottled up in the village, relying on steady platoon firing to do so.

All this while the village of Blenheim had been incessantly attacked by the Lord Cutts, who having found it impracticable to enter that place sword in hand, as the enemy were posted, had altered his method & attacked with his Fire only. The first of his lines which was posted near the enemies intrenchments continually discharged in Platoons & the other lines relieved this & each other successively.[17]

Sandby's account demonstrated how the lines were rotated while the following account of John Deane suggested this enabled them to keep supplied with ammunition. He also told how some of the attacking troops did get into Blenheim, but were unable to establish any sort of a position in there.

Att length the enemy making all the force they could upon us forced us to retreat and to quitt the village having lost a great many of our men, but we rallied againe, having received some fresh ammunition, resolving to give the enemy another salute. So that as soon as they perceived our designe they beat a parley.[18]

Bottled up in the village the French were unable to make use of their superior numbers while suffering dreadfully from the British platoon fire; eventually they surrendered.

The effectiveness of infantry against cavalry was also demonstrated in the centre of the battlefield where the Comte de Merode-Westerloo led an attack of French cavalry that was initially successful as it drove Marlborough's cavalry back.

I charged with all the men I could rally, and I had the good luck to defeat my adversaries and push them back to the brink of the stream – but I had no wish to recross it, for I could see they still had five lines of cavalry. However, I failed to notice that they had brought their infantry well forward and they killed and wounded many of our horses at thirty paces. This was promptly followed by an unauthorised but definite movement to the rear by my men.[19]

The actions of the British infantry at Blenheim against both infantry and cavalry demonstrated a continuing commitment to maximising the effectiveness of infantry firepower by getting close to the enemy, even if that meant having to endure the enemy's fire to do so.

The battle of Ramilles in 1706 was won by Marlborough's brilliant use of terrain to move his troops to gain local superiority over the French and is best known for the massive cavalry action that decided the outcome of the battle.[20] By comparison with Blenheim the surviving accounts of the battle supplied little information about how the British infantry fought. However, it was during the winter that followed that the next major change took place in the manner in which the infantry delivered their firepower. That winter Lieutenant General Ingoldsby was appointed commander-in-chief in Flanders while the troops were in their winter quarters and Marlborough and most of the general officers were in England.[21] Ingoldsby was the governor of Ghent, where thirteen British battalions were to spend the winter.[22] It is clear from correspondence that Ingoldsby was busy with the training of the infantry in something new. Unfortunately not all the relevant correspondence appears to have survived, such as the letters from Ingoldsby to which Adam Cardonnel, Marlborough's secretary, replied on 16 December 1706:

> I received yesterday by the Ostend Packet the honours of your letter of the 10th instant and this morning by way of the Brill that of the 19th and have laid them before my Lord Duke who approves entirely of what you are doing relating to the Exercise of the Foot. You see by the enclosed the method I have taken to acquaint the General of the Foot with it that he may have nothing to object to you on that score.[23]

It is clear from the need for Marlborough's approval and Cardonnel's remark about keeping the infantry's commander informed that something of some significance was afoot. The first clue to what was happening appears in a letter from Ingoldsby to Marlborough from Ghent on 31 December 1706.

> My Lord I have be-gon to exercise all the adjutants, sargants, and corporals, who are all-reddy pretty perfect, and mightelly pleased that your Grace has thought fitt to put them upon one exersise
>
> Itt is Imposable to tell your Grace the disorder thay weare in, not two regam^{ts} exersising a lik, nor anney one companney off Granadrs eable to exersis with the Battalyone so that if your Ldship had a mind to see the Line exersise, all the Granadrs off the armey must have stood still, and not to Regamts eable to perforum a like, which I hope is prevented, and will appeare to your sattysffacksion, iff I can have the recruits over in time.[24]

At the time of Ingoldsby's letter the last official drill issued to the English and Scots armies had been *The Exercise of the Foot with the Evolutions* that appeared in 1690 and was last issued in 1693 with Mackay's *Rules*. A further edition did appear in Dublin in 1701, but was simply a reprint of the 1690 version without Mackay's *Rules*.[25] This drill was written when battalions were armed with matchlock muskets and pikes. With their disappearance and replacement with flintlocks and bayonets it is perhaps not surprising that by the War of the Spanish Succession the drill of the infantry varied from regiment to regiment and even within regiments between the line companies and the grenadiers. It was to correct this state of affairs that Marlborough 'thought fitt to put them upon one exersise'.[26]

Ingoldsby's letter also demonstrates how new drill was disseminated amongst the regiments. First the regimental adjutants and NCOs were gathered together and taught the new drill. Once proficient they returned to their regiments and taught it to the other officers and soldiers.[27] It is clear, however, that Ingoldsby was doing more than just ensuring a uniformity of drill. He was also introducing something completely new, as his next letter to Marlborough, written from Ghent on 2 March 1707, makes clear: 'I suppose Maj^r Peniteere will give your Grace an acc^t how forward both officers, and souldiers are in the exercise you were pleas'd to cumande, to perforum which as well as the ffirings upon the Queens Berthday, I have contriv'd without toutching one grayne off her majys pouder, but what the souldiers brought with them into Garrison.'[28] This reference to 'ffirings' provides evidence of the first use of firings in the British army.

Prior to this date each platoon in a battalion had fired singly, in turn, along the length of the battalion. A firing was the grouping together of a number of platoons that could either fire one by one within the firing or altogether. The essential point was that these platoons were not grouped physically together, but distributed along the whole front of a battalion. Furthermore there were only three of these firings. This development overcame the main danger of the older system, which was stated clearly by Humphrey Bland some years later.[29] The problem with each platoon firing in turn along the line of a battalion was that whole sections of the line could be left unloaded and therefore vulnerable to a sudden attack, as had been seen at Killiekrankie and Fleurus. If the first platoon to fire in a wing was ready as the sixth platoon fired it meant that the four between them were still reloading and as little as one sixth of a battalion was ready to fire at any time. The adoption of firings meant that the platoons reloading, ready to fire or firing were distributed more evenly along a battalion. Bland was writing in the mid-1720s about the way the Dutch fired and it is clear that they had continued to fire in the same way throughout the War of the Spanish Succession. Among the papers of Willem Baron van Wassenaer, colonel of the First Dutch Guards Battalion, are instructions dating from 1713 on how firing was to be carried out.[30] They are, in substance, the same as Douglass's instructions.

It is also possible that there were other reasons for the change. The older system depended on each platoon reloading and being ready to fire again in the time it took the other five in a wing of a battalion to fire. With only three firings, reloading had to be carried out in the time that the other two firings took to fire. This suggests that with the increase in the speed of loading resulting from the introduction of the flintlock and the cartridge the reloading time may have been reduced to such an extent that platoons had found themselves loaded and ready to fire, but having to wait their turn while the other five platoons finished firing – not an easy thing to do in the heat of battle. Support for this possibility comes from Mackay's remark that just four platoons could keep up a continuous fire with matchlock muskets and bandoleers.[31] Concentrating the fire of a battalion into three firings also meant that a heavier fire could be delivered in a shorter time, overwhelming the enemy more quickly and avoiding a protracted firefight. Moreover, this form of firing could match, if not outweigh, the intensity of the initial fire of a French battalion and then be maintained while the French intensity fell off.

That Ingoldsby was successful in his enterprise is clear from an account of a review held on 30 May 1707.

> The Duke of Marlborough review'd all the British Corps, who exercised and fired four Rounds gradually before him, and that by the signal of the waving of a Pair of Colours for each Word of Command, performed by Colonel William Blakeney, on Top of our Pontons, posted a little in the Front thereof; attended by each Drum-Major with a Drum, in the Front of their respective Regiments, who, at each wave of the Colours, gave a tap on his Drum, answerable to and for each Word of Command; the which each Regiment observed to perform accordingly: And soon afterward he review'd each other Corps of the Army, who also in the like manner exercised and fired gradually before him.[32]

Another account of the same review described how 'all the English foote exercised by signall of coulers & beat of drium, and every brigade fired in platoons before his Grace; in which exercise the English gott great applause of the foreigners.'[33]

The first real test of this new method of firing the platoons did not come until June 1708 at Wynendael. A large French force attempted to intercept an important allied convoy taking ammunition and supplies to the allies besieging Lille. It was confronted by a much smaller allied force under the command of General Webb. Sir Winston Churchill described the following battle as 'a striking instance of the superior fire-discipline which was so marked a feature of Marlborough's infantry training'.[34] One contemporary account describes:

> The regiments and grenadiers making such a continual fire as forced their two wings on to their centre and obliged the whole to retire in the greatest confusion, notwithstanding all the efforts their officers could make by encouragement or violence to keep them up, so that they

only fired at a distance on our lines which was returned, advancing by platoons as at their exercise with all the order imaginable.[35]

Another account also draws attention to the precision with which the infantry delivered their fire: 'our foot made such a fire as never troops made more regular at exercise.'[36] The new firings clearly allowed the battalions to keep up a continuous, effective and sustained fire.

The following month, July, brought one of Marlborough's great victories, Oudenarde.[37] This was something of an encounter battle, with both sides feeding troops into the fight as they arrived. The theme of close and disciplined fire continued in the eyewitness accounts: 'Our two battalions of Guards, together with the two brigades of English ffoote ware come up, advanced upon the enemy who boldly bore down towards us, and having rec'd there fire without much damage, we gave them a merry salute, firing into there verry faces, the wch. they could not abide, but turned tayle and never faced more.'[38]

The theme of receiving the enemy's fire and getting close before returning fire and its effectiveness was clearly demonstrated here. The application of the controlled and disciplined nature of platoon fire was also described: 'Half our Army, immediately advanced on with undaunted Courage, and vigorously attack'd the Enemies Right Wing next to them, and most open, and elsewhere, with small Shot, as regular and gradual as the Time and Ground would permit.'[39]

Another description of the fighting at Oudenarde refers to a 'colour platoon', implying one central platoon, something not found in the platoon firing of Mackay or Douglass where the platoons were evenly divided between two wings.[40] The explanation for this and details of the way the new firings were organised were to be found in Ireland.

Following the winter spent training the infantry in Ghent Lieutenant General Richard Ingoldsby had been appointed as commander-in-chief in Ireland. There he found the troops 'very defective in their discipline, especially the foot' and consequently, as Robert Parker records, Ingoldsby wrote to Marlborough requesting that Parker be sent to Ireland 'in order to introduce among them the discipline practiced in Flanders'.[41] Parker had been the adjutant of the Royal Irish Regiment and consequently responsible for the training of his regiment. It was particularly appropriate for Parker to be summoned as Ingoldsby was the colonel of the Royal Irish. Moreover, some years later the regiment's then major and acting lieutenant colonel, Richard Kane, wrote: 'The Regiment of Foot that I serv'd in, is well known by the Title of the Royal Regiment of Ireland, from which Regiment I may without Vanity say, our British Infantry had the Ground-work of their present Discipline.'[42] This combination of circumstantial evidence, Ingoldsby's training initiative in Ghent, his choice of Parker and Kane's remark, suggests that it might have been in the Royal Irish that the use of firings was first developed. Moreover, as Parker seems from the following letter to have been instrumental in devising drill it is possible that he was the officer responsible for the idea.

On 13 September 1708 Parker wrote from Dublin to Lieutenant Colonel Sterne, acting as colonel of the Royal Irish in Ingoldsby's absence.

Dear Coll°

I have been labouring hard wth ye two Regim^{ts} in Town in showing them & ye ajud^{ts} our fireings, the Gen^{ll} is come from his progress & will see these Regim^{ts} perform in a day or two after which I shall be going for Corke and when ever the wether permits I must be wth ye Regim^{ts} there & at Kinsale.

According to yor directions I brought the Gen^{ll} to consent to our Marching in four Grand divisions and I have undertaken to form ye Square on ye March which is done in half ye time you are drawing up ye Bat^l . . . [at this point Parker gives a lengthy and detailed description of forming square on the march]. I thought fitt to let you know what I have don in this affair that I might have an opinion of you & ye Major on it.[43]

As already shown, the infantry in Flanders were taught the new exercise and firings by training the adjutants and NCOs first. Parker's letter shows that much the same process was followed in Dublin and it is tempting to suggest that it might have been him that carried out the training in Ghent. As Ingoldsby needed to bring Parker to Ireland to introduce the troops there to Flanders' practice, it suggests that Flanders' practice was developed in isolation in theatre in Flanders, that it was not written or published, and that it was developed and transmitted by word of mouth. This is not surprising as the British regiments in Flanders were not rotated in and out of theatre as they are today, thus there was no opportunity for the new firings to be transmitted from regiment to regiment through the army. Furthermore, the close proximity of the British regiments in Flanders to each other meant that everything could be achieved by word of mouth and there was no need for written instructions. There was certainly no published manual of the period that described the new organisation of platoons into firings. It was even possible that Parker did not have his own written version, or, even if he did, that the drill was transmitted by instruction and demonstration rather than by being copied. Houlding has suggested that the drill was copied in manuscript; however, this seems not to have been the case.[44] Parker described how 'in order to introduce among them the discipline practiced in Flanders . . . I continued two years disciplining the Foot of that Kingdom, in which time all the Regiments of Foot passed through my hands.'[45] It is clear that he instructed them directly.

Fortunately it is possible to examine in detail what the new drill was and how the new firings were organised as two manuscript versions of the drill survived. One had a first page that was headed 'The Exercise of Firelock and Bayonet with the sev[ll] Fireings of the Foot as they are to follow Each other according to the method appointed by his Ex[cie] Lieu[t] Gen[ll] Ingoldsby'.[46] The other has no such heading and is superficially different, but in substance it is exactly the same, which further supports the idea that this drill was not copied from a master manuscript, but rather that each officer took his own notes on the new drill.[47] The first bears the name of Bryan Mahoney who was an ensign and subsequently a lieutenant in Mountjoy's regiment until placed on half pay on the Irish establishment when that regiment was disbanded in 1714. The second bears the name of a Captain John Foster of Dulwich, who it has not been possible to identify.

Mahony's manuscript began with the exercise or drill for handling a musket and bayonet, or the manual exercise as it was known, listing each drill movement and how many individual movements each was comprised of. These movements were the same, with minor variations in wording, as those given in Foster's manuscript and in a publication titled: *The New Exercise of Firelocks & Bayonets; Appointed by his Grace the Duke of Marlborough to be used by all the British Forces*. This was not an official publication, but was stated to be 'By an Officer in Her Majesties Foot

Figure 5.1: A Battalion of infantry according to Mahoney's Manuscript

3(G)	1	2	1	2	1	2	3	2	1	2	1	2	1	3(G)
1	1	1	3	3	5	5	3	6	6	4	4	2	2	2

Front

Source: Cornwall Record Office, DD.R.H.839.

Guards' and was published in London in 1708.[48] It was also limited to the manual exercise and did not deal with the firings.

The key sections in both Mahony's and Foster's manuscripts were their descriptions of the organisation of a battalion into platoons and firings and how firing was to be carried out. Mahony provided a diagram that clearly shows a central or colour platoon, see figure 5.1.

Each box represents one of the fifteen platoons that a battalion was now to be divided into. The grenadier company was still divided into two platoons that took their places on the flanks of the battalion, indicated in the diagram above by (G). The hat companies were divided into thirteen platoons. The fifteen platoons were then divided into three firings, the first and second of six platoons each and the third of just three. The upper number in each box indicates the firing that a platoon was in. The lower number in each box indicated the order of firing of the platoons within each firing. Thus when the first firing fired the platoon marked 1 over 1 fired first, followed by the platoon marked 1 over 2 from the other flank of the battalion. Next came 1 over 3, then 1 over 4, 1 over 5 and finally 1 over 6. The second and third firings followed in the same manner. There was a slight difference in the way the grenadier platoons fired as they were to wheel 45° towards the centre so that their fire was directed more towards the centre of the enemy line. If firing on the march or advancing, the whole battalion was to halt when the platoons fired. If the battalion was retreating then the whole battalion halted and faced about while the platoons of a firing delivered their fire. The effect of this new method was that the firing of the platoons was more evenly distributed across the front of a battalion, as the first two firings consisted of almost every other platoon. In addition there were always at least three platoons loaded at any time, those of the smallest, third firing and because those were on the flanks and in the centre it maximised the protection they could give to the other platoons.

The most significant aspect of the new firings, however, was that rather than only firing in turn all the platoons in a firing could fire together in a single volley. Six platoons together represented in excess of 40 per cent of the firepower of a battalion. This could be followed very quickly by a second firing of the same size and even the smaller third firing, 20 per cent, was on a par with a rank of a French infantry battalion. Furthermore, due to the sustainability of platoon firing, this small third firing could be followed by the first firing again with another 40 per cent of the available firepower and so on. This sustainability was in part a product of the changes that had taken place over the preceding fifteen years or so as flintlock replaced matchlock and cartridge replaced bandoleer, leading to much quicker reloading.

As a variation on the above the commander of a battalion could choose to keep in the reserve the front ranks of the first and second firings. The reserved front ranks were then fired after the second firing. This would give four firings of approximately 27 per cent, 27 per cent, 26 per cent and 20 per cent. The orders for loading and firing continued to be 'make ready', 'present' and 'fire' but the distance between ranks for loading was reduced to a single pace from two. This reduction in space was probably the result of the abandonment of the matchlock and bandoleer making the loading process less risky. The benefit of it was that it further reduced, albeit slightly, the time taken to load, as the third rank now only needed to take two paces back instead of four.

A reduction in the reloading time of the few seconds it took to take two steps backwards may not seem very significant. However, when combined with the benefits of the changes in weapons and equipment it is what allowed a battalion to keep up a continuous fire based on three firings rather than the four platoons required by Mackay. This increase in the rate of fire increased a battalion's firepower by a third.

The effectiveness of the new firings was demonstrated at Oudenarde, while at the battle of Malplaquet in 1709, the fourth of Marlborough's great victories against the French, the British infantry demonstrated that they had not lost any ability when hand-to-hand combat rather than shattering volleys was required.[49] The fighting in the wood of Taisnières was described by Sergeant John Wilson:

[We] attacked the Enemy in the wood afores'd with a great deal of courage and resolution but were received by the Enemy with as great bravery. Wee beat them from that post and they beat us back again with as great courage and resolution as wee had them. Whereupon ensued an obstinate engagem't for the space of two hors in which there was a great effusion of blood on both sides; the Armys fireing at each other bayonet to bayonet. And after came to stab each other with their bayonets and several came so close that they knocked one another's brains out w'th the butt end of their firelocks.[50]

It was, however, at Malplaquet that a most remarkable event occurred, which gives perhaps the clearest evidence of the superiority of British platoon firing over French fire by ranks. Robert Parker of the Royal Irish Regiment was not a participant in the battle of Malplaquet, being at the time in Ireland, but he has left a most vivid account, presumably garnered from fellow officers. The regiment was the last British regiment to arrive on the battlefield and found itself in a relatively isolated position of the extreme flank of the army, opposite the wood of Sart. As the army advanced and the Royal Irish marched through the wood they found themselves in a clearing and confronted by a single French battalion. No other troops were involved in what followed.

Upon this Colonel Kane, who was then at the head of the Regiment, having drawn us up, and formed our Plattoons, advanced gently toward them, with the six Plattoons of our first fire made ready. When we had advanced within a hundred paces of them, they gave us a fire of one of their ranks: Whereupon we halted, and returned them the fire of our six Platoons at once; and immediately made ready the six Plattoons of our second fire, and advanced upon them again. They then gave us the fire of another rank, and we returned them a second fire, which made them shrink; however they gave us the fire of a third rank after a scattering manner, and then retired into the wood in great disorder: On which we sent our third fire after them, and saw them no more.[51]

This was a textbook action on the part of the Royal Irish. They closed with the French and did not fire until the French had. The French were clearly adhering to their usual practice of firing by ranks and the Royal Irish replied with whole firings. When Parker's regiment advanced they discovered that the enemy battalion had been the French Royal Regiment of Ireland. The British battalion had suffered four killed and six wounded while the French battalion lost 'near forty' killed and wounded. Parker gave an explanation for this victory and the disparity in casualties:

> The advantage on our side will be easily accounted for, first from the weight of our ball; for the French Arms carry bullets of 24 to the pound: Whereas our British Firelocks carry ball of 16 only to the pound, which will make a considerable difference in the execution. Again, the manner of our firing was different from theirs; the French at that time fired all by ranks, which can never do equal execution with our Plattoon-firing, especially when six Plattoons are fired together. This is undoubtedly the best method that has yet been discovered for fighting a Battalion; especially when two Battalions only engage each other.[52]

This extensive and detailed account contained a wealth of information, but has also been subject to some misunderstanding. Parker stated that the first and second firings of the Royal Irish consisted of six platoons. It has been assumed by Chandler, Nosworthy and others that the third firing also consisted of six platoons and that this event represented a clear example of platoon firing as described by Kane.[53] It is clear from the manuscripts of Mahony and Foster that the third firing would have been only three platoons. Three firings of six platoons each was a much later development, before which, as will be shown, there was a reduction to only fourteen platoons. Finally, in an echo of Mackay, the third firing was fired as the enemy broke and ran.[54]

Parker describes the battalion advancing on the enemy and not firing until fired upon, each rank fired by the French Irish being replied to with all the platoons of a firing giving fire together. He is clear in his view of the superiority of platoon firing over firing by ranks, which is perhaps not surprising as each French rank that fired, representing 20 per cent of the battalion, was replied to by a firing of 40 per cent of the Royal Irish. He also makes a very interesting comment about the relative effectiveness of British and French muskets. Edward D'Auvergene made a similar comment in his account of the campaign of 1692: 'Of the wounded a vast many dy'd afterwards, because our arms are stronger, and carry better balls than theirs.'[55] Undoubtedly a heavier musket ball travelling at the same velocity as a lighter one will inflict the greater damage. However, there are a number of other factors at play that determine the ballistic characteristics of a musket shot, such as the size of the charge of powder, the strength of the powder and the quality of the musket barrels, which would need to be considered in evaluating Parker's claim and which fall outside this work. But whatever the reason, there would appear to have been a belief that individual British musket shots caused more damage than French ones. If this belief was shared by the French it could have had a serious, deleterious effect on their morale. A hint that this might have been the case is found in Chandler, who cites a French dispatch after the battle of Steenkirk that reported French soldiers throwing away their matchlocks and taking up captured flintlocks.[56] That, however, could be because of the superiority of the flintlock to the matchlock firing mechanism rather than a superior ballistic performance.

The new system of firings was not without its problems. These arose when a battalion had to form a hollow square as a defence against cavalry. This required the grenadiers to be divided into four platoons and the rest of the battalion to be divided into four grand divisions of equal size that were divided in turn into four platoons each. This was relatively straightforward for the grenadiers, but the hat companies had to be reorganised from thirteen platoons into sixteen. This problem was touched upon in Parker's letter of 13 September 1708; however it is not clear if he is writing about four grand divisions being made the norm or just used on the march.[57] Each grand division formed a side of the square and became a firing of four platoons. The grenadier platoons either stayed outside the square and covered the corners or marched in and out of the square to fire, the right-hand platoon of each face, called the angle platoon, acting as a sort of gate for them. A square could be formed either from the battalion in line or on the march with the four grand divisions marching in column, one behind the other. This last manoeuvre as described in Mahony's manuscript is the same as that apparently devised by Parker. Once the square was formed the battalion commander had a number of options when it came to firing. First the angle platoons marched forwards while the grenadiers outside the square fired. They then marched into the square behind the angle platoon while it fired, before returning to its place. After that the other three platoons in each firing fired, the right-hand one first, then the left and lastly the centre one. As a variation on this the fire of the front ranks could be reserved. Alternatively, the three platoons of each firing could fire together by ranks, starting with the rear rank, followed in turn by the angle and grenadier platoons firing their three ranks together.

Given the complexity of two different arrangements of a battalion into platoons it is perhaps no surprise that British infantry battalions appear to have preferred to face French cavalry head on. At Malplaquet Matthew Bishop described what happened when his battalion was threatened by French cavalry; 'Then we had orders to wheel to the right. Had we not the French Horse would certainly have fallen upon our Rear. This happened at the Ground where we first made our Attack. But when we faced them, they backed their Horses as fast as they could.'[58]

Foster's manuscript book also contained a revision of drill issued by Lord Orkney on 23 October 1711 because 'For the better Regulating of her Maj[ties] Foot his Grace the Duke of Marlborough has thought fit I should give out the following orders.' Orkney's orders included the manual exercise, which contained minor changes, mostly in the wording of commands, the 'Evolutions', described as being 'according to the Explainat[n] in K W[ms] Book of Exercise', various regulations for garrison duty and the like and a new method of organising the firings.[59] A diagram showed twelve hat platoons and two of grenadiers: see figure 5.2.

Figure 5.2: A battalion of infantry after 1711, according to Foster

11(G)	1	7	3	9	5	13	14	6	10	4	8	2	12(G)
3	1	2	1	2	1	3	3	1	2	1	2	1	3

Front

Source: BL Add Mss 29477, f. 117v – 107r.

The first firing was composed of the platoons numbered 1 to 6, using the upper number, the lower number indicating the first firing. The second firing was platoons 7 to 10 and the third firing was the grenadier platoons, 11 and 12, and platoons 13 and 14 in the centre. The orders stated 'You fire your Platoons Right and Left as usual', referring to the order of firing within each firing.[60] The orders do not go into any detail about the different ways of managing the fire of the firings and the platoons, so it would seem that these remained unchanged.

This method represents an improvement on the previous method for a number of reasons. Firstly, this organisation meant a return to each company also forming a platoon, except for the grenadiers, which can only have simplified matters and made command and control easier. Secondly and most obviously, it is a lot easier to form a square as the twelve line platoons are simply divided into four grand divisions without the need to reorganise the platoons. Once the square was formed the grenadiers still marched in and out to fire, the three platoons on each face of the square formed a firing and fired in the order of the right-hand platoon first, then the left-hand one and finally the centre one. The third improvement was that fewer platoons meant bigger platoons. The first firing of six platoons represented almost half the battalion while the other two firings were roughly a quarter each. This meant that the all-important first firing was slightly bigger than before while the second firing was about a third smaller. The third firing was also larger than before, but two of its four platoons were the grenadier company divided in two, so it was still smaller than the second firing. In percentage terms the strengths of the firings were approximately 46 per cent, 31 per cent and 23 per cent.

The orders for the garrison of Ghent issued by Major General Cobham in 1712 contain no changes to the organisation and execution of firing; he did, however, include in the orders some illuminating observations about firefights:

All Commanding Officers must take great care when they march a Batt^n to attack an Enemy, to be moving so slow that their men may be in good ord^r & not out of breath when they come to Engage, they must always manage their fire well, & never begin to fire till they are very near it being very certain it is better to receive an Enemy's fire than fire at two [*sic*] great distance.[61]

Cobham emphasised the importance of a steady advance and of getting close to the enemy before firing, even if it meant receiving the enemy's fire. On the subject of dealing with cavalry attacks he advised that whether in square or line it was best to reserve the fire of the front rank while the second and rear ranks fired by platoon. The fire of the front rank was to be delivered at close range, 'a well managed fire at 30 or 40 paces distance will make their front rank not only stop short, but fall into confusion upon those which follows.'[62]

Cobham also gave details of a rather fanciful way of forming a battalion six deep into a total of twenty-eight platoons. His comment on this was telling. 'These sorts of figures are very handsome in exercise & very useful for ye instruction of soldiers, & it may happen may be of great use sometimes.' He followed this with his observations on what he considered practical on the battlefield.

I have seen much pains & trouble in firing Platoons advancing, & retreating but such will never happen, but at Exercise for it was never Done on real service but a Batt^n formed this way is ready to march either backwards or forwards together, if you beat ye enemy you can't overtake them in good order without ye fear of being flank't, & if they will beat you all the Precaution imagineable will not hinder some Confusion so as to put you by order so that fireing as it's call'd maintaining ground, & very quick is ye real service done by Platoons, & let ye maner & form of making Plattoons be never so convenient & handsome, quick firing & maintaining ground is ye real service of it, & indeed on all occasions to teach men to fire quick & sure is the best Exercise, not but all figures composed Handsomely shows a genious fill for great matters, it is very commendable in every offic^r & will meet with the applause of all men, & will enable those men to make enquiry into further matters that will at least make them great.[63]

Taken together with his comment about not firing at 'two great distance' this represented a clear statement of British doctrine for infantry combat as it had developed during the previous two decades. It amounted to getting in close, thirty paces or less, before one fired, fire quickly and accurately, hold one's ground and keep firing. Stated thus it was a simple doctrine, albeit one that was complex in execution. That it worked is clear from the success of British infantry on the battlefield. Sustained fire won the day at Wynendael in the face of a numerically superior enemy and kept another numerically superior French force bottled up in Blenheim. The short, sharp bursts of fire delivered at Oudenarde quickly decided the firefights in favour of the British infantry. Confidence in its firepower also allowed British infantry to face and see off French cavalry without resorting to forming square, as at Blenheim and Malplaquet.

There is no doubt that Marlborough was one of the finest generals of his day and one of the best ever produced by Britain. All his skill and talent in planning and manoeuvre would, however, have counted for nothing if his infantry had not been able to win the firefights and drive off enemy cavalry. That they could do so, frequently in the face of a numerically superior enemy, was due to the adoption of and adherence to platoon firing. Employed at often brutally close range, it simply overwhelmed the opposition with its weight of fire. Combined with continuing ferocity in hand-to-hand combat, British infantry under Marlborough became arguably the finest in Europe.

Chapter 6

Humphrey Bland and the Duke of Cumberland, 1714 to 1749

Following the battle of Malplaquet in 1709 and the end of the War of the Spanish Succession in 1714 the British Army was not involved in another major battle until Dettingen in 1743. During the intervening three decades there were minor engagements and campaigns, most notably against the Jacobites in 1715 and 1719. Mostly, however, the army was engaged in peacetime soldiering and its levels of readiness and competency, its fitness for service, suffered accordingly.[1] It was also a period during which little of any substance appeared to change in the way that the British infantry would fight, battalions would still form their companies into platoons organised in three firings. What changes there were, however, whilst subtle, would have both positive and negative effects on the effectiveness of the infantry in battle.

It was a time when professional British soldiers started to put pen to paper for the first time since Orrery and Turner were published in the 1670s.[2] It was also when, in 1728, the first official drill regulations since the 1690s were published.[3] Taken together with the regulations, the works of Bland and Kane gave a picture of how British infantry, indeed the whole army, intended to fight battles.[4]

Accounts of battles became more numerous, allowing analysis of the way the British infantry conducted themselves during the War of the Austrian Succession, 1740 to 1748, and that home affair of the Jacobite Rebellion of 1745 to 1746. The manuscript of Lieutenant Colonel John La Fausille, written after the war, was the first example of a retrospective analysis of combat by a British officer and offered the opportunity for deeper understanding of what happened at Dettingen and Laffeldt and the doctrinal approach of the infantry.[5]

When writing about the tactics and doctrine of the British Army in the mid-eighteenth century modern historians invariably turn to Humphrey Bland's *A Treatise of Military Discipline*. Houlding describes it as being of 'commanding influence in the army'.[6] In the preface Humphrey Bland laid out his aims and his reasons for writing. He pointed out that there had been nothing written on the art of war by a British author for fifty years. He went on to say that as there were then so few old officers with experience of war he felt it necessary to write what he knew of military matters for those 'who are yet to learn'.[7] Bland's *Military Discipline* was thus a statement of how things were at the time of writing. It contained nothing that would be considered innovative by his fellow officers; if anything it looked backwards. It was also very comprehensive, which probably explains its widespread appeal at the time and its endurance.[8] For the historian it allows developments since the War of the Spanish Succession to be identified.

Prior to the publication of Bland the drill for handling, loading and firing the musket was simply referred to as the 'exercise of the firelock and bayonet'. In Bland this was, for the first time, referred to as the 'manual exercise', in order to differentiate it from the platoon exercise that then appeared. Prior to the introduction of the platoon exercise, possibly sometime around 1720, that part of the exercise of the firelock and bayonet that was concerned with loading could be carried out either move by move, with a separate command for each move, or by each soldier in his own time when the orders for loading and firing were reduced to 'make ready, present, fire'. The platoon exercise was intended specifically for the soldier loading in his own time. Most of the movements for these two exercises were the same, but there was one significant difference. In both exercises the soldier, having faced to the right of his unit, primed the pan of his musket with the musket pointed to the front of his unit and held level in the left hand at about waist height. With the manual exercise the soldier then faced to the front and brought the musket upright in a position known as 'recover'. He then faced to the left and brought the musket down, holding it in his left hand with the butt down and the muzzle up near his right shoulder ready to insert the cartridge in the barrel. This was the movement known as 'cast about to charge'. After loading his musket the soldier would face to the front and come to the recover position again. In the platoon exercise, after priming, the soldier stayed facing to the right and simply rotated his musket in his left hand to bring the muzzle up to near his right shoulder where he could load the musket. It was effectively the same position as that for loading after casting about, but without the 180° turn to the left with the recover in the middle of it. This simple expedient cut the loading time by several seconds and also required less effort on the part of the soldier.[9] Curiously the official regulations issued in 1728, the year after the publication of Bland, made no mention of the platoon exercise. However, in the next official regulations, of 1756, the platoon exercise was the only way given of loading a musket.

In his instructions for the platoon exercise Bland also reintroduced locking, last seen in Mackay's *Rules*.[10] Bland observed that this avoided the awkward position of the middle-rank man having to stoop.

Bland goes into considerable detail on the organisation of platoons into firings. It is here that some difficulties begin to arise in identifying precisely how it was intended to organise a battalion for platoon firing in the 1720s. Lord Orkney's orders of 1711 had laid down an organisation of fourteen platoons.[11] At that time a battalion had one grenadier company and twelve hat companies, meaning that each hat platoon was made up of a single company while the grenadier company formed two platoons. Bland's *Military Discipline* included a diagram of a battalion drawn up that clearly showed that structure.[12] In 1717, however, the establishment of battalions in England had been reduced by one company. Despite this, an order book for Handasyde's regiment showed a battalion in 1723 still divided into two grenadier platoons and twelve hat platoons, see Figure 6.1.[13] This organisation was also shown in the 1728 regulations and meant that eleven hat companies had to form twelve platoons.[14] In Ireland the establishment was reduced to just nine hat companies in a battalion and the order book for Handasyde's, then serving in Ireland, also showed an eleven-platoon organisation, presumably in an endeavour to adhere to the more practical method of platoons and companies being the same, see Figure 6.2.

Early in his book Bland stated that the hat companies of a battalion should be divided into three grand divisions, each divided into three,

Figure 6.1: : A Battalion in 12 Platoons Besides Grenadiers Divided into four Grand divisions three Platoons in each Grand Division

1	3	1	2	3	4	2	4
3	1	2	1	2	1	3	3	1	2	1	2	1	3

Front

Source: National Army Museum, NAM6807.205.

Figure 6.2: The Method of Fireing a Battalion in 11 Platoons Including Granadiers in three Fireings

9(G)	1	5	3	7	11	8	4	6	2	10(G)
3	1	2	1	2	3	2	1	2	1	3

Front

Source: National Army Museum, NAM6807.205.

four or five platoons. With the grenadiers, as usual, divided into two platoons, this left the eleven hat companies to be divided into nine, twelve or fifteen platoons.[15] Subsequently, however, Bland provided diagrams for battalions formed with two grenadier platoons and ten, thirteen or sixteen hat platoons.[16] He then went on to write of his diagrams that they made everything clear and 'I believe there will want no further Explication for the Comprehending of it.'[17] Several pages later he adds that these plans are for battalions of four hundred, five hundred and six hundred men respectively, resulting in platoons of between thirty-three and forty-six men.[18] All of the organisations that Bland gives, bar one, are at odds with the contemporary organisations in the order book of Handasyde's and the 1728 regulations, both of which have twelve hat platoons.

This organisational variety is thoroughly confusing and difficult to make any sense of. However, Bland did write: 'The rule laid down in these Plans, for disposing the Platoons of the different Firings in the manner here mention'd, may be varied, if the Commanding Officer thinks proper.'[19] What Bland was giving the reader were examples, and within his writing were the principles that guided how battalions were to be divided into platoons, according to circumstance. With regard to the size of platoons he wrote that they should not be fewer than thirty men, because less than that did not produce sufficient fire, or more than forty-eight because that was the most a single officer could manage.[20] This is entirely in keeping with his statement about the numbers of platoons varying according to the size of battalions. In this remark on command considerations he was harking back to the first half of the seventeenth century.[21] The 1728 regulations also suggested that other arrangements were possible when they stated: 'supposing the Battalion to be told off in fourteen Platoons, including two of Granadiers'.[22]

If Bland was confusing in his description of the various permutations of the organisation of platoon firing, he was clearer when he discussed practical tactics and doctrine. Here he came down firmly in favour of the use of four grand divisions and the dividing of a battalion's hat companies into twelve or sixteen platoons. As he wrote, if a battalion was divided into any other number of platoons it was necessary to reorganise the platoons before grand divisions and squares could be formed.[23]

Bland helpfully laid out the reasons why platoon firing, with the platoons of each firing distributed along the front of a battalion, was the best way to fire, giving four reasons. Firstly, it spread the fire of each firing across the enemy battalion. Secondly, if a battalion was attacked while some platoons were loading then the fire of no part of the battalion would be particularly weakened. His third reason is something of a reiteration of the second, which was that if the platoons of a firing were all together it would leave that section vulnerable while loading. Lastly he suggested that this way of firing 'makes the Exercise the more beautiful' and, rather more importantly, got the men used to having firing going on both sides of them without joining in themselves.[24]

In his descriptions of how to carry out platoon firing Bland wrote of the platoons both firing in turn within their particular firing and all the platoons of a firing firing together. As detailed in Mahoney's drill book he also had the grenadier platoons wheeling slightly inwards before firing.[25] After firing, the men were to reload without orders and, when finished, to bring their muskets to the shoulder, that is, held vertically against the left shoulder, the butt at about waist height. When advancing Bland had the whole battalion halt while each firing fired; likewise when retreating he had the whole battalion halt and face about while each firing fired. He also described an alternative way of firing advancing and retreating, which involved the battalion continuing to move while each firing fired and the men marching with their muskets at the recover position and at half cock. In this position the musket is held vertically in front of the body with the right hand at the trigger guard at about chest height. This was the position immediately before bringing the butt to the shoulder and levelling the musket to fire. Bland disliked this as it made it particularly difficult to stop the men firing out of turn. He wrote:

> In Advancing towards the Enemy, it is with great Difficulty that the Officers can prevent the Men (but more particularly when they are Fired at) from taking their Arms without Orders, off from their Shoulders, and Firing at too great a Distance. How much more difficult must it be to prevent their Firing, when they have their Arms in their Hands ready Cock'd and their Fingers on the Trickers.[26]

When it came to dealing with cavalry Bland advised the same way of firing, whether a battalion was in line or square, which was to keep the front rank in reserve and fire the second and rear ranks by platoons.[27] He went on to say, however, that because of the intervals in cavalry formations there was usually sufficient time for all a battalion to reload between individual cavalry attacks, in which case it was unnecessary to keep a reserve.[28] As with earlier writers he stressed the importance of not firing until close range, twenty-five or thirty paces, and also of being able to present, but not actually fire.[29] He also described how firing by ranks was executed, and dismissed it as old fashioned and a relic of the days when pikes were used, but made no mention of this still being the preferred method of the French Army.[30] Bland was confident of the infantry's ability to deal with cavalry and stated: 'If Foot could be brought to know their own Strength, the Danger which they apprehend from Horse would soon vanish; since the Fire of one Platoon, given in due Time, is sufficient to break any Squadron.' He continued in words that anticipated the battle of

Minden: 'one battalion of well-disciplined Foot may despise the Attacks of a whole Line of Horse.'[31]

When he wrote of how to engage enemy infantry Bland continued the long-held doctrine of reserving a battalion's fire until close range and after the enemy had fired. Unlike earlier writers, however, he spelt out this doctrine, rather than leaving it to be extrapolated from the evidence. He advised that the sight of seeing troops with their fire reserved still advancing on troops that had fired would often cause those who had fired to run away.[32] If the enemy also reserved their fire Bland advocated preventing them from firing by giving a battalion's fire and immediately charging them, under the cover of the smoke, with the bayonet. His belief was that the shock of the fire and the immediate attack would result in victory with 'a very inconsiderable Loss'.[33] Bland also included in his work a description of how Dutch infantry conducted platoon firing. The Dutch fired their platoons from the flanks to the centre, alternating between the right and left flanks, thus giving it its name of alternate fire. Bland describes how the Dutch used alternate fire while advancing towards the enemy, but reloaded so that when close to the enemy they could give them the fire of the whole battalion, 'as the English do'.[34] What was absent from Bland's work was any mention of sustained firefights. Within Bland's work there was an expectation that a single round of close-range fire from a battalion followed by an immediate attack with the bayonet would be sufficient to bring victory.

Brigadier General Richard Kane's book was not published until after his death. The writer of the preface says of Kane: 'With great Contempt he read some Books, which pretended to Teach the whole Military Art; and often assured his Friends, that those mean Performances provoked him, to attempt something on the same Subject, which, if not perfect, might be free from those gross Errors and glaring Absurdities, which abound in them.'[35] This may be a reference to Bland's *Military Discipline*; indeed it is difficult to think that it could refer to anything else for the simple reason, as Bland himself said, that there were no other books. Kane himself is also scathing of the 1728 regulations. After quoting its title in full he called it a 'poor performance'.[36]

Kane is particularly adamant concerning the division of a battalion into four grand divisions. This is, he wrote, 'the Groundwork of all our Performances, of which our *Martinet* gives but a faint Idea'.[37] Although

Bland wrote initially of dividing a battalion into three grand divisions he also wrote of four when it came to how to form a square. The 1728 regulations contain no mention at all of forming grand divisions, which makes it seem likely that Kane's 'Martinet' is a reference to the official regulations. These were drawn up by a committee of very senior and distinguished officers and approved by the king, George II, who took a great interest in his army. It is therefore perhaps not surprising that Kane's ideas were not published until after his death.

Kane was also flexible in the number of platoons to be formed by a battalion. His preferred number was sixteen hat platoons in addition to the grenadiers, but he also wrote that twelve was possible for a weak battalion, particularly one on a reduced peacetime establishment. He divided the platoons into three firings but as he considered it 'absolutely necessary' to have a reserve he held the front rank as a reserve or fourth firing, leaving the second and rear ranks to carry out the firings.[38] The front ranks of the two central platoons, however, were not reserved, but were to fire with the rest of their platoons. This was so that the battalion commander, out in front of the battalion, had somewhere safe to stand when the reserve fired.[39]

Kane insisted that all the platoons of a firing should fire together and not one at a time, according to their order in a firing, which he describes as normal practice at reviews: 'they are not to keep popping by single Platoons.'[40] He required the full weight of six platoons' fire to be delivered together.[41] Kane described how the simultaneous firing of six platoons scattered along a battalion frontage could be achieved by the battalion commander making use of drum beats to transmit commands. The

Figure 6.3: A battalion in eighteen platoons according to Kane

| 3G | 1 | 2 | 1 | 2 | 3 | 1 | 2 | 3 | 3 | 2 | 1 | 3 | 2 | 1 | 2 | 1 | 3G |

Front

Key: G=Grenadiers, 1=1st firing, 2=2nd firing, 3=3rd firing

Source: Kane, Campaigns, *pp. 111–13.*

— 102 —

platoon officers and sergeants were simply to ensure their men acted as ordered by the battalion commander. In particular he mentioned ensuring that the soldiers 'level well their Arms, so that their Fire may have Effect on the Enemy'.[42] Kane does seem to suggest that extended firefights might be necessary; describing the battalion going through its firings, he wrote: 'And thus the Colonel continues his Firings standing, without Intermission between them.' If the enemy were not broken by that fire he wrote that the battalion should be advanced closer by the commander who then 'continues his Firings as fast as he can, until he obliges them to give Way'.[43]

Like Bland, Kane writes that infantry in line fighting cavalry should fire by platoons, but in contrast to Bland Kane wrote that when in square each side of the square was to fire by ranks.[44] Unfortunately he did not explain his reasons for his preference. Kane also completely omits any mention of the bayonet in attack or defence. Another officer writing in 1744 deliberately omits anything on firings, writing that they 'have long ago been very clearly and fully laid down by Mr. Bland', but mentions firing by ranks as one way of firing.[45] Despite the comprehensive nature of Bland it would seem that there was still a considerable amount of variety of opinion over the details of how a battalion of infantry should fight. This was not helped by the brevity of the 1728 regulations, which would have left officers with no alternative but to consult Bland on the finer points of drill. What is clear is that the underlying principal of close-range firing by platoons organised into firings and the subsequent assault with the bayonet against infantry, if necessary, was still the basis of the way British infantry intended to fight.

A further change to the process of loading and firing made its first appearance in the 1740 edition of the 1728 regulations. Until then, officially at least, muskets had been primed from a small flask before a cartridge was opened and loaded into the barrel. The 1740 edition allowed for the musket to be primed direct from a cartridge, thus saving valuable seconds in the loading process.[46] During the mid-eighteenth century wooden ramrods were gradually replaced by steel ramrods and despite some early problems with them bending or being too brittle and breaking they also seem to have speeded up the rate of fire.[47] Houlding suggests that these changes, combined with the platoon exercise, increased the rate of fire of the infantry from two to three rounds a minute.[48]

While Kane probably wrote his book around 1730 it was not published until 1745 and, although he shed a little light on the way British infantry were intended to fight, it was with Bland and the 1728 regulations to guide them that they embarked upon the War of the Austrian Succession.

La Fausille's manuscript, written around 1750–2, contained a considerable amount of information that cast light upon the battlefield practices of British infantry during the War of the Austrian Succession in a manner that a theoretical drill book could not. Not least he identifies the French contribution to British success. He first emphasised the importance of preventing 'the men from throwing away their Fire to no purpose, or at too great a distance, as our men, being then Novices, did at the Battle of Dettingen', explaining that the first discharge of fire in a battle is the one that does the greatest execution as it was properly loaded. As well as happening at Dettingen he added that long-range fire almost happened again at Fontenoy. He then stated that 'the French generally begin to Fire at a great distance.'[49] Amherst, later to be commander-in-chief in North America recorded that at Fontenoy the French opened fire at 'about 80 yards distance'.[50] Citing Laffeldt as an example, La Fausille described how the British infantry continued to advance, ignoring the French fire; the French then hurried to reload, doing so without using the ramrod, but simply dropping the open cartridge into the musket and then banging the butt on the ground to get the cartridge and ball to drop into the breech. The effect of loading in this manner, now commonly referred to as tap-loading, is that the balls do not travel far or with any great force – in fact, if the ball lodges in the barrel some way short of the breech, it can result in the barrel bursting. La Fausille added, 'this Preserved many of our men at the Battle of Laffelt.'[51] He then described how they advanced against the French, ignoring their fire, until they came up to the hedge and ditch in front of the French. The British then fired and 'leaping in among them immediately after it, thus struck them with such a terror, that they gave way'. He made the observation that British battalions were able to attack in this manner three times and lost fewer men than allied battalions who tried to rely entirely upon firepower to defeat the French.[52]

La Fausille observed that once an engagement had begun the pressure of combat 'rarely affords the men time to Prime, Load and Ram down their Cartridge properly'. That tap-loading was a common practice in British infantry regiments was clear from his advice on what to do after an enemy had been broken. First the battalion was to be put in order and then it was to 'fresh Prime, Load or Ram down the charge of such as are Loaded'.[53] Ramming tap-loaded charges and freshly priming muskets would have ensured that the battalion's next fire was as effective as any first fire: it was effectively starting again.

Bland also wrote about tap-loading in his manual, reinforcing that it was a common practice. He advised that loading quickly was facilitated by ensuring that the cartridges were made so that after being placed in the barrel a thump on the ground with the butt end of the musket would make them drop to the breech. Like La Fausille he did not greatly approve of it and listed his objections. First, if the barrel was dirty, the cartridge could stick part way down, risking the barrel bursting. Secondly the paper of the cartridge could get between the powder and the touch-hole. Thirdly, the power of the shot could be greatly reduced so that 'the Ball will either drop within two or three Yards, or not have Force enough to do much Execution.' He added that if the men 'are not press'd too close by the Enemy, the Ramming down of the Cartridge should not be omitted in Service'.[54]

Despite Bland's objections there are clear indications in order books that tap-loading was not only acceptable, but was planned for in the preparation of ammunition. An order of February 1743 to the British Army in Europe instructed that if any unit had balls too big for their muskets they were to hammer them 'on every side, to reduce them to such a size as they may go easily down in a Cartridge, allowing for the fouling of a piece by often firing'.[55] It would appear that, while the dangers of tap-loading and the benefits of properly loaded muskets were well understood, at short range the benefit of an increase in the speed of loading, and thus the rate of fire, outweighed any loss in effectiveness. Loading without using the rammer could have shortened the loading time by as much as half. This meant that the well-loaded first shots of the firings could be fired with shorter intervals between each firing as the first firing to fire would have reloaded in half the usual time. This would have increased the intensity of the firing and thus its effect on an enemy.

The first battle of the war, Dettingen, 1743, was also the last occasion upon which British troops were commanded in the field by their monarch, in this case George II. The British with their Hanoverian and Austrian allies were outmanoeuvred by the French and found themselves trapped between the river Main and forest-covered hills with the French in front, behind and across the river. Fortunately, errors by the French gave the British and their allies a chance to fight their way out when the French force blocking their march launched an unnecessary attack.[56]

It is generally stated that the platoon firing of the infantry pretty much fell apart with every man firing in his own time, despite which the British and their allies were able to achieve a notable victory over the French. The main source for this assertion is a letter from Lieutenant Colonel Russell of the Guards in letters to his wife.

> That the Austrians also behaved well is also true; that except one of their battalions which fired only once by platoons, they all fired as irregular as we did; that the English infantry behaved like heroes, and as they were the major part of the action, to them the honour of the day was due; that they were under no command by way of Hide Park firing, but that the whole three ranks made a running fire of their own accord, and at the same time with great judgement and skill, stooping all as low as they could, making almost every ball take place is true; that the enemy when expecting our fire, dropped down, which our own men perceiving, waited till they got up before they would fire, as a confirmation of their coolness as well as bravery, is very certain; that the French fired in the same manner, I mean like a running fire, without waiting for words of command, and that Lord Stair did often say he had seen many a battle and never saw the infantry engage in any other manner is as true.[57]

Russell is clearly stating that the British infantry did not fire by platoons as practised in Hyde Park. The London-based Guards' regiments drilled in Hyde Park and the term Hyde Park became synonymous with doing things strictly according to regulations. In another letter Russell wrote: 'our men and their regimental officers gained the day; not in the manner of Hyde Park discipline, but our foot almost kneeled down by whole ranks, and so fired upon 'em a constant running fire.'[58] He goes on to say that each man fired as an individual, and that Lord Stair stated that was what always happened in a battle. The extent to which this sweeping statement, which could be read as applying solely to the French, can be relied upon is open to question. Lord Stair had been the army's commander-in-chief until his position was usurped when George II took personal command and there is little doubt that Stair was sulking.[59] Similarly Russell was in no mood to pay compliments to the line battalions as the Guards had been with the rearguard of the army and saw no action. In fact Russell wrote to his wife that his view of the battle was from a hill two miles away.[60] More reliable are the accounts of those in the infantry who were directly involved, including a young James Wolfe with Duroure's regiment. He is clear on the point that his battalion and several others opened fire at far too great a range.[61] Colonel Duroure, acting as adjutant general, wrote that the British infantry fired 'not by Platoons but with perpetual Volleys from Right to Left, loading almost as fast as they fired without ceasing, so that the French were forced to retreat'.[62] La Fausille described how, once some battalions began to fire, firing broke out right along the line of British infantry even though in places the French were even out of cannon shot.[63] He also recounted how, when a battalion commander asked a general whether he should order his battalion to fire by platoons or ranks the general advised him to keep his men in good order, try to hold their fire to a very close range and he would be delighted to see either fire by platoon or ranks as he 'never did yet but on a Field day or at a Review'.[64] However, at least one British infantry battalion seems to have managed to fire correctly, by platoons, in firings. An officer in the Royal Welch Fusiliers described how they advanced to within sixty paces of the French before firing:

Our people imitated their predecessors in the late war gloriously, marching in close order, as firm as a wall, and did not fire till we came within sixty paces, and still kept advancing; so that when we had soon closed with the Enemy, they had not retreated: for when the smoak blew off a little, instead of being among their living we found the dead in heaps by us; and the second fire turned them to the right about, and upon a long trot.[65]

This describes the battalion continuing to advance after giving the first firing and on emerging from the smoke of their fire finding the French had taken heavy casualties. The battalion's second firing then caused the enemy to run. This feat was then repeated against three other French regiments, including a Guard's regiment that retreated before the fusiliers could fire. This officer was clear in his views about the reasons for the success of his regiment, emphasising the importance of getting close to the enemy before firing: 'What preserved us was keeping close order, and advancing near the enemy ere we fir'd. Several that popp'd at one hundred paces lost more of their men, and did less execution, for the French will stand fire at that distance, tho' 'tis plain they cannot look men in the face.'[66]

In his official report Colonel Duroure not only gave his account of what happened, but also made mention of how the infantry had been ordered to fight. It was 'judged that the whole fire had been given without Orders, against the Directions to preserve ours, and first to receive the Enemy's, then giving ours and charging with Bayonets'.[67] A clear statement that if Dettingen had been won by firepower alone that had not been the intention.

At Dettingen the French cavalry enjoyed an initial success against the British infantry. The French Household cavalry broke through the first line of British infantry, but did not cause it to retreat. Rather the words of Bland about the superiority of infantry over cavalry were vindicated when the grenadier company of Huske's 32nd, in the second line, held off the cavalry while the battalion finished forming.[68] Then, trapped between the first and second line of infantry, the cavalry were shot to pieces.

For events at Fontenoy in 1745 there is a French account of cavalry attacking British infantry. 'Our Cavalry, which advanced before them immediately, could not sustain the terrible Fire made by that Line of Infantry . . . Several of our Squadrons rallied, but were again repuls'd by the prodigious Fire of the Enemy's Infantry.'[69] Although Fontenoy was a defeat for the allied army under the Duke of Cumberland the British infantry more than held their own against both French cavalry and infantry.[70]

Following Dettingen the infantry had trained hard in their battalion firings, as shown by an order of 1 December 1744: 'The Regt which fired ball against the wall of ye Capuchin's near the Nonnen Bosh, are to do so no more, but to find some other place, if they have occasion to fire anymore.'[71] Whilst not a great deal of detail of the infantry battle at Fontenoy has come down to us, the notable exception to this is the firefight between the British and French Guards early on in the battle, when the benefits of such training were clear. Three battalions of British Guards were on the right of the first line of the British infantry attacking the French position. In an incident immortalised by Voltaire they came face to face with the French Guards, the Swiss Guards and the Regiment Courten. According to Voltaire, Lord Hay, a captain in the First Guards, stepped forwards and invited the French to fire first. A French officer responded, saying that they never fired first.[72] The truth, as related by Lord Hay, was more prosaic. He saluted the French, toasted them from his hip flask and told the French he hoped they would not swim the nearby Scheldt as they had the Main at Dettingen, a reference to their rout at that battle.[73] It is unclear who did fire first. Voltaire suggests that the French infantry were so stunned by the British fire that they did not fire at all.[74] An account in a British newspaper stated that the French fired first.[75] Whether they fired first or second the effect of the British fire was devastating. Voltaire says that the fire was by platoons and it seems most likely that the Guards fired twice by firings at a range of less than thirty yards. The total strength of the three guard's battalions at Fontenoy was approximately 1,970 rank and file, meaning that the French received approximately 3,900 rounds of musket fire.[76] Voltaire records this fire as causing a total of 912 killed and wounded, giving the Guards a hit rate of about 23 per cent.[77] By contrast the three battalions of Guards suffered a total of 736 killed and wounded for the whole battle.

British participation in the War of the Austrian Succession was interrupted by the Jacobite Rebellion of 1745 when Prince Charles Edward Stuart, with French support, landed in Scotland and raised a Scottish army to attempt to recover the Crown for his father. The eyewitness descriptions of combat that survive from that domestic affair allow a far more detailed analysis of how the British infantry fought than has so far been possible. From the beginning it was recognised that the threat posed by Highland forces was quite different from that of conventional European forces. Their tactics had been described by Lieutenant General Hugh Mackay who had been beaten by them at Killiekrankie.

> Their way of fighting is to divide themselves by clans, the chief or principal man being at their heads, with some distance to distinguish betwixt them. They come on slowly till they be within distance of firing,

which, because they keep no rank or file, doth ordinarily little harm. When their fire is over, they throw away their firelocks, and everyone drawing a long broad sword, with his targe (such as have them) on his left hand, they fall a running toward the enemy.[78]

Lieutenant General Henry Hawley wrote a similar account of the Highlander's tactics, adding that they normally formed four deep, with their best men in the front rank, but that by the time they reached their enemy they were twelve or fourteen deep.[79] The Duke of Cumberland added further detail when he gave his orders on how the Highlanders were to be fought. His orders explained that the object of the Highlanders firing 'at a distance' was to draw their enemy's fire, adding that after firing they lay down to avoid that return fire. This enabled them to charge home with swords against unloaded muskets.[80]

Mackay's attempts to overcome the Highland tactics ended in defeat.[81] Hawley's response was to advise firing by ranks, the fire directed at the centre of the attacking body of Highlanders, starting with the rear rank, but not firing until the range was 'ten or twelve paces'. He deemed it necessary to wait until the range was so short because the speed of the advance would prevent reloading. Cumberland's orders were more comprehensive as he allowed for the enemy advancing slowly as well as for the Highland charge. First he specified that a battalion must be in eighteen platoons. If the advance was slow he ordered that firing should be by half firings, that is three platoons at a time, in the case of a rapid advance the fire of the whole battalion was to be reserved until the range was ten or twelve yards. He makes no mention of firing by ranks, so it would seem the whole battalion was to fire together.[82]

The first infantry to meet the Jacobite army were those of the scratch force of Lieutenant General Sir John Cope at Prestonpans on 21 September 1745. A considerable amount is known concerning events at Prestonpans because there was a subsequent inquiry into the defeat of Cope's little army, although the main interest of the inquiry was the conduct of the senior officers, not the tactics employed. What is clear is that there was no attempt to fight the Jacobite army in anything other than a completely conventional way. The infantry was described as completely formed and having been divided into platoons and firings.[83] When the

Jacobites attacked first the dragoons broke and then the infantry gave what was described as ragged fire and also broke and ran.[84]

At the battle of Falkirk, 17 January 1746, the British army was led by Lieutenant General Hawley and, following the defeat of his cavalry, most of his infantry turned and ran in the face of the Highland charge and a raging storm with rain and sleet.[85] However, some detail is available of how the infantry battalions that did stand fought the Jacobites. In particular the description by a sergeant in Barrell's regiment described how the front rank knelt while the centre and rear rank fired continually.[86] This is confirmed by a private in Barrell's who referred to the battalion keeping a reserve, that is the front rank.[87] A description of the Royal Scots that appeared in a Dublin newspaper described them firing on attacking Highlanders, the rear rank first, then the centre rank and the front rank when the enemy were within a few paces. This was sufficient to repel the attack.[88] There is a suggestion that while the front rank was held as a reserve, the centre and rear ranks fired by platoon rather than whole ranks, but on the whole those battalions that stood appear to have adhered to Hawley's advice.[89]

Prior to the battle of Culloden the Duke of Cumberland assembled his army at Aberdeen. There the infantry were carefully trained for the forthcoming confrontation with the Jacobite army and the Highland charge in particular. On 2 April 1746 Cumberland ordered: 'The Royal North British Fuzileers to be out in the Park tomorrow at 11 o'clock there to practice the motions of alternate firings by platoons from ye right and left to ye centre reserving the fire of ye front rank & Grenadiers.' These were followed by the Royal Scots, Price's, Barrell's and 'Every Regiment to take their turns afterwards.'[90] This method of firing was a departure from the normal practice of firing by platoons organised into firings. In some ways this was similar to what Bland advised for dealing with cavalry, with the front rank reserved, but alternate firing was something that he advised against. He described the way the Dutch conducted alternate firing when advancing and although he thought it could be very effective against a stationary enemy he considered it to be vulnerable to a sudden counter-attack while the platoons were reloading. He emphasised that it was necessary for a battalion firing in this manner to advance slowly, 'to give the Men Time to load their Arms before they approach too near the Enemy'.[91] This would seem to make it unsuitable as a method of dealing with the fast-advancing Highlanders.

However, the suggestion that a battalion could be left vulnerable while men reloaded also indicates that the whole fire of a battalion could be delivered very quickly in this manner, something that would be desirable against Highlanders closing quickly. Should that fire not stop an attack then the fire of the reserved grenadiers and front rank could be delivered at a range of only a few yards. This intention of delivering the maximum available fire in a short time at close range is borne out by a passage in a contemporary history of the rebellion that described the infantry at Culloden as firing 'according to Orders, viz. the 2d and 3d Rank, as they were within 30 Yards, and the 1st, just as they were at the Muzzles of their Guns'.[92]

In addition to a different form of firing the infantry also received instruction in a new way of using the bayonet. From its introduction the bayonet had been treated in the same manner as the pike and for combat it was held in exactly the same manner as the 'charge for pike' position. The soldier turned his body to the right with the musket held horizontally under the chin across the chest. The left hand supported the musket under the chin while the right arm was fully extended and the right hand held the musket butt. Drill for fighting with the bayonet was limited to simply thrusting the musket forward, bringing the right hand to the right shoulder and extending the left arm, all with the musket held horizontally at shoulder level. It would seem improbable that soldiers in hand-to-hand combat only plied their bayonets in this manner and it is possible that this lack of drill, when compared to the extensive instructions for musketry,

Figure 6.4: Platoon Firing at Culloden

G	1	3	5	7	9	11	13	15	16	14	12	10	8	6	4	2	G

Front

Front rank and Grenadiers held in reserve; second and third ranks of platoons firing in the sequence indicated from the flanks to the centre might be partly responsible for the idea that firepower was more important than the bayonet. However, the amount of instruction required for an activity is not necessarily an indication of its relative importance.

The drawback with this drill when fighting a Highlander armed with a sword in the right hand and a targe on the left arm was that any thrust with the bayonet was easily caught on the targe and the musket was also easily knocked aside by the targe, leaving the back of the soldier exposed to the sword. The solution to this problem was simple and introduced by the Duke of Cumberland: 'his Highness took the pains to confer with every Battalion of Foot, on the proper Method of using the Musket and Bayonet to Advantage against the Sword and Target.'[93] He simply instructed the soldiers to reverse the position so that they faced to the left of their unit with the right hand under their chin and their left hand on the musket butt. The intention was that any thrust with the bayonet would then tend to come at a Highlander's exposed right side instead of the left that was covered by the targe.[94] Although Cumberland is usually credited with devising this drill, it is described in an article in the *Gentleman's Magazine* for January 1746.[95]

Cumberland's army came face to face with the Jacobite army of Charles Edward Stuart on Culloden Moor on 16 April 1746. What followed was Cumberland's army simply, efficiently and professionally going about its business, particularly the infantry. The Jacobite army was organised in two lines, the front consisting of the Highland units, with the Lowland units and French regulars in the second line. It was the Highlanders in the front line that attacked, moving forward in three large bodies. The body which moved towards Cumberland's right flank did not make contact. Three times it advanced, trying to provoke the infantry into firing too soon, but, as Cumberland wrote in a letter to Lord Loudon: 'On our right tho they came on with great fury, our Men did not take their firelocks from their shoulders tho they advanced three times within less than an hundred yards of us.'[96] It was also probable that the Jacobites were inhibited by the presence of three squadrons of cavalry on that flank.

On the other side of the battlefield the other two bodies of Highlanders coalesced into one single mass that struck the battalions of Barrell and Monro. Because of the surviving accounts and an accurate list of the strength of Cumberland's army it is possible to examine in some detail the combat that ensued.

Barrell's regiment took the brunt of the Highland charge. The strength of Barrell's that day was 373, all ranks, of whom 325 were carrying muskets in the three-deep platoons.[97] At this time infantry battalions consisted of nine hat companies and one grenadier company. Given the low strength of Barrell's, it is probable that it was organised into a total of twelve platoons, giving a platoon strength of twenty-seven men.[98] This would mean that the centre and rear ranks of the ten hat platoons contained 180 men and the reserve had 145 men. If they fired as related, the platoons would have commenced firing at thirty yards in what one eyewitness described as a 'running fire', followed by the reserve who 'received them with their fire upon the Points of their Bayonets'.[99] They appear to have only fired once before the Highlanders reached them, a total of 325 rounds.

Monro's regiment was the largest battalion on the field with a total strength of 491 men and 426 men in the platoons.[100] An account by a corporal in the regiment states: 'we fired at about 50 yards Distance ... they still advanced, and were almost upon us before we had loaden again. We immediately gave them another full fire.'[101] This probably means that the platoons of the centre and rear ranks fired twice, almost certainly tap-loading to get in a second round, followed by the reserve. Thus 236 men fired twice and 190 fired once, a total of 662 rounds. The corporal of Monro's continued that 'the Front Rank charged their Bayonets Breast high, and the Centre and Rear Ranks kept a continual Firing ... most of us having discharged nine Shot each.'[102] Monro's suffered a total of eighty-two killed and wounded in the battle, allowing for which the battalion could have fired approximately two thousand rounds at ranges well under fifty metres.

To the right of Monro's was Cambell's Royal Scots Fusiliers. Although not subsequently involved in hand-to-hand fighting, part of the Highland charge crossed its front. With 412 men in its platoons, and assuming its reserve did not fire, it is likely that it fired about 220 rounds at the Highlanders, if it only fired once. The initial fire received by the front of the Highland charge was probably in excess of one thousand rounds, many at point-blank range. The corporal of Monro's wrote that this 'made hundreds fall'.[103]

It was at this point that Cumberland's new bayonet drill came into play and numerous letters and accounts speak of its effectiveness. Cumberland himself wrote: 'our Men fairly beat them & drove them back with their

Bayonets & made a great slaughter of them.'[104] According to another account: 'the Soldiers mutually defended each other, and pierced the Heart of his Opponent, ramming their fixed Bayonets up to the Socket.'[105] Another eyewitness claimed: 'there being scarce one Soldier in Barreyl's Regiment who did not each kill several Men; and they of Monro's which ingaged did the same.'[106]

Some Highlanders passed around the left flank of Barrell's and between Barrell's and Monro's, overrunning two artillery pieces in the gap. Pairs of three-pounder cannon had been placed between the battalions in the front line and these undoubtedly added many casualties, the guns next to Barrell's firing their last shots of grape at only six feet.[107] The Highlanders who passed Barrell's then came under fire from regiments in the second line. Subsequently these moved forward to support Barrell's and Monro's. In particular Edward Wolfe's regiment marched to the left of Barrell's and placed itself at right angles to the front line where it commenced firing. The account of an officer of that regiment says that the battalion fired five or six times. The strength of the regiment was 324 in the platoons and if this firing was carried out with the front rank and grenadier platoons reserved it would have fired between nine hundred and one thousand rounds into the Highlanders at close range. Ligonier's, Bligh's and Sempill's regiments also added their weight to this fire with a total of 1,157 muskets in their platoons. There is no indication of how many rounds they fired, but if, like Wolfe's, they fired five rounds each that would have been another 3,200 rounds.

All in all it would appear that the Highlanders received between six and seven thousand rounds from the battalions of British infantry, many at ranges well under fifty metres. The strength of the Highlanders who attacked the British left-flank battalions was about 2,500.[108] According to the officer of Monro's left-flank grenadier platoon: 'we laid about 1,600 dead on the spot.'[109] The figures for rounds fired would seem to be reasonably robust, as the various sources are consistent. It would also seem that most, if not all, were fired at ranges under fifty metres and that a considerable proportion were fired at much closer ranges. The area where the greatest doubt is to be found is in the numbers of casualties actually inflicted by this fire. However, a return of approximately 1,600 casualties for six or seven thousand rounds is a hit rate of roughly 22–26 per cent, which is in keeping with the 23 per cent suggested for Fontenoy. Even if the casualty figure is high and includes casualties from other parts of the battlefield a figure of one thousand casualties still gives a rate of 14–16 per cent. It would be unwise to place too much reliance on these figures, but they do give an indication of the capability of British musketry to inflict high casualties at the short range that they seem to have preferred to engage at. Every soldier with a musket had twenty-four rounds at Culloden, yet Wolfe's battalion fired only five or six rounds a man.[110] It would seem most likely that they stopped firing because there was nothing left to fire at.

Following the conclusion of the Jacobite Rebellion the British Army returned to Europe and on 11 October 1746 was engaged with its allies in the battle of Rocoux. Contemporary accounts of this defeat at the hands of the French tell us nothing about how the British infantry fought, but do tell that they fought well.[111] On 2 July the following year the allied army was again beaten at Laffeldt.[112] On this occasion one detail in a letter from a British officer sheds a little light on infantry combat doctrine. The letter confirms La Fausille's statement that some British battalions attacked the French three times in the fight for possession of the village of Laffeldt. The officer gives the example of Wolfe's regiment to illustrate how the British battalions fought.

> Wolfe's Regiment carried into the field 24 rounds a man. This they made use of. Afterwards they had a supply of 8 rounds a man more. After this was spent, they made use of all the ammunition amongst the dead and wounded, both of their own men and the enemies. When no farther supply could be had, they formed themselves immediately to receive the enemy upon their bayonets, and being ordered to retreat did it with the utmost regularity.[113]

Wolfe's battalion was probably involved in trying to repel at least four French attacks on Laffeldt as the village repeatedly changed hands. With firing minimised in the assault it would appear that Wolfe's men fired in excess of thirty rounds each in defence or six or seven rounds a man against each French attack. This represents a considerable amount of sustained firing and paints a different picture to the short, sharp bursts of fire followed by the vigorous use of the bayonet that seem to have been the preferred method. It may be that the nature of this fighting, in and around a village – hedges are referred to in several accounts – forced the infantry into extended firefights. However, it clearly demonstrates that when necessary British infantry was capable of considerably extended periods of sustained fire.

Following the effective end of the war and while peace negotiations were in progress the Duke of Cumberland and the army were camped at Eindhoven. The organisation of firing was further developed and new instructions were issued on 27 August 1748. La Fausille recorded the form of these in a diagram, figure 6.5, and further details appear in a publication of 1757 that included Kane's works.[114]

According to these instructions a battalion was to be divided into two grenadier platoons and sixteen hat platoons. Although Bland, Kane and the 1728 regulations allow for other numbers of platoons according to the size of the battalion, the Duke of Cumberland was insistent on forming eighteen. As early as 17 May 1744 he had ordered all battalions to form sixteen subdivisions, eight half divisions and four grand divisions, besides the grenadiers.[115] In his first orders for fighting Highlanders he again stated that battalions were to form eighteen platoons.[116] This may have

Figure 6.5: Directions for Firings in Battalion by Platoons, Sub-Divisions & Firings given by HRH at Eyndhoven, August the 27th NS 1748

1	1	1	3	3	3	5	5	5	6	6	6	4	4	4	2	2	2
3	1	2	1	2	3	1	2	3	3	2	1	3	2	1	2	1	3
G	1		5		3		7		4		8		2		6		G
	1			2			3			4							

Front

Top line: firing by platoons, number in firing, (alternating right and left to the centre), over number of firing. Middle line: firing by sub-divisions, order of firing, alternates right and left with the right hand sub-division of each grand division first. Bottom line: battalion grand divisions (not used for firing).

Source: Cumberland Papers, Orderly Book Extracts, 2/2 f. 61v (M).

been fine for the battalions of Guards, in 1744 they averaged at about 660 men in each battalion, not far short of the establishment of seven hundred privates, giving thirty-six men to a platoon.[117] The relatively small size of line battalions, compared to the theoretical establishment, can be seen from the morning state of the battalions at Culloden, where the battalions averaged about 367 privates. Forming eighteen platoons would have given a platoon strength of twenty, far below what Bland recommended as a minimum.[118] In the case of Barrell's regiment this figure would have been eighteen, yet the commander of one grenadier platoon wrote that he 'had 18 men killed and wounded in my platoon'.[119] Furthermore, if the grenadier company accounted for a tenth of the battalion strength, as one of the ten companies, and formed two platoons, then eighteen men would have been the platoon size again. As the officer is clear that he had eighteen men killed and wounded in his platoon, and not that all of his platoon were killed or wounded, it suggests that, as recommended by Bland, the grenadier platoons had been supplemented by hatmen. This further suggests that the number of platoons was fewer than eighteen, as has been discussed above.

Prior to the directions issued in 1748 there was no suggestion that the subdivisions could be used as a fire unit, they were simply for manoeuvring. In the absence of any contemporary discussion of the development of the new directions the possibility arises that the new departure of using of subdivisions – that is, pairs of platoons – as firing units was to overcome the problem of platoons that were too small to be effective on their own. As before the platoons were divided into three firings, the platoons of which could either fire singly, one after the other, or all together in a whole firing. However, before these directions could be tested in battle the War of the Austrian Succession was concluded.

There is no doubt that platoon firing was not an easy procedure to execute effectively. This was clearly demonstrated at Dettingen, the British Army's first major battle in three decades. There, inexperience caused the infantry, described by La Fausille as novices, to open fire spontaneously at far too great a range.[120] Although the same thing nearly happened again at Fontenoy, from then onwards the infantry carried out their firing most effectively. That effectiveness was improved by a number of changes from the days of Marlborough. Locking up made firing easier for the men and may have improved accuracy as a consequence. The platoon exercise, priming from the cartridge and steel ramrods all contributed to shortening the loading time, which could be further shortened under pressure by tap-loading. Working against these improvements, however, was the change in battalion organisation that meant platoons and companies were no longer synonymous. However, in Europe the difficulties and complexities were overcome and the experienced infantry fighting there were able to realise the full potential effectiveness of their firepower.

The importance of experience was clearly demonstrated during the Jacobite Rebellion. Of the fifteen battalions at Culloden that destroyed the Jacobite army five battalions had been at Dettingen, another eight at Fontenoy and four had been at both. It was also experience that taught that it was better to brave the enemy fire and get close before firing and then closing with the bayonet than to give in to instinct and fire as soon as the enemy was in range. As La Fausille pointed out, it was the apparently more dangerous course of action that led to the fewer casualties.[121]

What is also clear from both the theory and the practice of British infantry combat doctrine during the War of the Austrian Succession is that it is still basically the same as that developed during the English Civil War. What was also demonstrated during the Jacobite Rebellion was that the infantry were capable of adapting the detailed execution of their doctrine to suit circumstances and the nature of a specific enemy, but that they did so without compromising the underlying principles of maximising short-range fire and following it with effective use of the bayonet. Nor should the importance of the bayonet be underestimated. Perhaps because of the small amount of attention paid to it in the drill books, modern writers appear to have missed the significance of its use and rather emphasised the infantry's commitment to firepower. That it was an essential element of the way the infantry fought is clearly stated by Duroure in his comment on how it had been intended to fight at Dettingen and La Fausille in his remarks on Laffeldt. What British infantry generally did not do was get into long, sustained firefights where fire alone would decide the outcome, though when necessary they were more than capable of it, as at Laffeldt.

Chapter 7

The Seven Years War in Europe

The mid-eighteenth century saw a considerable amount of theoretical consideration of the conduct of war and tactical doctrine. Authors such as Saxe, Folard and Santa Cruz wrote extensively on their theories of the best way to conduct war. In Europe the military successes of Frederick the Great resulted in the widespread imitation of all things Prussian, particularly in the art of war. In the Seven Years War, 1756–63, it also saw what has been described as the first worldwide war.[1] One consequence of this was that for the first time significant numbers of British soldiers found themselves fighting far from their habitual European campaigning grounds. Within Europe, however, the British Army was again pitted against the French. Amongst military historians, even British ones, the emphasis has been on studies of Frederick and his army. Studies of the British Army, in the European theatre, have been largely limited to biographies and narrative histories. In what little analysis there is of combat modern historians, such as McLynn and Black writing about Minden, have again credited its victories to the firepower of the infantry.[2]

In mid-eighteenth-century Europe the military debate on doctrine was between the advocates of *l'ordre profonde*, or columnar tactics, and those of *l'ordre mince*, or linear tactics. Supporters of the column believed in cold steel and shock tactics and included such writers and military theorists as the Spanish Marquis de Santa-Cruz and the French Chevalier de Folard.[3] Another influential figure was the very successful French general, Field Marshal Maurice, Comte de Saxe. His *Reveries* was published in English in 1757, following his death in 1750, although it had been written in 1732 under unusual circumstances.[4] Saxe had been extremely ill and suffering from a fever when he put pen to paper to counter the boredom of his illness. Saxe maintained, from personal experience, that infantry fire was largely ineffective, although he shared the belief that fire should be reserved until the enemy had fired first. His preference was for the combination of shock tactics and cold steel, with firepower in a supporting role rather being relied upon to provide victory.[5] Ironically he was subsequently an eyewitness to the terrible effectiveness of British infantry firepower at Fontenoy.

Following the War of the Spanish Succession there had been little development in France in infantry tactics and the method for delivering firepower remained unchanged. A form of platoon firing had been introduced in 1707, similar to the alternate form of platoon firing, but it was only used in defensive positions.[6] Much of the responsibility for this stagnation lay with the officer class.[7] Nosworthy has written that there was an 'attitude among the nobility making up the officer class. This was the belief that what was most important in an officer was valor and honor; if the troops were brave enough and led by a daring fellow, any situation could be won.'[8]

The French experience of British firepower in the War of the Austrian Succession, however, made a considerable impression. After Dettingen Marshal Noailes wrote to Louis XV: 'Their infantry was closed and held themselves brazenly, they conducted a fire so lively and so sustained that the old officers never had seen anything like it, and so superior to ours one could not make any comparison, this resulting from our troops being neither exercised nor disciplined as to be suitable.'[9]

While the French continued to believe cold steel was their métier they did take steps to improve the infantry's firepower. They began 'locking up' and levelling their muskets according to the range, and in 1750 three methods of delivering fire became regulation: fire by ranks, platoon fire and *billebaude*, or voluntary fire, where each soldier fired individually in his own time. Fire by ranks was finally abolished in 1753. During the Seven Years War, however, French infantry only occasionally managed to employ platoon fire, usually resorting to voluntary fire.[10]

Perhaps the most influential figure in the development of warfare in the mid-eighteenth century was Frederick the Great. Initially Fredrick was an exponent of shock action and cold steel, preferring his infantry to attack with the bayonet and without firing. However, during the course of the Seven Years War it was the Prussian infantry's ability to generate a considerable volume of fire that gained the attention and admiration of British officers. A Dutch officer wrote that the 'Prussians have certainly brought quick-firing to a greater degree of perfection than the troops of any other nation', but added that they did not rely on it and preferred the bayonet.[11]

Among the British admirers of the Prussian army's firepower was James Wolfe, who, at the beginning of the Seven Years War was the lieutenant colonel of the 20th Foot and effectively in command of it. An order of his from 1753 shows how British officers were determined to do what they could to improve the effectiveness of their battalions' firepower. At a review of the 20th and the 13th regiments the Duke of Cumberland had expressed the opinion that the 13th fired faster than the 20th. The colonel of the 20th, Lord Bury: 'Commanded that we practise the same platoon exercise that they do; for to the differences between their platoon exercise and ours, his lordship ascribes their superiority in this point . . . he desires we may begin to practise this platoon exercise as early as possible.'[12]

By the phrase platoon exercise Wolfe was referring to the process of loading a musket, rather than the manner of delivering fire. Regrettably his order did not explain what it was the 13th were doing that made them faster. It is possible that, as regulations often codified what had already been developed, this was a forerunner of the changes that would be brought in officially with the 1756 platoon exercise.

With the threat of a French invasion of Britain in January 1755 Wolfe wrote a set of instructions for the battalion on how it was to fight if the French landed. These included a clear allusion to the Prussian methods of firing; 'As the alternate fire by platoons or divisions, or by companies, is the most simple, plain and easy, and used by the best disciplined troops in Europe, we are at all times to imitate them in that respect.'[13] It is usually assumed that this is Wolfe the innovator at work, giving him the credit for the introduction of more effective Prussian ideas of delivering fire.[14] However, one of the captains of the 20th was the young Duke of Richmond. Richmond had travelled abroad before joining the army and had met Frederick the Great. Although Wolfe's military junior he was a person of considerable influence, being acquainted with the Duke of

Cumberland, with Henry Fox as his brother-in-law and later serving as aide-de-camp to Prince Frederick of Brunswick.[15] A clue that Richmond rather than Wolfe may have been behind the innovations introduced to the 20th is found in a letter from Wolfe to Richmond after the latter had become lieutenant colonel of the 33rd: 'I have great hope of your success in bringing about such reformations, as you think wanting in your Corps ... & as your Grace has seen & brought away many excellent things from the Armies upon the Continent, they may, by your help, become general among our Troops, & improve them.'[16]

Alternate fire, as has been shown, was used in the War of the Spanish Succession until superseded by the organisation of platoons into three firings. Cumberland had made use of alternate fire against the Highland charge at Culloden, but thereafter was insistent on the forms of firing laid down in 1748. Of these, firing by subdivisions came closest to alternate fire. However, instead of each subdivision firing in turn from the flanks to the centre, alternating between the left and right halves of a battalion, first the right-hand subdivision of each grand division fired from the flanks to the centre, alternating between the halves of the battalion, and then the left-hand subdivisions did the same.[17] There is no known explanation of exactly why Cumberland objected to alternate fire, but that he did was made clear in a letter he wrote when he heard that it was being practised by troops in 1757:

> I must desire that you will acquaint Sir John Ligonier, for the Army in general; & to all General officers commanding Corps, Sir John Mordaunt not excepted, that I am surprised to hear that my orders as to the Fireing and Posting of the officers, approved & confirmed by His Majesty, are changed according to the Whim & Supposed Improvements of every fertile Genius; and that therefore, it is my positive order, that ... they conform exactly to those Standing orders.[18]

In this letter Cumberland is making reference to the new platoon exercise of 1756 which perpetuated Cumberland's 1748 firings.[19] It is notable that with the Duke of Richmond leaving the 20th in 1756 Wolfe was quick to comply with the new regulations for all that he might complain about them. In his orders for an exercise issued in 1756 he instructed that: 'The two regiments shall conform to the practice of the army in their firings, and in their telling off the battalion.' He further added that: 'The firing of the infantry shall begin by platoons followed by that of subdivisions, then by grand-divisions, as they approach nearer and nearer the enemy, so that this last firing may cease when they are within a few paces of his line.'[20]

Leaving aside for the moment the arguments concerning alternate fire, Wolfe's orders of December 1755 also contain a wealth of information on the steps that could be taken to improve a battalion's general combat readiness and firepower, regardless of how it was finally delivered. There were clear instructions that stressed the importance of both marksmanship and the use of the bayonet: 'they are to be taught to fire at marks at different distances, and in different situations, to be fully instructed in the use of their bayonet' and 'to fire, kneeling and standing, to the front, to the rear, and obliquely, and from one rank to six deep'.[21] Quite how firing was to be carried out in six ranks is not explained, but it could simply be a reference to a unit parading six deep before forming into three ranks to fire. An explanation of oblique fire, however, is to be found in *The Complete Militia-Man* of 1760.[22] Firing at an angle to either side of a battalion presented no difficulty for the front- or centre-rank man. In oblique firing, however, the rear-rank man, instead of presenting his musket to the right of the man in front of him, presented his musket to either the right or left of the men standing on either side of the man in front of him. The platoon exercise was to be practised under different circumstances as was the use of the bayonet in attack and defence, suggesting that there was a lot more unofficial drill for the use of the bayonet than that contained in the regulations.[23] The use of the bayonet was reiterated when Wolfe ordered: 'If the firing is ordered to begin by platoons, either from the wings or from the center, it is to proceed in a regular manner, till the enemy is defeated, or till the signal is given for attacking them with the bayonets.'[24]

The regularity of the firing was also something Wolfe emphasised: 'There is no necessity for firing very fast; a cool well levelled fire, with the pieces carefully loaded, is much more destructive and formidable than the quickest fire in confusion.'[25] Although the Prussian method of delivering fire was admired and imitated it would appear that British officers did not share the Prussian view that speed was everything.

Wolfe also had instructions for dealing with any attack by a column of infantry. He instructed that his soldiers were to carry 'a couple of spare balls' and if attacked by a column, and time allowed, that part of the battalion facing the head of the column was to load the extra balls and then when 'the column is within about twenty yards they must fire with a good aim, which will necessarily stop them a little'.[26]

One section of Wolfe's orders that began, 'There are particulars in relation to fire arms that the soldiers should know' is of particular interest because of the light it sheds on some of the minutiae of firing a musket. It pointed out that the power and accuracy of a musket did not improve the more powder was used, but that the best size of charge was discovered through experience, something very necessary when soldiers were issued with powder, ball and cartridge paper to make their own ammunition. In relation to this the size of cartridges was also an important matter. Muskets became fouled with powder residue after repeated firing and if a cartridge was too big it could be difficult to ram home the ball. Too large a gap between powder and ball could result in a barrel bursting. Conversely, if a ball was rammed home too hard it could inhibit the powder from burning completely, thus reducing the power of the shot.[27]

In April 1756 new regulations were issued, first just dealing with the platoon exercise, but subsequently expanded in the 1757 regulations to cover all aspects of drill.[28] Under these regulations battalions continued to be organised for firing as had been laid down by the Duke of Cumberland in 1748. There were, however, some significant changes in the way the soldiers loaded their muskets. Previously, after firing, each soldier brought his musket up to the recover position, with the musket held vertically in front of him, the lock at about neck height. The front rank rose from their kneeling position and the middle and rear ranks stepped back to a distance of six feet between each rank before reloading.[29] According to the *New Exercise* the ranks were to be at one pace or two feet distance both to fire and reload. This saved the few seconds of time taken up opening and closing the ranks to load and to fire. Furthermore, instead of first coming to the recover with the musket it was instead to be brought from the present position for firing straight to the position for priming, again saving a few seconds.[30]

Another difference, albeit an apparently slight one, concerned the use of the rammer. Prior to the issue of the *New Exercise* of 1756 the 1728 regulations still applied to the loading of a musket, which were themselves unchanged where the rammer was concerned from the 1708 regulations. It took two motions to pull the rammer from the stock of the musket, then after turning it round and shortening it so that the rammer head was at the muzzle, it took three motions to use it to thrust the cartridge down the barrel. This was followed by withdrawing it to an arm's length and then ramming 'down the charge with ordinary force'. It took a further three motions to pull the rammer out of the barrel – unless it was a steel one rather than a wooden one, in which case it took only two motions.[31] The additional weight of a steel rammer and its greater strength meant that it could be treated with more vigour as it was less likely to break.

The change from wooden to steel rammer was not without its opponents. General Hawley was blunt in his opinion in his article *Chaos*, which he appears to have written in 1726 when he was Colonel of the 33rd Foot: 'The iron rammers the Foot are coming into are very ridiculous . . . if they have not some alloy of steel they stand bent and cannot be returned. If they have the least too much steel then they snap like glass; in wet weather or in a fog they rust and won't come out.'[32]

Despite these objections the changeover continued, but was slow as can be seen from an order of 22 April 1748, 'Lord Harry Beauclerk's Regt. [31st] to send to the Train [of Artillery] tomorrow to compleat their iron Rammers'; they were to be followed by the Guards and all the line regiments according to seniority.[33]

The instructions in the 1757 regulations were that the rammer was to be drawn from the musket stock in two motions and then to 'Ram down the Cartridge quick, and with good force; at the rebound of the rammer catch it close at the muzzle.' One further motion was sufficient to get it out of the barrel. A footnote in the regulations states: 'The Firing quick depends chiefly upon the quick Loading, and that chiefly upon the dexterity of drawing the Rammer, the ramming down and returning the Rammer. This Part of the Exercise therefore requires great practice and Attention.'[34] This increased vigour and speed in the use of the rammer was only possible because of the introduction of the more robust steel rammer.

A battalion was arranged for firing as had been laid down by Cumberland in 1748, with two platoons of grenadiers on the flanks and the hat companies divided into sixteen platoons, eight subdivisions and four grand divisions. The only difference from the 1748 arrangement was that the grand divisions were now fire units as well as units for manoeuvring. While this *New Exercise* improved on the platoon exercise it did nothing to address two significant problems that had caused difficulties with the various firings from the 1730s onwards.

When the form of the firings and the division of a battalion into fourteen platoons had been fixed under Marlborough in 1711, a battalion had consisted of one grenadier company and twelve hat companies. With the division of the grenadier company into two platoons, one on each flank, the hat companies were left to form one platoon each.[35] In 1717 the number of hat companies had been reduced to eleven, as was still the case in 1727 when Bland's *Military Discipline* was published and the following year when the 1728 regulations were issued. Although Bland contained details for a variety of numbers of platoons the 1728 regulations still specified fourteen.[36] In the 1730s, however, the number of hat companies was further reduced to nine, but without any compensatory alteration in the number of platoons. In fact, as has been seen, under the Duke of Cumberland the number of platoons increased so that the nine hat companies had to form sixteen platoons.

The inevitable confusion caused by breaking up the companies into a different number of platoons was further exacerbated by the way the officers of a battalion were distributed around the battalion for command and control purposes. This was done entirely according to seniority and with no regard for the position of the men in an officer's company. As was spelt out at length in the *New Exercise* and reinforced with the authority of both Cumberland and the king: 'By the above scheme the Colonel and Lieutenant colonel are in the Front, and the eldest Captain in the Center of the Rear; a Captain commands each Grand Division, the Senior Lieutenants command every other Subdivision, and the remaining eight platoons are commanded by Lieutenants and Ensigns.'[37] The effect of this was that soldiers were frequently formed with men from other companies and more often than not were under the command of officers they did not know and who did not know them.

For some years officers had questioned the existence of two separate sets of arms drill, the manual exercise, which included all the drill involving the musket, and the platoon exercise, which was for use in the platoons, in action, on the battlefield.[38] The question asked was why was there a need for two drills? This had the potential to confuse a soldier in battle, particularly as the manual required the soldier to cast about the musket to his left side, whilst the platoon required him to load with the musket to his right. With the issue of the 1756 regulations the manual exercise was restricted to those parts of the musket drill that were not part of the loading and firing drill. Loading and firing were now carried out solely according to the platoon exercise.

The new platoon exercise was not, however, without fault and one change was made between the exercise as first issued in April 1756 and as issued in 1758 in a second, 'entirely corrected and enlarged' edition. Initially the position for priming the musket required it to be held at chest height, the muzzle a little higher than the butt and resting in the crook of the left elbow and between the thumb and forefinger of the left hand, the forefinger resting of the feather spring of the lock.[39] This had two obvious drawbacks: it was uncomfortable, with the elbow raised unnaturally high and supporting the weight of the musket, and the muskets of each rank were liable to get in the way of the rank in front. In the revised version the musket was held in the left hand at the point of balance with the muzzle raised above the head of the man in front.[40]

With the ranks standing two feet apart for loading, there was no longer any need for the second and rear rank to close forward in order to lock up for firing. Instead the front-rank man knelt, pushing his right foot backwards three feet. The second-rank man stepped back a foot with his right foot, placing it just behind the right foot of the front-rank man. This allowed him to fire over the head of the front-rank man. The rear-rank man stepped to the right with his right foot so that it was behind the left heel of his right-hand man. This allowed him to aim his musket between the second-rank man to his front and the one to his right.[41] The main consequence of these changes was that it became possible to form the men with the elbows just touching, reckoned as twenty-one inches to each file.[42] Prior to this the files had been half an arm's length apart, which is approximately a nine-inch gap.[43] The effect of this was to increase the density of the distribution of muskets in a battalion. The effect of the fire of a platoon of thirty-six men was concentrated in seven yards rather than ten as previously. While this would not have resulted in more casualties amongst the enemy it would have concentrated them in a smaller area.

John Houlding states that the 1756 regulations reduced the platoon exercise from sixty-three to twenty-four motions, making it easier to learn and increasing the rate of fire by at least one round every two minutes.[44] Houlding does not say what the rate of fire was, and the effect of reducing the number of motions on the loading time was minimal. The loading time of a musket was certainly decreased by the elimination of the ranks opening and closing and the new priming position. But the number of motions that the loading process was divided into made no difference to the requirements of the process itself. This was something that Douglass commented on in the 1740s in relation to a new platoon exercise developed by Colonel Blakeney. He wrote: 'Lastly the author pretends shortening ye exercise by leaving out ye words of command . . . although ye words are left out yet ye number of motions are not decres'd.'[45] In other words, it does not matter how the process of loading a musket is divided up, it is only by such things as priming from the cartridge instead of a flask, going straight to the priming position from the present and by adopting the more robust steel ramrod or by tap-loading that the process can be speeded up.

Despite these regulations reiterating the 1748 firings, there continued to be moves to change to alternate firing, in the face of considerable high-ranking opposition in the shape of the Duke of Cumberland. As has already been discussed in connection with its use at Culloden, alternate fire could deliver the fire of a battalion very quickly.[46] An article apparently written in 1757, although not published until 1759, offers a possible explanation for the objections to alternate fire. 'We have imbibed a notion that our safety depends upon reserving the greatest part of our fire, and therefore we use our men to fire by single platoons.'[47] Another officer gave a similar explanation: 'The square toes of the army tells us that half the regiment ought to be constantly shoulder'd. I have often heard this maxim, but never heard a reason for it.'[48] In a reiteration of this the 'foot exercise' of 1757 as found in *A System of Camp Discipline* includes, 'In the firings by grand Divisions the Officers must give a little more Time betwixt each Fire, that one half of the Battalion may always be loaded.'[49] This would seem to chime with the arguments against alternate fire offered by Bland who thought its use left a battalion too open to attack.[50]

But just as much as alternate fire was objected to, so too were there complaints about the authorised methods of delivering fire. One officer wrote in the *London Magazine*: 'But at present five or six different methods of firing in a battalion are constantly taught and practised. But, pray, why so many? Since they cannot all be good.'[51] Firing platoon by platoon was objected to on the grounds that it took far too long and left the men standing with muskets loaded waiting their turn. The same officer recorded how high he could count between a platoon finishing loading and its turn to fire coming round. Unfortunately he did not say how fast he counted other than to say it was 'with moderate quickness'. He claimed he had counted from up to 180 to 260, which, assuming two counts to the second, gives a time delay of from 90 to 130 seconds; even at three counts a second this gives a time delay of at least 60 seconds. He went on to say: 'The reason generally given for firing by these platoons is that a constant fire should always be kept up.'[52]

If firing by individual platoons was too slow then firing by firings or subdivisions was also criticised. Here the objections were based upon the difficulty of coordinating the fire of units that were separated from each other, some by the whole width of a battalion. This was thought to be particularly difficult when more than one battalion was firing at a time and even more difficult in battle: 'In regard to firing by firings, I should think that it must also be impossible for the scattered divisions, in action, to hear their signals, whether they be given by drums, or voices; and, as the battalion is divided into three fires only, perhaps the fire could not be perpetual.'[53]

This was something that Wolfe had stated when introducing alternate fire to the 20th:

As the alternate fire by platoons or divisions, or by companies, is the most simple, plain and easy, and used by the best disciplined troops in Europe, we are at all times to imitate them in that respect, making every platoon receive the word of command, to make ready and fire from the officer who commands it; because in battle the fire of the artillery and infantry may render it difficult to use any general signals by beat of drum.[54]

The officer who questioned firing by platoons in the *London Magazine* also argued that perpetual fire was possible with subdivisions and even grand divisions, which was eight or four fire units, and which raised the question: why fire by individual platoons? To demonstrate that perpetual firing with four fire units was possible he gave the example of the 2nd Troop of Horse Grenadiers who had done just that.[55] This was a particularly interesting example to use as this was a cavalry unit. At that time all cavalry units were required to be able to fight on foot if necessary.[56] He also informed his readers that Marshal Saxe said a good soldier could fire four times a minute, or every fifteen seconds, and that the Prussians had eight platoons in a battalion. These, he informs us, were 'only one word of command behind that which it follows'.[57] By this he means that if, as with British infantry, the words of command to fire a volley were 'make ready, present, fire' then the officer commanding the second platoon to fire would order 'make ready' as the first ordered 'present'. This would have resulted in something like a two-second delay between platoons firing, meaning that each platoon fired every sixteen seconds.

This officer made the case for a battalion's fire to be delivered in four firings. Another did the same, but adding that in a firing it was not absolutely necessary for the platoons to fire perfectly together.[58] The view that a constant fire could be kept up using four fire units was challenged in an article commenting upon the 'Observations on the present methods of firing' article: 'He imagines, that four platoons are able to keep up a constant succession of firing; whereas he will find, upon experiment, that just double that number will come nearest the mark he aims at, viz. to keep up an uninterrupted succession of fire, and thus to discharge the greatest quantity of ball in the least time possible.' The author of this article went on to recommend to his readers *The Complete Militia-Man*, 'where he will find the best system of firing we remember to have seen'. [59]

The Complete Militia-Man was an extremely useful publication because it was written for civilians taking commissions in the militia and thus contained explanations that would not have been necessary for regular officers. The criticism of the authorised firings was repeated: 'In my chapter *of the firings*, I have differed entirely from the practice of the army, because I was willing to recommend nothing to the Militia, but was essential and practicable upon real service.'[60] The anonymous army officer who wrote this was in agreement with the other two equally anonymous officers in stating that fire should be reserved to close range, 'Experience informs us that the fire of musketry at a distance does very little execution', but that once firing had started it could not be delivered too quickly. However, he maintained that it was necessary to have eight fire units.

> It is scarce possible to reserve your fire too long, before you begin; but I am certain, that after you do begin, it is impossible to make your succession of fire too quick. Let me therefore advise the gentlemen of the Militia, if they ever engage an enemy, not to fire by platoons, but by subdivisions, or companies, provided they have eight companies in their battalion.[61]

What is noticeable about this discussion in the pages of various English publications is that it is entirely concerned with the best way to deliver a battalion's fire. There is no discussion anywhere of the relative benefits of firepower as against cold steel, or column versus line. The debates that took place in Europe appear to have completely passed by the British officer corps. Although it is not explicitly stated anywhere, it is tempting to consider that they were perfectly content with their tactical doctrine and it was only improving the execution of that which was of interest to them.

Some officers were so convinced of the difficulties of the official firings and of the superiority of alternate fire that they introduced it to the troops under their command. This is what occurred in 1757 on the Isle of Wight where General Mordaunt was preparing a force for an amphibious assault on France. Two of the battalions under his command were the 20th, under Wolfe, and the 33rd, under the Duke of Richmond. Perhaps under the influence of those two officers, Mordaunt effectively tore up the regulations, as the Duke of Richmond wrote in a letter to his brother:

> General Mordaunt has done a thing in his army, which if it is followed by the rest the whole nation will be obliged to him for it. He has dared to follow common sense and to put into execution what every body has long since thought right. He has broke through all the absurd regulations that General Napier has been puzzling the army with since he has been Adjutant General. He has abolished the manual exercise both old and

new, and draws up all the regiments as Kingsley's [20th] used to do, by companies with their own officers.

This is truly great and you have no idea how much it has already improved the other regiments. This is against all order, and some persons are amazed that Sir John Mordaunt will undertake it.[62]

In doing this Mordaunt was risking the wrath of the Duke of Cumberland, who was campaigning in Germany, albeit with an army that contained no British troops. Not surprisingly Cumberland heard about Mordaunt's actions and wrote to the Secretary at War in no uncertain terms, insisting that the regulations should be adhered to.[63]

However, Cumberland had just been badly beaten by the French at the battle of Hastenbeck and at the convention of Kloster Zeven was forced to accept humiliating terms by which his army was disbanded.[64] As a result Cumberland resigned all his positions, leaving the way clear for the proponents of alternate fire.

Using Wolfe's *Instructions*, Richmond's letter to his brother, which states categorically that they were drawing up 'all the regiments as Kingsley's [20th] used to do', and *The Complete Militia-Man*, it is possible to examine precisely how alternate fire was organised and executed and to analyse its effectiveness. In keeping with the Prussian practice the core of alternate fire was eight fire units. In order to simplify the organisation of a battalion these were to be eight of a battalion's ten companies. Of the other two companies one was the grenadier company. Previously this had been divided into two platoons, one on each flank of the battalion. With the company now the basic fire unit it was no longer possible to divide the grenadiers in that manner. Instead they were posted as a complete company on the right of the battalion whilst the other, tenth company was posted on the left and referred to as a piquet. This term applied to any detachment of soldiers, as Richmond explained in his letter: 'The whole comp[any] of Grenadiers on the right and a detached company or picquet on the left.' In addition to a company acting as a single fire unit it was also divided into two platoons that could also be used as fire units if necessary. One further detail, found in both Wolfe's *Instructions* and Richmond's letter, is that each company retained its own officers with it instead of them being distributed around the battalion according to seniority.[65]

Figure 7.1: The order of firing of eight companies using alternate fire

1	3	5	7	8	6	4	2

Front

According to *The Complete Militia-Man* the first and second companies to fire, being at opposite ends of a battalion, were to 'make ready' when the battalion commander instructed the battalion to 'take care to fire by subdivision'. When the order was given to commence firing the officer commanding the first company, on the right of the battalion, then gave the orders 'present', followed by 'fire'. The next company to the left was to fire third, after the second company to fire, which was on the other flank. The commander of this third company gave the order 'make ready' as soon as the first company fired. On hearing that first company fire the commander of the second company to fire also gave the orders 'present' and 'fire', at which point the company to its right, which was to be the fourth to fire, would 'make ready'. Meanwhile, back on the other flank of the battalion, the officer commanding the third company to fire, hearing the second fire, gave the orders 'present' and 'fire', which was followed by the fourth company firing.[66] As the commander of the third company to fire took his timing for the order 'make ready' from the first, which was next to him, and had only to listen for the second company firing, this largely dealt with the difficulty of the separation of the successive companies firing.

Rather than having the grenadier company on one flank and a piquet company on the other, as practised in the regular army, *The Complete Militia-Man* had the grenadier company divided into two platoons, one on each flank. Of these, the right-hand platoon was to 'make ready' after the fourth company fired and to fire after the fifth, followed by the grenadier platoon on the left flank. The remaining four companies followed in a like manner.[67] It would seem likely, however, that the firing sequence used by the regular battalions did not include the grenadier and piquet companies. According to Richmond the battalions formed with 'The whole comp[any] of Grenadiers on the right and a detached company or picquet on the left. The remaining eight companies form the battalions and have all their own officers with them, and practise no other firing but by companies from right and left.'[68] Wolfe's *Instructions* also suggest that the grenadier and piquet companies operated semi-independently of the main body of the battalion, covering and protecting the flanks or pursuing a beaten enemy.[69]

The rate of fire or of reloading is difficult to determine; there is no record of any officer making use of a watch to time the firings. However, taking the various comments suggesting that four rounds a minute was possible, that eight fire units could keep up a continual fire and considering the description of the giving of orders for alternate fire in *The Complete Militia-Man*, some estimation is possible.[70] Four rounds a minute suggests a reloading time of fifteen seconds, but a unit had to be reloaded before an officer could give the first order of 'make ready', followed by 'present' and 'fire'. Allowing time for the front rank to kneel, this sequence could take approximately five seconds, reducing the loading time to ten seconds, which would seem extremely difficult to achieve.

If the firing sequence in eight fire units is considered, the first company to fire was expected to make ready again after the seventh company had fired so that it could fire again after the eighth. This gave it the six intervals between it firing and the subsequent six companies firing in which to reload. Each interval was long enough for a company commander to give the orders 'present' and 'fire' and for his company to do just that. It was also long enough for a company to make ready, with the front rank kneeling, the second and rear ranks taking their proper position and the muskets being cocked. If this interval was three seconds, that gave each company eighteen seconds from firing before it had to be reloaded again and prepared to 'make ready'.

These figures are, of course, approximations, but they do suggest strongly that a battalion was quite capable of delivering all of its fire approximately every twenty seconds. Allowing for a battalion on campaign being a little under its official establishment of seventy men to a company, perhaps sixty men, then eight companies would discharge 480 rounds. Standing in three ranks with a frontage of twenty-one inches a man and with a three-foot interval between companies, they had a total frontage of approximately one hundred yards. If the rate of hits already seen at Culloden and

Fontenoy is allowed, then a battalion of British infantry employing eight companies firing alternately, could, at the preferred range of thirty yards, inflict between 100 to 120 casualties on an enemy every twenty seconds. That is one casualty for every yard of frontage every twenty seconds.

Arguing against the possibility of this sort of effectiveness a Dutch officer wrote:

> It is observed that, at the battle of Fontenoy, the French had about six thousand killed and wounded. Now, on the side of the allies . . . there were but twenty thousand combatants. It is known, these fired away all their cartridges, to the number, perhaps, of thirty-six each man: but we will suppose each man fired no more than twenty: here were four hundred thousand shot discharged. And if, at the same time, we suppose, that only five hundred men suffered from the artillery, it is plain, here were seventy-three shot to one person killed or wounded. If we consider, besides, how many might suffer from the bayonet, the disproportion will also be considerably increased.[71]

This argument, however, was effectively dealt with by the author of *The Complete Militia-Man*.

> First, let me assure you that the fire of a regiment, unless it be very near, is far from being so terrible as those who are not experienced are apt to imagine. One would think that almost every ball must do execution; but this is so far from being the case, that, in a general engagement, not one ball in a hundred does any mischief, till the armies come within twenty or thirty paces of each other. For this reason, if you have any desire to triumph over your enemies, or the least regard for your own safety, you will be very cautious not to throw away your fire.[72]

The inaccuracy of musket fire at any sort of distance was well known and was highlighted by La Fausille as contributing to the defeat of the French during the War of the Austrian Succession.[73] The British infantry was clearly still adhering to the doctrine of close-range fire delivered with efficiency and accuracy. Whilst other nations might have been debating the competing merits of firepower and cold steel, British infantry was still balancing firepower with the use of the bayonet. Wolfe's comments have already been noted above.[74] *The Complete Militia-Man* contained directions to march up close to the enemy – in this case specifically naming the French – fire and then 'charge your bayonets, march briskly up, and rush, like lions, into the broken ranks of the enemy.'[75]

In connection with the bayonet it has been suggested that Wolfe was responsible for the introduction to the British Army of a new form of bayonet drill.[76] Rather than being held breast high as the pike had been, this new method saw the bayonet held much more comfortably at waist height. Unlike alternate fire there was no mention of this in direct connection with Wolfe, or Richmond, in any contemporary writing. However, it did make an appearance in several of the manuals that were written specifically for militia units. One of these was written for the Norfolk Militia and in his introduction its author acknowledged the assistance received from officers of Wolfe's and Richmond's regiments.[77] It was not until the 1764 regulations were issued that this bayonet drill became authorised for use by the regular battalions, although it would seem unlikely that something like this was in use by the militia, but not the regulars.

On the question of dealing with cavalry the Duke of Richmond's letter tells us that amongst other things General Mordaunt abandoned 'such absurdities as squares etc.'[78] Wolfe's *Instructions* are silent on the matter. *The Complete Militia-Man* repeats advice that had been given since Mackay's *Rules*.[79]

> If ever you are attack'd by cavalry, your safety, as in the former case, depends entirely on reserving your fire; for if you should foolishly throw it away whilst they are at a distance, they will instantly put spurs to horses, and drive in among you: but if, on the contrary, you do not fire at all, you may be certain they will never come within fifty yards of you with their whole body.[80]

In 1755, at the same time as the British Army had been striving to improve its platoon exercise, the French Army also further developed its own version of platoon firing. A French battalion was to form in three ranks rather than four and its twelve companies were divided into six platoons that fired alternately from the centre to the flanks. There was to be a two-second interval between each platoon firing. The French, however, saw platoon firing as an essentially defensive tactic, continuing to prefer to rely on shock and cold steel in the offensive.[81] Consequently they did not develop the aggressive combination of firepower and the bayonet in the attack used by British infantry. There was also an apparent problem with the quality of French musketry. A British paymaster, George Durant, wrote that the French were bad marksmen because they believed a musket ball in flight falls. As a consequence they had a tendency to aim high. Whilst this is true with regard to the laws of gravity, it was in fact necessary to aim low with a musket – and the closer the target, the lower the aim. This was because a musket kicked up as it was fired, throwing the shot high.[82] Durant went on to write that consequently few British soldiers were hit below the chest while muskets being carried at the shoulder were hit above soldiers' heads.[83] In Germany in August 1761 Corporal Todd of the 30th described an attack against French infantry who 'fired a whole Volley upon us . . . but scarce Kill'd a man, their shott flying over us'. He continued to describe how, in their normal manner, the British battalion continued to advance until within pistol shot before firing, which caused the immediate retreat of the French.[84]

In Germany in 1759 British infantry was ordered by Lord George Sackville to form according to the 1749 firings, in sixteen platoons, exclusive of grenadiers. At first sight this appeared to be a retrograde step, but the orders added further details. Each company was to be a subdivision, or two platoons, with two companies to a grand division. This organisation is not possible with an establishment of nine hat companies, unless the extra company was deployed as a piquet. That these orders established, as at least local regulations, the organisation and firings practised under General Mordaunt is clear from the part dealing with firing: 'It is recommended to the commanding officers to practice chiefly the alternate firing, firing from right and left by grand divisions, subdivisions and platoons. His Lordship expects that the regiments will strictly conform to this order and he shall not see for the future one regiment practising differently from another, and of course producing confusion in the service.'[85] It was with this organisation that British infantry entered the Seven Years War in Europe.

Leaving aside the various British amphibious raids on the French coast, there was, initially, limited participation in the Seven Years War in Europe by British infantry. Their first engagement was at Minden where the six British battalions that won the day were the only British infantry present. At Corbach just four battalions were engaged, whilst at Warburg it was primarily the British cavalry that was engaged. At Klosterkamp there were eight battalions with two grenadier battalions formed by combining the grenadier companies of those battalions. At both Vellinghausen and Wilhelmsthal there were seventeen British battalions, but some sixty or more other allied battalions. Despite this numerical inferiority it is arguable that in all their engagements British infantry punched above their weight.

At the Battle of Minden on 1 August 1759 the six British battalions present performed in such a manner that their feats that day are still annually celebrated by their descendant units. An allied Army under Prince Frederick of Brunswick had lured a French army into battle on unfavourable ground. Whilst the battle was still in its early stages the British infantry, in the centre of Frederick's army, misunderstood their orders and immediately set off, supported by three Hanoverian battalions, marching directly towards the centre of the French army. The 12th, 37th and 23rd regiments formed the first line, followed by the 25th, 51st and 20th with the Hanoverians on their left flank. In an unusual deployment they were faced by sixty-three squadrons of cavalry formed in three lines in the centre of the French army.[86] A detailed account of what followed was given by a British officer in the 12th, which, as the front right battalion, saw the hardest of the fighting: 'When we got within about 100 yards of the Enemy a large Body of French Cavalry galloped boldly down upon us; these our Men by reserving their fire until they came within 30 yards immediately ruined.'[87]

Yet again the infantry held their fire until the enemy were within the preferred range of thirty yards. It would be reasonable to assume that under such circumstances the battalions fired all their companies together, something that appears to have been practised even if it does not appear in the regulations. Corporal Todd reported practising all the usual forms of firing and 'vollies'.[88] If not a reference to whole battalion firings it is difficult to know what else this might refer to.

The British battalions were then charged by fresh cavalry, the Gens d'Armes, who 'we almost immediately dispersed without receiving hardly any mischief from the harmless Creatures'. The next French attack was made by seventeen infantry battalions, which the 12th and 37th wheeled to face. There followed a sustained firefight for about ten minutes before the French were driven off.[89] It is highly improbable that the British infantry fired without a break for ten minutes. At three or four rounds a minute that would have used up most, if not all, the ammunition carried by the infantry, usually twenty-four rounds a man. It is more likely that they fought a quick succession of firefights as enemy battalions were beaten and replaced by others. The next French attack was carried out by battalions of grenadiers and the description sheds light on the French infantry's apprehension about getting into a firefight with British infantry.

> The next who made their appearance were some Regts of the Grenadiers of France, as fine and terrible looking Fellows as I ever saw. They stood us a tug; not with standing we beat them off to a distance, where they galded us much they having rifled barrels, and our Musquets would not reach them. To remedy this we advanced, they took the hint, and ran away.[90]

A final attack– the officer of the 12th said by infantry, others cavalry, and perhaps some confusion is understandable in the light of what had passed – partially broke the front three battalions, but was beaten by the three battalions in the second line. By the end of the battle the 12th had suffered 302 rank and file killed and wounded out of 480 and eighteen officers killed and wounded out of twenty-seven. 'With this remnant we returned again the charge, but to our unspeakable joy no opponents could be found.'[91]

There is insufficient information to analyse this action in terms of rounds fired, rates of fire and casualties caused. There is no doubt, however, that it represented an unheard-of achievement by infantry. The French general, Contades, summarised what had happened and its implications for the French Army:

> As to the cannon, those of our enemy fired quicker, and did more execution than ours. Our musquetry, indeed, fired faster and oftener, being discharged sooner, and at a greater distance; but the enemy reserved

their fire till they discharged it in our teeth; by which means they did thrice the execution; and then rushing in with their bayonets, prevented our troops from giving any more; and I cannot help mentioning, what if I had not seen it, I should have thought incredible, that one single column of infantry penetrated and broke through three lines of cavalry. This column consisted principally of the English regiments, whose intrepid behaviour in this battle, it will be prudent to conceal from the troops designed to invade Great Britain from France, less they should be intimidated by it.[92]

This is a clear recognition of the battlefield doctrine of British infantry, an admission of its capabilities and a confession that the French could not match it.

The battles of Corbach, Emsdorf and Warburg in 1760 are best known for the successful exploits of the British cavalry, which more than made up for Minden, where they had sat inactive while the French army fled the field. Their commander, Lord Sackville, was subsequently court-martialled and cashiered. Later that year, on 16 October 1760, at Klosterkamp an attempt to launch a surprise attack on the French ultimately failed, but only after the allied infantry involved had expended all their ammunition. In this engagement the fire of the British infantry was said to have been 'so rapid and deadly that three French brigades were almost wiped out of existence'.[93] The engagement lasted from before dawn until noon. One small hint as to how the British infantry at least might have been able to sustain a fight for so long when the standard issue of ammunition was twenty-four rounds comes from the diary of Corporal Todd. Prior to taking the field in 1761 he recorded how, on 1 June, after going through all the 'firing Motions' and having all the arms and ammunition checked it was ordered that more cartridges should be made up so that every man would have sixty rounds.[94] On 9 June it was further ordered that the battalions should have 'plenty of Ammunition ready made up in the Tummerils [tumbrils]'.[95] These were in addition to the sixty carried by each man, as in August Todd recorded thirty being taken from each man, 'they having carried with them 60 as before Order'd'.[96] Whether carrying sixty rounds had been the case at Klosterkamp or was a consequence of it is unclear.

On the evening of 15 July 1761 Corporal Todd and his battalion were engaged in the opening round of the battle of Vellinghausen. The French attacked the Marquis of Granby's British corps and Todd described how the eight British battalions 'performed wonders & Maintain'd their ground against four times their Number'.[97] No doubt their sixty rounds a man helped. The French attack on the allied army under Ferdinand the following day has been described as 'one of the feeblest ever fought by the French army'.[98] Todd, however, has left some interesting detail about the fight seen from his level. After the first evening's fighting he recorded that they were ordered to check their muskets and to ensure every man had a good flint and was properly loaded. Much of the fighting the following day was in woods and amongst thick bushes where they had frequent recourse to their bayonets.[99]

The Seven Years War came to an end in 1763 and in 1764 a new set of regulations were issued for the British Army. There were some minor changes to the loading and individual firing in the platoon exercise. The use of the rammer was further quickened as it was drawn from the stock in two motions, turned and put into the barrel without first being shortened against the body. After ramming it was similarly just turned and replaced in the stock without shortening.[100] It would appear that having the men in each rank standing so close that they touched the men beside them left too little room for ease of loading. The files were now to be four inches apart while the distance between the ranks for firing remained at two feet.[101] On the order 'make ready' the second-rank men stepped slightly to their right, only moving their right foot. After firing they brought the left foot towards the right for reloading. The rear rank took a larger step to the right and followed it with the left foot. They also stayed stepped to the right to reload, but after reloading both ranks stepped back to the left behind the front-rank men.[102] While this meant that each file had a frontage of twenty-five inches instead of twenty-one it probably made loading easier and thus slightly quicker. This was still closer together than had been the case during the War of the Austrian Succession.

With regard to the instructions for delivering the fire of a battalion, the use of firing by individual platoons and by firings had disappeared. Firing was now limited to alternate fire by subdivisions – exactly as described by Wolfe, Richmond and in *The Complete Militia-Man* – or firing by grand divisions. The only difference was that the number of hat companies was reduced to eight after the war and the grenadier company was once again divided into two platoons, one on each flank.[103]

During the Seven Years War in Europe the infantry of the British Army had continued to demonstrate their effectiveness and to seek to improve their performance. This was not done, however, as a result of any great debate about how battles should be fought, whether cold steel was superior to firepower, or column to line – the doctrinal debates in Europe seem to have passed by almost unremarked. Instead there was a continuing adherence to the doctrine of close-range fire followed by the prompt and effective use of the bayonet. In doing so they changed the method of delivery back to something like it had been at the start of the War of the Spanish Succession, which was alternate fire by companies. Bland's objection to this had been that it left parts of a battalion unloaded and thus too exposed to attack.[104] The introduction of firings had meant that a part of a battalion's fire was always available along the whole front. Changes in drill and the adoption of other measures, such as the steel rammer, had the effect of reducing the loading time to the point where the dangers highlighted by Bland were neutralised. This allowed a return to the much simpler alternate fire method, which was far easier to control and less likely to break down in confusion. This in turn increased the effectiveness of that fire.

Chapter 8

The French and Indian War

Whilst a part of the British Army was campaigning in Europe a significant part was experiencing the less familiar expanses of North America. The nature of the environment required the army to adapt to campaigning over huge distances through wilderness landscapes and presented many new challenges to an army more accustomed to campaigning in Europe.[1] It was also faced with fighting against not only French regulars, but a very different enemy in the form of Native Americans (known as Indians at that time) and French-Canadian irregulars. However, despite the very different nature of such warfare, the bulk of the recent scholarly history written about this war is concerned with the narrative of events rather than any analysis of those differences and their consequences. An example of this is Anderson's *Crucible of War*.[2]

Historians of the Seven Years War in North America – or the French and Indian War, as it usually referred to in North America – have tended to look most frequently at the campaign in 1759 under Major General James Wolfe. This is not surprising as it was the decisive campaign that led to not only the defeat of the French and the capture of Quebec, but to the expulsion of France from Canada and the establishment of British control there. In addition to Wolfe's strategic achievements Stuart Reid has also sought to analyse his wider contribution to the British Army and concludes: 'In the longer term it was Wolfe's volley and bayonet tactics, first described in December 1755, which formed the cornerstone of British infantry tactics in the Peninsular War and at Waterloo . . . his influence on the development of the British Army, and in particular on its infantry tactics, was perhaps his real legacy.'[3]

This assessment of Wolfe has been reiterated most recently by Saul David: 'He left, moreover, an important legacy: the simple but effective battle tactic – a close quarter volley, followed by a bayonet charge – that British infantrymen would use to sweep all (or almost all) before them for much of the next hundred years.'[4]

Both writers are referring to Wolfe's influence on conventional warfare as represented by the battle of Quebec, where, according to Fortescue, the British infantry delivered 'the most perfect volley ever fired on a battlefield'.[5] Wolfe's part in the development of tactics in the European theatre has already been discussed, but the Quebec campaign was his first independent command where he could influence tactics free of outside interference or objection.

By comparison scant attention has been paid to the demands and challenges of the irregular warfare that had to be faced. The campaigns in North America saw the establishment, albeit temporarily, of the first light infantry units in the British Army. These were raised specifically to counter the threat posed by the Indian allies of the French and their own French-Canadian irregulars. Perhaps because their contribution is not seen as decisive, or perhaps because their existence was temporary, their tactics and methods have been little studied. Fuller's *British Light Infantry in the Eighteenth Century* is dated and demonstrates a limited availability of material.[6] Gates's *The British Light Infantry Arm* touches on the subject in his first chapter, but the French and Indian War is outside the main scope of his work.[7] More recently there has been a useful publication by Osprey, but the limited size of this publication means that it can only serve as an introduction to the subject.[8]

The most comprehensive recent treatment of the development of light infantry and Indian fighting is in Brumwell's *Redcoats*. He deals with all aspects of the war in North America and addresses the nature of irregular warfare and the tactical evolution of the redcoats.[9] His account of the development of British light infantry and its experiences is thorough, but in keeping with most military historians he neglects the procedures by which this form of warfare was conducted, making it difficult to identify any underlying tactical doctrine. He writes: 'The mixture of regular and irregular warfare which characterised these campaigns demanded diverse combat skills; the resulting fusion of Old and New World techniques created troops capable of fighting in both the conventional fashion of

Flanders and in a more flexible manner that owed little to the traditions of Dettingen and Fontenoy.'[10]

What he does not do is give any description of those combat skills and techniques or the doctrine underpinning them, although he does claim that the '"American Army" acquired an ethos and tactical doctrine that set it apart from other British and European armies'.[11]

It was clearly understood that the nature of warfare against Indians was different from anything experienced in Europe or even the Highlands of Scotland. What would seem not to have been appreciated was just how different it was. Writing after the war, Colonel (later Brigadier) Henry Bouquet summarised the tactics of the Indians:

The first, that their general maxim is to surround their enemy.

The second, that they fight scattered, and never in a compact body.

The third, that they never stand their ground when attacked, but immediately give way, to return to the charge.[12]

This type of warfare was far removed from Europe where solid lines of infantry three deep and manoeuvring in an open landscape could fire shattering volleys at ranges of thirty yards.

Just how different this was became apparent when Major General Braddock's expedition against Fort DuQuesne was thoroughly defeated on 9 July 1755 at the battle of Monongahela. Braddock was aware that the army's usual tactics would need to change in order to combat the Indian threat and he took steps to do that. In March he had issued instructions on how the battalions were to conduct their firing.

One company was nominated as a second grenadier company and was to be posted on the left of the battalion while the grenadier company took the right. The eight remaining companies were retained intact and either formed single fire units or were divided into two platoons. When firing, the right hand of the eight companies fired first, followed by the left-hand company, and so on, alternating right and left towards the centre. The two grenadier companies fired last, but not until the first companies to fire were loaded again. The firing was to be 'as fast as possible'. Orders were to be given by the officer commanding a company.[13] This method of delivering fire was nothing more or less than the alternate-fire system that had been introduced by Wolfe to his regiment just two months earlier and is here in use some three years before Mordaunt introduced it to his command on the Isle of Wight.

On the march and in order to secure the numerous wagons from attack by Indians the main body of the infantry marched on each side of the wagons, company by company and in two files. In case of attack the infantry were to simply face outwards forming a two-deep line on each side of the road. An advance guard preceded the main body. A few miles short of Fort DuQuesne the advance guard was engaged by a force of Indians and French infantry. 'The French . . . threw themselves behind trees as soon as they saw the English & began to fire their muskets. The Indians . . . took up their positions at the base of each tree with their customary shrieks.'[14]

After giving an initial platoon volley the officer commanding the advance guard,

> observing their Confusion and being apprehensive of a second Attack of the same kind, immediately ordered the Men to draw back, and posted them singly behind Trees, in the Indian Manner; where probably they would not only have maintained themselves, but might have done execution against the Enemy, had not the General, who came up from the Rear upon the first Fire, upbraided them for Cowards, and with his Sword drawn forced them in a Manner to return to their Ranks.[15]

The consequence of this was that rather than holding their ground until the main body could be organised to meet the attack, the advance guard and their supports were driven back onto the main body, causing considerable confusion. The Indians then encircled the whole British column and continuously fired from cover at the British infantry standing in the open in rank and file.

> They having always a large marke to shoute at and we having only to shoute at them behind trees or laid on their Bellies. We was drawn up in large Bodies together, a ready mark. They need not have taken sight at us for they Always had a large Mark, but if we saw of them five or six at one time [it] was a great sight and they Either on their Bellies or Behind trees or Running from one tree to another almost by the ground.[16]

Some attempts were made to close with the Indians with the bayonet, but these came to nothing as the Indians shot down the officers and avoided any close contact. Some of the American provincial troops took cover behind trees to return the Indian's fire, but many of these were shot from behind by the wild volleys that came from the British infantry whenever they caught a glimpse of a target.[17] One British soldier claimed that it was these Americans who caused what casualties were inflicted on the enemy.[18]

Remarkably the British infantry held their ground for about three hours, only finally breaking when they ran out of ammunition.[19] According to a contemporary newspaper report the soldiers told their officers that it was pointless shooting at trees and bushes, but that they would fight their enemy if they could see him.[20] The French and Indians had also made a point of picking off the officers, which contributed to the lack of fire control and the general state of confusion and, ultimately, panic.[21] As the French themselves reported: 'The Indian mode of fighting is entirely different from that of us Europeans, which is good for nothing in this country. The enemy formed themselves into battle array, presented a front to men concealed behind trees, who at each shot brought down one or two, and thus defeated almost the whole of the English.'[22]

In the aftermath of this defeat one British officer complained that Braddock had given orders to fire by platoon, which was inappropriate for the situation they had found themselves in.[23] Braddock was mortally wounded in the battle and unable to defend himself. However, this lack of control of the infantry's fire, along with an ignorance of the nature of the enemy, was also identified by the French as contributing to the result. 'If on terrain without real problems, such a disaster could happen to brave and well-disciplined troops, through an inability to direct fire & ignorance of the nature of the enemy they were engaging, then this provides a good lesson that these two aspects of warfare should receive close attention.'[24]

At the time much of the blame for the defeat was laid on the behaviour of the rank and file.[25] Wolfe, still in Britain, wrote that 'the cowardice and ill-behaviour of the men far exceeded the ignorance of the chief.'[26] Stanley Pargellis has argued more recently that the blame lay with Braddock's failure to apply basic military precautions when on the march through enclosed country, be it in Europe or North America.

This allowed the column, in the first instance, to be surprised and then to be unable to react correctly to the attack.[27] However, even if the British had not been surprised and had been able to form an ordered two-deep line against the attack, it is unlikely that they would have defeated the French and Indians. As the two French reports quoted above make clear, European-style combat procedures were rendered impotent in the face of the irregular procedures. It was impossible for the British infantry to apply their traditional combat doctrine of first disrupting the enemy with effective musketry and then dispersing him by means of the bayonet. Monongahela was a victory of individual aimed fire from cover over massed volleys delivered from in the open.

The effectiveness of irregular warfare was also demonstrated a few months later on 8 September 1755 in an engagement between British provincial forces and a French force of regulars, Indians and Canadians. The French were making a pre-emptive strike against a force advancing to attempt the capture of Fort St Frederic. The ensuing fight was a long, confused affair that ended in victory for the provincial forces and the establishment of Fort William Henry while Fort St Frederic remained in French hands. During the battle the irregulars on both sides made full use of the available cover, even the French regulars: after firing, a few platoons 'went into the Indian way of Fighting, squatting below the Shrubs, or placing themselves behind the Trees'.[28]

The British Army's response to the difficulties of this sort of warfare was twofold. One measure was to endeavour to train the regular battalions in the rudiments of irregular warfare or bush fighting. The second measure was the introduction of their own light troops to take on the French irregulars on their own terms. One of the first and perhaps the most famous of these was Rogers' Rangers. This was not a regular British Army unit, but formed of Anglo-Americans. It was one of several ranger units, most of which proved themselves unreliable and ill-disciplined. Consequently British commanders determined to form their own light infantry subject to regular army discipline. However, many of the officers of the regular light infantry served with Rogers and learnt their bushcraft from him. Rogers subsequently wrote down his rules for irregular warfare and these can be said to have formed the basis for the operational methods of British light infantry.

He first required that rangers carried sixty rounds of powder and ball. This was necessary because they spent considerable periods away from bases where they might resupply. He wrote extensively about the tactics of warfare in the woods, including a number of points that dealt specifically with combat methods. If the enemy was firing, he advised: 'fall or squat down, till it is over, then rise and discharge at them.' When advancing against an enemy his instructions were for the rangers to keep well apart from each other and move from tree to tree in two lines, the first some ten or twelve yards ahead of the other. After the first line fired the second was to pass through and fire in turn while the first line reloaded. By this means the two lines could advance whilst keeping up a constant fire on the enemy. If receiving an attack his instructions were: 'In general, when pushed upon by the enemy, reserve your fire until they approach very near, which will then put them into the greatest surprise and consternation, and give you an opportunity of rushing upon them with your hatchets and cutlasses to the better advantage.'[29] There are two features of these instructions that stand out. One was the requirement for keeping up a constant fire; the other was the use of firepower backed up by close-quarter combat.

Captain Knox added further details about the ammunition of the rangers. He described them as carrying a bag which 'contains bullets, and a smaller shot, of the size of full-grown peas: six or seven of which, with a ball, they generally load'. This was also a practice of the French irregulars who are described as always loading with six or seven 'buck shot' as well as a normal ball.[30]

Bouquet also had his views on training light infantry: 'They will be taught to handle their arms with dexterity; and without losing time upon trifles, to load and fire very quick, standing, kneeling or lying on the ground. They are to fire at a mark without a rest, and not suffered to be too long in taking aim.'[31] The emphasis had shifted to the effectiveness of the fire of the individual rather than a battalion, company or platoon. This new emphasis was also seen in other proposals concerning the development of light infantry.

One of the first proposals for forming light infantry from amongst the regular infantry came from Major George Scott in early 1758. He wrote to Lord Loudon, who had arrived in North America in July 1756, replacing Braddock as commander-in-chief, with proposals on how they should be equipped. He recommended a firelock that was shorter and lighter than the standard Long Land Pattern musket with its forty-six-inch-long barrel. Apart from being less of a burden a shorter, lighter musket was also quicker to bring to the aim and easier to keep on target, thus improving accuracy, particularly against briefly seen or moving targets. Furthermore the barrel was to be blackened, which served two purposes. It prevented the position of the firer being given away by sunlight reflecting off it and it also prevented reflected sunlight dazzling the firer. The musket was still to be provided with a bayonet, but it was to be short and light and in the form of a knife, making it a dual-purpose item. Scott maintained that in the absence of cavalry in North America it did not need to be as long as the usual seventeen inches. The advantage of the lighter bayonet was the reduction in weight of the musket at the muzzle end, thus improving aiming.

Ammunition, in the form of cartridges, was to be carried in a tin cartridge box that would protect the ammunition from the damp. In a significant change Scott proposed a return to using priming horns, abandoned in the 1740s, instead of priming from the cartridge. These were to be filled with finer pistol powder, His argument was that the finer powder was easier to ignite than the slightly coarser powder used in muskets and that priming from a horn would avoid any loss of powder from the cartridge, ensuring the musket got a full load. He claimed that as much as half the powder in a cartridge was sometimes lost in priming, with the consequence that the resultant shot had neither its intended force nor range.[32] The return to the use of priming flasks could be seen as a retrograde step, their abandonment had speeded up the loading process. However, since, according to Bouquet, light infantry were to load without 'losing time upon trifles' and were not handicapped by standing in closely packed ranks and files it is possible that there was no real loss of speed in reloading.

Loudoun, however, had already authorised the raising of what was the first regular light infantry regiment in the British Army, the 80th under Thomas Gage. A list of items supplied for equipping this new unit specifies a cost for 'cutting and finishing' the 540 firelocks supplied – that is, shortening them and possibly blacking the barrels as well. In addition 540 shot bags and powder horns were supplied.[33]

In May 1758 Major General Jeffrey Amherst arrived in North America at Halifax, Nova Scotia, where he was making preparations for his assault on the French fortress of Louisbourg. He ordered the formation of light infantry from amongst the regular battalions, which were placed under the command of Major Scott. The men drafted from 'the regiments, that have been any time in America, are to furnish such as have been most accustomed to the woods, and are good marksmen; and those from Europe are to furnish active marchers, and men that are expert at firing ball'.[34]

Amherst subsequently ordered that this light infantry were to exchange their long and heavy Long Land Pattern firelocks for the lighter, shorter firelocks carried by the artillery.[35] In his instructions for how they were to fight, the influence of Rogers was clear: they were to 'generally fight in a single rank' and avoid huddling together, thus presenting their enemy with a target. They were apparently expected to load their muskets from powder horns, rather than just priming, as they were instructed to be careful not to overload their guns and to have tow or paper ready cut to serve as wadding in the place of the paper of a cartridge.[36]

Early in 1759 Amherst – by then the fourth commander-in-chief in North America in as many years, following Braddock, Loudoun and Abercromby – issued further directions for the equipment of the light infantry. In particular he stated that they were not to carry bayonets, instead they had a 'tomahock'.[37] Wolfe, however, once at Quebec, ordered the light infantry to carry them again, 'as the want of ammunition may sometimes be supplied with that weapon', adding that lack of ammunition was no excuse for a man to leave his post and that at night the bayonet was preferable to fire.[38]

Steps were also taken to train the regular battalions so that, if not as specialised as the light infantry, they could at least hold their own against the Indians and French-Canadian irregulars. The Duke of Cumberland had insisted to Lord Loudoun that all American recruits to the army should be taught according to regulations.[39] Wolfe had commented: 'My Lord Loudoun . . . did adhere so literally and strictly to the one – two and the firings by the impracticable chequer, &c., that these regiments must necessarily be cut off one after another unless they fall into some method more suited to the country and the kind of enemy they have to deal with.'[40] This is somewhat harsh on Wolfe's part and it must be remembered that he was writing to Lord Sackville, a man of considerable influence and was promoting himself. In fact Loudoun did take measures to suitably train his infantry for bush fighting. In respect of the newly formed Royal American Regiment he wrote to the commanding officers of its three battalions in December 1756 insisting that the soldiers were trained to fire at marks and to learn to load and fire kneeling and lying on the ground.[41]

One of Loudoun's brigadiers, John Forbes, wrote of the necessity for training troops in the specialist nature of bush warfare. He believed that, when attacked, untrained troops would be killed or flee, whereas a trained and experienced bush fighter would take cover 'behind some tree stumps or stone, where he becomes his own Commanding Officer, acting to the best of his judgement for his own defence and General Good of the whole', thus squarely placing the emphasis on the individual soldier rather than a unit.[42] In a letter to Bouquet he recognised the need to adapt to the local form of warfare: 'And I must confess in this country, we must comply and learn the Art of War from Enemy Indians or anything else who have seen the Country and Warr carried on in it.'[43] It was possibly Forbes who introduced the order 'tree all' into the regulars' repertoire. If ambushed or otherwise surprised this order resulted in the men immediately seeking cover individually behind trees or rocks. From there they could return fire, again individually.[44]

In 1758 Forbes led an expedition to capture Fort DuQuesne, which was abandoned by the French in the face of his advance and renamed Fort Pitt by Forbes, who died soon after taking possession of it. Prior to the expedition setting out, Forbes had spent considerable time and trouble training his command. A letter to him from Bouquet speaks of the need to buy two or three hundred barrels of gunpowder in order to train provincial recruits and 'to drill our troops in forest warfare'. The same letter also spoke of the need to provide the provincials with lead in bars. This was because some of them were armed with rifles, weapons that were not of a military calibre, and it was thus necessary for the provincials to cast their own balls for these.[45] The rifle was a more accurate weapon than the issue musket, but the necessity for the balls to be a tight fit, in order to grip the rifling that imparted spin to the ball, thus improving accuracy, meant that they were slower to load. A few were issued to marksmen amongst the regulars, but they were most commonly found in the hands of Indians and irregulars. The rifle seems to have had little impact on the warfare of the day and was not seen in any number in the British Army until the formation of the 95th Rifles during the Napoleonic wars. It did not reach the hands of the ordinary redcoat until the mid-nineteenth century when the development of the Minie ball overcame the loading problem.

The training of Forbes's men included 'running & firing in the Indian Manner'.[46] The Reverend Thomas Barton who accompanied the expedition has also left a description of how this firing was organised. For battle the men formed in a single rank and were divided into platoons of twenty. There was no attempt to coordinate the fire of the different platoons, but within each platoon the men fired individually, starting with the right-hand man, followed by the left-hand man and then alternating right and left until the fire reached the centre of the platoon. Before the fire reached the centre the first men to fire were reloaded and ready to fire again. By this means a continuous fire was maintained across the front of each platoon in the same manner as it was by companies in battalions using the alternate-fire system.[47] Bouquet's order book for the same expedition adds the detail that each platoon was to be commanded by an officer or a sergeant.[48]

Also in the summer of 1758 Amherst was leading his army against the important fortress and port of Louisbourg. It is clear that Amherst had little respect for the Indians and their way of war, calling them cowards and barbarians and expressing astonishment that they had managed to beat Braddock. However, he clearly understood how they fought and how to beat them.

> Their whole dependence is upon a tree, or a bush, you have nothing to do, but to advance & they will fly, they never stand an open fire or an attack. Our irregulars and light Infantry are certainly of great use & should always accompany an Army in this Country, as these troops drive them out of their shelter, harass them continually & beat them in their own way.[49]

Amherst's orders to his regulars for a field day dealt with an advance by four battalions led by an advance guard of two platoons. If attacked the left hand of these two platoons was to fire 'singly', that is each man individually. This was to be followed by the right-hand platoon firing 'the whole together', after which the left-hand platoon was to begin firing again as before. It is difficult to see what Amherst thought this mix of firing styles might achieve. It is possible that he thought the individual firing would protect the platoon firing a single volley from the attentions of irregulars who fought as individuals whilst the sheer power of a platoon volley might overwhelm or, at least intimidate, an enemy and prevent them from advancing while the following battalions deployed. These four battalions were to form two lines, with the flank subdivisions wheeled outwards to protect the flanks. After the two leading battalions had fired the second line was to pass through and fire in turn.[50] To pass through each other would require the battalions to be in a very loose order and possibly in a single rank. This is very much like Rogers's fire-and-movement tactic, but on a much larger scale.

In early December 1758 Forbes left Fort Pitt to return to Philadelphia where he died the following March. In his absence Bouquet gave instructions to Colonel Hugh Mercer who was charged with the defence of the fort. In these he wrote: 'Your best marksmen only should fire from the Fort, The other to load for them; Each man having two muskets.'[51] In this order there is an echo of Field Marshal Saxe. In his *Reveries* he had advised that the most effective fire could be achieved in a similar method with one man firing while four loaded for him.[52] In both cases the result was to make the most effective use of the best individual marksman available.

By June 1759 Amherst had replaced Abercromby as the commander-in-chief in North America and was assembling his army at Fort Edward. There, both newly arrived provincial troops and the regulars were kept busy, firing at marks and practicing 'forming and dispersing in the woods, and in other exercises adapted to the peculiar method of carrying on war in close-covered countries'.[53] However, this was the year in which the outcome of the war was decided and that happened in open and relatively conventional battle against the French.

It has already been shown above that early in 1755 Braddock had ordered his troops to make use of the alternate system of delivering a battalion's fire and that at the same time Wolfe had been introducing alternate fire to his battalion in England. This was clearly contradictory to the regulations then in force, which, for the delivery of fire, were the regulations authorised by the Duke of Cumberland in 1748. Prior to becoming colonel of the 14th Foot in 1753 and a major general in 1754, Braddock's entire career had been in the Coldstream Guards and thus very much under the eye of the Duke of Cumberland, who seems to have been instrumental in getting Braddock his North American command.[54] Whilst the influence of the Duke of Richmond on the young Lieutenant Colonel Wolfe has been considered, a different explanation offers itself for Braddock's innovation. During the War of the Austrian Succession Frederick the Great had acquired a considerable reputation for his successes against the Austrians, much of which was due to his infantry. In 1754 a translation of the Prussian infantry manual was published in London that contained detailed instructions on how the Prussians executed alternate fire, using eight fire units in a battalion.[55] The two battalions with Braddock had come from the Irish Establishment and were thus well below full strength.[56] They had been brought up to strength by drafts from other battalions and recruiting in America. It would seem probable that Braddock, recognising that these battalions lacked cohesion and training, tried to keep things simple by introducing the far less complex Prussian alternate fire instead of Cumberland's complex system of 1748.

Braddock's replacement, Loudoun, has already been noted as adhering strictly to regulations, but it has to be borne in mind that the 1756 platoon exercise had just been issued and that Loudoun had been given very specific instructions about adhering to them. Loudoun's successor, Major General Abercromby, had gone out to America with Loudoun and so was operating under the same understanding. When Abercromby replaced Loudoun as commander-in-chief in early 1758 he also received assistance in the form of the arrival of new senior officers. To lead the attack against Louisbourg was Major General Amherst, assisted by Brigadier James Wolfe; Brigadier Lord Howe was to assist Abercromby in his attack on Fort Carillon.

In July Abercromby launched his attempt against Fort Carillon. It ended in disaster. Lord Howe was killed in an opening skirmish and Abercromby hurled his regulars forward in a frontal assault, without artillery support, against French fieldworks protected by an abatis of felled trees. The regulars were shot down without reaching the French and Abercromby was forced to retreat. Abercromby was recalled and command passed to Amherst in September 1758.

Although Amherst formed light infantry and took measures to adapt his regulars to irregular warfare he appears to have taken no steps to alter the drill that the regulars would use against the French regulars they would meet at Louisbourg, other than to order that they should load their muskets with two balls.[57] The assault on Louisbourg was preceded by an amphibious landing under fire in which Wolfe played a conspicuous role in achieving a successful landing. The assault on Louisbourg itself was an almost European siege and Louisbourg surrendered on 26 July 1758.

Amherst had served on the Duke of Cumberland's staff, but he was quick to put aside the 1748 firings and introduce alternate fire to the army now under his command.[58] In April 1759 he had ordered each battalion to form a light infantry company, but in May he withdrew those and the grenadier companies of each battalion in his command, then in Albany, to form composite light and grenadier battalions. The remaining eight companies were:

> at all times to be told off in four grand divisions, eight subdivisions, and sixteen platoons; and this must be done without breaking the companies, if the numbers be nearly equal, except in[to] the platoons, that each company must be subdivided to form two platoons. The Officers will be posted, as much as the service will permit, to the companies they belong to.[59]

By specifying that the companies, so long as they were all roughly the same size, should form the basic fire unit and only be divided to form two platoons, all with their own officers, Amherst was placing considerable emphasis on the benefits of the natural cohesion to be found in companies where the men lived together and were commanded by officers they knew.

Meanwhile, at Louisbourg, Wolfe was preparing his army for the attempt on Quebec. Captain John Knox of the 43rd recorded the preparations. It would appear that there was some concern amongst battalion commanders about 'a new system of discipline'. This could have been a reference to either the introduction of alternate fire by Amherst or the new 1757 regulations or, indeed, both. When this issue was raised with Wolfe he is reported to have responded with: 'Pho, pho! – new exercise – new fiddlesticks; if they are otherwise well disciplined and will fight, that's all I shall require of them.'[60]

One of the battalions not familiar with the new exercise would appear to have been Knox's. Prior to setting out to join Wolfe's army in May

1759 they had spent twenty-two months manning various garrisons in Nova Scotia.[61] Whilst in garrison they had done what they could to maintain military efficiency, but it is no surprise that such things as the 1757 regulations and the new fashion for alternate fire had passed them by. However, prior to leaving their garrisons to join the main army Knox recorded: 'The 43d regiment are at exercise every morning, and discharge ammunition cartridges; in the afternoon the men are employed in firing at targets, in which they are encouraged by presents from their Officers, according to their several performances.'[62] The practice of individual marksmanship is a constantly recurring activity amongst all troops throughout the war in North America.

Once with Wolfe's army, the 43rd appear to have been quickly introduced to the new method of delivering a battalion's fire. Knox described firing alternately from right and left to the centre by platoons, sixteen in all, and then by subdivisions, each platoon or subdivision under the command of its own officers. Whilst this was another description of the conduct of alternate fire, Knox added two interesting observations. First he described its effectiveness. The exercise was carried out in a field of wheat and he wrote: 'I never saw grain closer cut down by the reap-hook, or scithe, than this was.' Knox also recorded that 'the method we were ordered to observe did not admit of any confusion, though we fired remarkably quick.'[63] This was the unbiased view of a professional officer that alternate fire was accurate, effective and could be delivered quickly and without confusion, confirmation of its superiority to Cumberland's 1748 firings.

Nor was the use of the bayonet neglected: in a passage redolent with the contempt of a seasoned professional, Knox described a demonstration by a sergeant from another regiment of what he called 'a new method of pushing bayonets', which caused considerable mirth amongst the men. It may have been new to Knox, but this new drill was nothing less than the old style of charging a musket and bayonet like a pike. It would appear that the 43rd had long since given that up, presumably in preference for the new style of holding the musket and bayonet levelled at waist height. Knox described how the sergeant held the firelock 'which he poked out before him, in like-manner as an indolent hay-maker turns hay with a forked pole'. His verdict was 'I thought it ludicrous'.[64]

In July 1759 Amherst gave orders that his infantry were to form and fight in just two ranks 'as the enemy have very few regular troops to oppose us, and no yelling of Indians, or fire of Canadians, can possibly withstand two ranks.'[65] This development appears to have been general throughout North America as Wolfe's army used it at Quebec and the following year Amherst recorded exercising infantry in both three- and two-deep lines.[66]

The analysis of the effectiveness of the new bush-fighting techniques for regulars, light infantry and rangers reveals that success against the French and Indian irregulars did not come quickly and that there were many other factors involved besides actual combat techniques. However, British infantry at least began to be able to hold their own against irregulars so that they could engage the French regular forces in the engagements that would decide the outcome of the war. Accounts of Wolfe's campaign against Quebec are full of accounts of the continuous low-intensity warfare that epitomised irregular combat. One account confirms the individual nature of both the firing and the close-quarter combat. A soldier of the 35th described a skirmish where he saw an Indian aim at him, but miss; he then aimed at the Indian and missed in turn, whereupon the Indian threw his tomahawk at him, but missed, and the soldier threw it back and missed. The soldier was then attacked from behind and hit in the back with a tomahawk, but escaped.[67]

On another occasion at Quebec: 'An Indian Swam over . . . with an intention as we suppose to Scalp a Centry, but on the Centry running up to him and presenting his piece to his breast he got down on his knees threw away his knife and deliver'd himself up.'[68]

Gradually the British infantry began to acquire a degree of ascendancy over their irregular opponents. One officer recorded that small parties were constantly attacked by the enemy who was always repulsed, but not without casualties. He added: 'These skirmishes had indeed the good effect of using our men to the woods, and familiarising them with the Canadians and Indians, whom they soon began to despise.'[69] By October 1759, after the fall of Quebec, an NCO was able to record that 'By this time our small reconnoitring detachments began to appear terrible among the skulking parties of Canadians and Indians.' He described how the Indians would not face them in the open, but would lie in ambush at the edges of woods, firing and then rushing out to attack. At length the Indians 'learned us to be as good hunters as themselves' so that a small number of British were often able to see off larger numbers of Indians. He gave as an example an incident where a sergeant with a corporal and twelve men was cut off from his regiment by a large body of enemy irregulars. Four days later the party returned having lost only two men.[70]

The competence of the British infantry in Indian fighting was most notably demonstrated at the fight at Bushey Run on 5 and 6 August 1763. The Treaty of Paris, signed on 10 February 1763 had brought an end to hostilities between Britain and France, but in North America an Indian uprising, Pontiac's War, broke out on the western frontier. Colonel Bouquet was leading a relief column to Fort Pitt when his convoy was surrounded and pinned down by Indians near a stream that gave its name to the battle. Bouquet and his men took up a position on a hill where they constructed a makeshift breastwork with bags of flour. Of the first day of the battle Bouquet remarked on 'the cool and steady behaviour of the Troops, who did not fire a Shot without orders, and drove the enemy from their Posts with fixed Bayonets'. Robert Kirk of Montgomery's Highlanders wrote that when charged with bayonets the Indians ran away, but, as Bouquet wrote, only to return to the attack. On the second day of the fight British casualties were mounting and Bouquet's force was short of water. He therefore contrived to lure the Indians into an unfavourable position. He weakened part of his defensive perimeter, which the Indians mistook for an indication of retreat and attacked vigorously. However, Bouquet had used the withdrawn infantry to make a flanking move against the Indians. As they attacked they were caught in the open where they received the full fire of four companies followed by a bayonet charge. Bouquet referred to the 'irresistible Shock of our Men, who rushing in among them, killed many of them, and put the rest to flight'.[71] Kirk wrote: 'we met them with our fire first, and then made terrible havock amongst them with our fixt bayonets.'[72]

Platoon fire was also shown to be effective against Indians under the right circumstances. During some of the low-level skirmishing at Quebec, 'the Rangers, Light Infantry and advanced parties continued popping with the enemy . . . Captain Campbell . . . ordered a part of his Company to fire a volley at them, when the firing almost ceased.'[73] Again, in 1761 during a campaign against the Cherokee, in the midst of skirmishing between light infantry and Indians, a regularly formed battalion took decisive action: 'A close Fire from the Regiment for some Minutes, and Orders punctually executed of throwing a Platoon of Fire into every Bush where the least smoke appeared, saved the Lives of a number of brave Fellows, drove the Indians back to great Distance.'[74]

Whilst success against Indians and French-Canadian irregulars enabled the British Army to prosecute the war, it was in open battle against French regulars that the outcome of the war was decided. In July 1759 British forces were besieging Fort Niagara when a French relief force approached. This force of some 800 French regulars and militia and 300 Indians was opposed by 464 British regulars, mostly of the 46th, under the command of Lieutenant Colonel Eyre Massey at La Belle Famille. Seeing that the French had regulars Massey ordered his front rank to fix bayonets, an indication that bayonets were considered inappropriate against irregulars, presumably because of the difficulties of getting in close enough to use them and the negative effect on accuracy of the weight of a bayonet on the muzzle of the musket. In another indication of the influence of irregular warfare Massey ordered his whole line to lie down. Massey estimated that the French, who advanced in column along a road, fired twice in their advance, about five hundred rounds; then, when his men 'could almost reach them with our Bayonets' he gave the order to fire. Massey described the troops that met the French head on as a grand division and wrote that it fired seven rounds standing. As he wrote that he 'gave the Word for the Whole to Fire', it would seem most likely that he fired as a grand division. With his light infantry, 108 men, covering his left flank this grand division probably numbered about 225, supported by the grenadiers of the 46th and a piquet of the 44th, about 125 men, who were covering the right flank. At the same time his grenadiers outflanked the French 'and by their pouring in all their fire, on the Enemy's Flanks, kill'd great numbers, and in my opinion was the occasion of breaking them'. Massey's force then advanced and fired another eight rounds, 'by constant firing', making fifteen in all, and then charged with the bayonet.[75]

Massey's force was considerably outnumbered – by about two to one without counting the Indians accompanying the French. Massey's own Iroquois allies did not engage the French until they were already retreating. Because he had detached his grenadiers and light infantry to cover his flanks the main assault of the French pitted approximately 800 French against 225 men directly to their front and perhaps 125 on Massey's right flank. When numbers were evenly matched British battalions appear to have usually found it necessary only to fire once or twice before charging with the bayonet. Here, outnumbered four to one, the main body of the 46th fired seven times, perhaps fifteen hundred rounds. If the grenadiers and piquet on his right did the same that would have been another seven or eight hundred rounds and, although Massey reported that half the grenadiers were killed or wounded, he expressed the view that this fire into the French flank was decisive. The initial fire of the British infantry was clearly sufficient to stop the French attack in its tracks, probably helped by the French advancing in column so that the head of the column attracted the main weight of the British fire. The heavy casualties suffered by the grenadiers might have been a consequence of them facing the long flank of the French column from which fire was returned while the main British body faced the relatively narrow head of the column. The disparity in numbers meant it took longer, perhaps two or three minutes – less if tap-loading – to deliver the fire to cause sufficient casualties to break the French. Massey had to rely on his firepower in order to avoid being overwhelmed by French numbers. When the French began to retreat, a further eight rounds per man were fired and Massey's reference to 'constant fire' suggests that he switched from volleys of the whole body together to firing by subdivisions or platoons. When Massey was sure that the French were sufficiently broken he then sent them on their way with a bayonet charge.

The battle that effectively decided the outcome of the war in North America was fought on the Plains of Abraham, in front of Quebec, on 13 September 1759. Wolfe had contrived to land his army upstream of Quebec under cover of darkness and Montcalm, the defender of Quebec, marched out to meet him. The decisive action was between six of Wolfe's battalions and seven of Montcalm's. In Wolfe's six battalions facing Quebec there were a little more than seventeen hundred muskets and Montcalm's numbered a little under two thousand, but supported by about fifteen hundred irregulars. Five other British battalions were covering Wolfe's flanks and rear.[76] At least one of Wolfe's battalions was drawn up in two ranks, Anstruther's 58th on the extreme left of the line.

An account by a soldier in that battalion also recorded that the files were three feet apart. No other account mentions this and it is possible that the 58th was forced to spread itself so thin in order to cover the ground between the main line and the position of the battalions protecting its left flank. Elsewhere, although not specifically mentioned, it seems probable that the infantry were formed two deep with files at a more conventional spacing, in accordance with Amherst's general orders.[77]

As the French advanced they began firing at the British line from about a hundred yards away or more; this fire was steadfastly ignored.[78] According to Knox, the 43rd at least was ordered to lie down.[79] At least four of Wolfe's six battalions reserved their fire until the French were less than forty yards away. One battalion, the Louisbourg Grenadiers, are recorded to have waited until the range was less than twenty yards.[80] Wolfe had ordered that the muskets should be loaded with two balls.[81] Townshend, commanding the battalions covering the left flank described the fire of the British line: 'it was regular proved effect and constant – they were routed in three discharges', while Lieutenant Fraser with the 78th wrote that the firing continued for six or eight minutes.[82] Johnson with the 58th wrote: 'we poured in such a discharge; and which we continued, with such a regular briskness, as was visible to all, by the good effect it produced.'[83] Humphreys with the 28th wrote that the firing 'was so well continued, that the enemy everywhere gave way'.[84] Knox recorded 'a well timed, regular, and heavy discharge of our small arms, such as they could no longer oppose, hereupon they gave way, and fled with precipitation', adding:

The forty-third and forty-seventh regiments, in the center, being little affected by the oblique fire of the enemy, gave them, with great calmness, as remarkable a close and heavy discharge, as ever I saw performed at a private field of exercise, insomuch that better troops than we encountered could not possibly withstand it: and, indeed, well might the French Officers say, that they never opposed such a shock as they received from the center of our line, for they believed every ball took place, and such regularity and discipline they had not experienced before; our troops in general, and particularly the central corps, having levelled and fired,- comme une coup de canon.[85]

This firing was followed by a general advance with the bayonet, or, in the case of Fraser's 78th Highlanders, the broadsword.[86] The fighting was not over – some French fought a rearguard action as they withdrew into Quebec – but the battle was won, although Wolfe himself was killed in the moment of victory. The French commander, Montcalm, was also killed and Quebec surrendered on 18 September 1759.

The battle of Quebec was won by a classic combination of firepower and the bayonet. The French attack was met at a range of less than forty yards with the fire of approximately seventeen hundred muskets, each loaded with two balls and wielded by soldiers who were arguably better shots than any British soldiers before. Townshend's three discharges would have delivered about five thousand rounds, or ten thousand balls, at the two thousand French attacking the British line. All the eyewitnesses are clear that the firing was continued after the initial volley. Three of them make use of the word 'regular', suggesting that after an initial full battalion volley the firing continued by subdivisions employing alternate fire. It is perhaps little wonder that one French officer wrote: 'Our troops gave the first fire, the British the second, and the affair was over.'[87]

In April 1760 the French attempted to recapture Quebec and Murray, commanding the British defenders, decided to meet the French in battle, outside Quebec at Sainte Foy. The British were heavily outnumbered and this, combined with tactical errors by Murray, resulted in defeat. The British battalions had been forced to form in two ranks with three feet between files in order to cover their front, but this was too thin and they were overwhelmed by French numbers, particularly when their supporting artillery began to run out of ammunition.[88] A small spotlight was thrown on the character of infantry combat in this battle when Lieutenant Eubele Ormsby of the Grenadier Company of the 35th was subsequently tried by court martial, accused of cowardice.[89] Ormsby's company was involved in fierce fighting for control of a windmill on the British right flank. He described how the company first fired in a regular manner with the front rank kneeling. Other soldiers described the subsequent advance to the windmill in confusion and small bodies, and how Ormsby had directed them where to fire. One told the court martial that he lost all his ammunition and went to get more, but without saying how or from where – presumably the officers of the court knew and this was not considered worthy of mention. Another said he had fallen behind the company in order to change his flint.

From the record of this court martial small snippets of information can be gleaned about the minutiae of the management of British infantry fire. The company was divided into two platoons that at times operated separately, although in close proximity to each other. There appears to have been some means for soldiers to replenish their ammunition, although this could simply have been taking it from the dead and wounded. When a soldier needed to change a flint he appears to have just fallen out and got on with it. Ormsby was cleared by the court martial.

Following the battle, Quebec held out until relieved by the Royal Navy. On 8 September 1760 Montreal surrendered and the war with France in North America was over. In the absence of cavalry and the limited participation of artillery, save in siege warfare, it was a war won by the infantry. Following serious initial setbacks the infantry had adapted to a completely new form of warfare: irregular bush fighting. It learned from allies and enemies and achieved at least parity – and occasionally superiority – over enemies raised knowing only that form of warfare. This was done, however, without any change in the infantry's traditional combat doctrine. The efficiency of the firepower of a battalion was replaced with the efficiency of the individual. The adaptability of the infantry allowed individual marksmanship to replace volume and speed of fire as the prime desirable quality. In the case of the light infantry this objective was pursued with the assistance of specially adapted firelocks and other equipment and specialist training. The object was still to overwhelm and disrupt the enemy with firepower and then to close with the bayonet, broadsword or tomahawk to disperse him and drive him off. This was not always easily achieved, particularly when actually getting to grips with an enemy such as the Indians who would simply retire in the face of superior firepower, but the end result was the same. When the infantry could get at their irregular opponents with the bayonet, as at Bushy Run, the Indians had no answer to it.

When it came to more conventional, European-style combat the infantry were arguably better than ever. Not only did they adopt the alternate-fire system with all its advantages of speed and simplicity, but they were, at the least, competent marksmen and the effectiveness of their fire can only have been increased, particularly at the short ranges they continued to prefer. The British, as Knox put it, 'do not expend their ammunition at an immense distance; and if they advance to engage, or stand to receive the charge, they are steady, profoundly silent and attentive, reserving their fire until they have received that of their adversaries, over whom they have a tenfold advantage'.[90]

The campaigns in North America also saw the appearance of the two-deep lines as part of the tactical repertoire of British infantry. Its success against the French at La Belle Famille and Quebec was an early forerunner of the way the infantry would fight under the Duke of Wellington in the Peninsular War. However, despite this increased reliance on firepower the infantry also retained their penchant for close-quarter combat. At both La Belle Famille and Quebec it was the bayonet that completed the work that firepower had begun and sealed the victory. Even at Sainte Foy a French officer remarked how the British infantry had 'advanced upon us with their bayonets, which, according to custom, threw us into confusion, and compelled us to give up the contest'.[91]

Chapter 9

Conclusion

Amongst modern writers of military history there is a widely held consensus that the infantry of Britain's armies of the seventeenth and eighteenth centuries repeatedly achieved a high level of effectiveness and superiority over their enemies in firepower and relied on that firepower to win battles. Although that assessment is justified by the narrative of the history of the British Army, there has not, until now, been a sufficiently searching investigation to explain how that superiority was first achieved and then maintained over such a long period.

That explanation is now established and it identifies the tactical doctrine and battlefield combat techniques of British infantry and analyses their effectiveness, starting with the English Civil Wars and then tracing a continuous line of development of doctrine and technique up to 1765, in the immediate aftermath of the Seven Years War. In identifying that line of development, previously unrecognised aspects of doctrine and technique have been discovered, and times pinpointed when key changes were brought about, such as the introduction of the organisation of platoons into firings. As a consequence of this detailed analysis some long-held misconceptions have been identified and corrected, such as that concerning the form that platoon firing first took.

At the start of the period under consideration the first armies to engage in the English Civil Wars did so in a completely textbook manner, employing long-established methods of delivering musket fire. At Edgehill in 1642 it was found that the level of fire generated, although sustainable, was insufficient to force a conclusion in a firefight between infantry regiments. There was subsequently a very rapid, nationwide change, which appears to have started within weeks of Edgehill, to delivering the infantry's fire in very short, sharp bursts at very close range, followed by an immediate assault. This was found to be a very effective technique against both cavalry and infantry and became used almost to the exclusion of other, earlier ways of delivering fire and meant that infantry could defend themselves against cavalry without resorting to squares or other all-round defensive formations.

It is likely that this development owed something to the techniques introduced by Gustavus Adolphus of Sweden in the 1630s, but British infantry developed those techniques and took them to a new level. This development occurred in isolation and was not matched by anything similar in Europe, where the use of this new method of fighting by troops from Britain achieved dramatic results. When English armies took to the field in the years immediately after the Civil War they employed this technique against Spanish troops at the battle of the Dunes in the presence of French allies. After the restoration of the monarchy, at Ameixial they again used it against Spanish troops, this time in the presence of Portuguese allies. The impact on friend and foe alike was considerable and nothing quite like it had been seen before on a European battlefield. It was not, however, adopted by any other European army and there are a number of possible reasons for that. It did not solve the issue of combining effective fire with sustainable fire, which was the real problem. It might simply not have suited the way other armies chose to fight, but it might also be a reflection of the limited influence of Britain and its army in the second half of the seventeenth century. Chandler describes the British infantry of the 1680s as 'amateur and immature'.[1]

One of the key developments in the way British infantry delivered its firepower occurred in 1689 following the Glorious Revolution and the accession to the thrones of England and Scotland of William III. It has long been assumed that the introduction of platoon firing to British infantry took place in Flanders where the Duke of Marlborough was leading an English contingent as part of a Dutch army. It is now possible to demonstrate that platoon firing was also almost simultaneously introduced to the Scottish Army and to William's English troops campaigning in Ireland. Furthermore, the precise form that it took has also now been identified and it is different in many aspects from the form that platoon firing is usually stated as having first taken. For instance, the platoons were not at first organised into firings. The great benefit of this new technique was that it allowed the same organisation and formation to deliver fire in a manner that was both sustainable and effective, and at a rate that could easily be controlled. As such it was a perfect development for British infantry with their preference for close-range fire followed by an assault and it also proved effective against cavalry.

During the course of the Nine Years War the pike was replaced by the bayonet, the matchlock musket by the firelock (or flintlock) musket and the cartridge replaced the bandoleer. By the start of the War of the Spanish Succession a battalion, now consisting of twelve companies or platoons of hatmen and two platoons of grenadiers, could fire one of its platoons every few seconds and still have the first platoon that fired reloaded and ready to fire again by the time all the others had fired. Over the course of half a century the firepower of British infantry had effectively doubled.

If the original form of platoon firing was different from the form that is usually described, it is now possible to say when that more usually recognised form, which organised the platoons into firings, was introduced. It is also possible to demonstrate that it was still not organised quite as is usually described. The introduction of firings took place in Ghent, where the British infantry were quartered during the winter of 1706–7. Organised by Major General Ingoldsby, there is some evidence to suggest that the idea had its origins in the Royal Regiment of Ireland. Whatever its exact origins it is clear from manuscript evidence that it did not at first take what might be called the classic form referred to by modern historians, in which a battalion formed three firings, each of six platoons. In their first form the firings made use of fifteen platoons, six in the first two firings and three in the third. It was this form that was employed in the oft-quoted engagement at Malplaquet in 1709 between the two 'rival' Royal Regiments of Ireland in the British and French armies. By the end of the War of the Spanish Succession a battalion was forming in fourteen platoons with a first firing of six platoons and the second and third of four platoons. This is the form described in the official drill manual of 1728.[2] The form with eighteen platoons is just one of the many variations suggested by Humphrey Bland in 1727 and appears in Kane's book of 1745.[3] It only becomes the usual form at the insistence of the Duke of

Cumberland in the 1740s. It would appear that the belief that the early form of platoon firing was as described by Kane has arisen because Kane's book was a history of the War of the Spanish Succession. It has been assumed that the attached drill was of the period of that war whereas it represents the views Kane held in the 1730s.

The organisation of platoons into firings was undoubtedly an effective development, but part of its strength in the form it took at the end of the War of the Spanish succession was because each platoon was also a company. This meant that each platoon was of a big enough size for its fire to be effective and that the men were under the command of their own company officers. Subsequently, however, the number of companies was reduced from thirteen to ten, which meant that companies had to be broken up to form platoons. Furthermore, Cumberland insisted not only on the increased number of platoons, but also that officers were posted to platoons by seniority, meaning that men were frequently commanded by officers they did not know. These changes made the management of a battalion's fire a far more complex business and the effectiveness of firings began to be questioned.

Leaving aside these difficulties, however, it is informative to compare the orders given by Montrose for the battle at Tippermuir in 1644 and the remarks made by La Fausille on how the infantry fought at Laffeldt in 1747.[4] Although divided by over a century, they are, in essence, the same. Both describe defeating the enemy by the close-range delivery of fire followed by an immediate assault.

Despite early difficulties with platoon firing at Dettingen, caused by inexperience and a lack of training, it served its purpose well through the rest of the War of the Austrian Succession. The exceptions were the battles of the Jacobite Rebellion of 1745–6 when the complexities of firings were not able to cope with the rapidity of the Highland charge. Instead Cumberland reverted to using alternate fire in order to deliver the fire of his battalions more quickly and this was used to devastating effect at Culloden. Against a more conventional enemy the use of standard platoon firings continued to be effective.

By the start of the Seven Years War, however, the adherence to the use of platoon firings was being widely questioned and challenged by officers such as James Wolfe. They were advocating the adoption of the

Prussian version of platoon fire, which was simply a version of alternate fire using eight fire units, platoons, companies or subdivisions. Eventually, following the resignation of Cumberland the British infantry was free to adopt this system and it became part of the official regulations in 1765 after being in widespread use during the Seven Years War. In essence it was little different from the alternate fire in use before 1706, and so raises the possibility that the introduction of firings was a mistake, given that the army subsequently returned to using alternate fire.

Bland spelt out the objection to the early form of alternate fire. As it involved twelve companies, with six companies firing in succession in each wing, an unacceptably broad portion of the front of a battalion could be left unloaded at any time, and thus vulnerable to attack.[5] The advantage of organising the platoons in firings was that the available fire was spread across the whole battalion rather than being concentrated at just one point in each wing. This worked well when platoons were whole companies and there were just fourteen platoons. As the number of platoons increased and the number of companies was reduced the whole process became increasingly complex and the firepower of an individual platoon decreased. That there was some recognition of this is clear from Cumberland's introduction of subdivisions comprising two platoons as a fire unit. The advantages of alternate fire by companies over the use of platoons in firings were that it was simpler, companies remained together under their own officers, there was no complex order of firing, and the basic fire unit became larger. Furthermore, Bland's objections were no longer valid for two reasons. Firstly, the rate of fire of the infantry had increased dramatically with improved drill, priming from cartridges and steel ramrods, which meant that the companies were unloaded for a shorter time. Secondly, only eight fire units were involved, rather than fourteen, which meant that, proportionately, any unloaded part of a battalion's front was smaller.

Throughout all the changes and argument about the best way to deliver effective fire two things did not change. One was the range, thirty yards or less, at which it was preferred to open fire. The second was the use of the bayonet to finish what firepower had started. Those arguments that did occur were simply about the best way to deliver the fire of a battalion; the doctrinal debates going on in Europe appear to have passed by the British Army with little effect.

There is no doubt that British infantry throughout the period under consideration was largely successful on the battlefield, often against considerable odds. On the few occasions when they were beaten there were often other factors at play and they soon recovered from those setbacks. Examples of this were Prestonpans, against the Jacobites in 1745, and Monongahela, against irregulars in 1755.

This success was largely due to the infantry's efficiency with firelock and bayonet and their adherence to their tactical doctrine. A factor of some importance in achieving this success was the character of the soldiers themselves. The doctrine that they executed required a considerable amount of confidence and the counter-intuitive recognition that it was safer to ignore the fire of the enemy and reserve a battalion's fire until the range was reached at which it would have the most and the quickest effect. They could also display considerable resilience if not downright stubbornness. At both Marston Moor and Naseby Royalist infantry put up very stubborn resistance. The battle of Fontenoy may have been a defeat, but the British infantry were not beaten, as French cavalry discovered to their cost. At Monongahela the infantry only broke after three hours when all their ammunition was expended, saying they would fight if they could see their enemy. At Minden the 12th Foot had suffered 302 rank and file killed and wounded out of 480 and eighteen officers killed and wounded out of twenty-seven, and yet were still prepared to fight.

If the infantry's performance at Dettingen was initially less than ideal it is perhaps not surprising. The last major battle for the British Army had been Malplaquet in 1709, thirty years earlier, and thus the vast majority of the army had never seen action – the small minority who had were senior officers who had been junior officers in 1709. Nonetheless, as the actions and comments of officers like Wolfe make clear, the army was at least familiar with the theory of their doctrine – what they had to do was relearn confidence in it. Relearn because although the techniques for the delivery of an infantry battalion's fire underwent a number of changes between 1642 and 1765 the underlying tactical doctrine did not. This can be summarised as reserving fire until within a range of thirty yards, then delivering fast and accurate fire to overwhelm the enemy's resolve, before driving them off with a vigorous bayonet charge.

Since this doctrine had lasted and been effective for such a long time, the question arises: did it continue after the period covered by this book? All the indications are that it did. Lawrence Spring in his work on the American War of Independence clearly establishes the combined use of firepower and the bayonet by the British Army.[6] The actions of British infantry in stopping and defeating French columns at La Belle Famille and Quebec are precursors to any number of battles in the Peninsular War and Waterloo.

Indeed it is worth considering the words of one modern British infantry NCO: 'The sight of men jumping out of the Warrior with incoming fire hitting the vehicles yet still no hesitance to go forward is because of the self-belief in their ability, and the knowledge that the only way to stop the incoming fire is to fire back and close with and kill the enemy.' CSM Falconer was writing of his time in Basra in 2004 and yet he expressed an underlying doctrine that would be recognised by any British infantryman from 1642 to 1765. He also wrote about the 'confidence that the soldiers had in the system and themselves'.[7]

The long-term success of British infantry in combat was the result of the adherence to a simple but very effective combat doctrine. It was born in the nationwide strife of the English Civil Wars. It was honed and improved in the cockpit of Europe. It was adapted to overcome Scottish Highlanders and North American Indians. Changes in the practices and procedures of its application sought only to improve the delivery and effectiveness of that doctrine. The professionalism and confidence with which it was applied made Britain's redcoats a force that repeatedly succeeded against numerically superior enemies.

With the understanding of doctrine and practice established it is now possible to look again at well-known narratives and understand why events unfolded as they did. The apprehension of the French about getting into a firefight with British infantry becomes understandable. The defeat of the Jacobites at Culloden, instead of a heroic defeat, begins to look like an inevitability. The brutal effectiveness of British infantry in combat is revealed.

Notes

Chapter 1

1 Frank McLynn, *1759: The Year Britain became Master of the World* (London, 2005).
2 McLlynn, *1759*, p. 276.
3 The Hon J. W. Fortescue, *A History of the British Army*, vol. ii (London, 1899), p. 381.
4 Fortescue, *History of the British Army*, vol. ii, , pp. 508–12; Piers Mackesy, *The Coward of Minden: The Affair of Lord George Sackville* (London, 1979).
5 Rex Whitworth, *Field Marshal Lord Ligonier* (Oxford, 1958), pp. 154–60.
6 John Houlding, *Fit for Service: The Training of the British Army, 1715–1795* (Oxford, 1981), p. 272.
7 Stuart Reid, *Wolfe: Career of General James Wolfe from Culloden to Quebec* (Staplehurst, 2000), p. 133.
8 For example; Matthew H. Spring, *With Zeal and with Bayonets Only* (University of Oklahoma Press, 2008).
9 There were three distinct periods of war, 1642 to 1646, 1648 and 1649 to 1651.
10 Houlding, *Fit For Service*, pp. 45–57.

Chapter 2

1 Colonel Drummond to Colonel Monck, 15 June 1658 in C. H. Firth, (ed.), *The Clarke Papers* (London, 1899), vol. iii, p. 154.
2 H. L. Blackmore, *British Military Firearms, 1650–1850* (London, 1961), p. 24. Bore size refers to the number of balls that can be made for a firearm from a pound of lead. Thus a 12-bore musket fired a lead ball weighing one-twelfth of a pound.

3 Walter M. Stern, 'Gunmaking in Seventeenth Century London', *Journal of the Arms and Armour Society*, 1:5 (1953–6), p. 64.

4 William Barriffe, *Military Discipline: Or the Young Artillery Man* (London, 1635).

5 Roger, Earl of Orrery, *A Treatise of the Art of War* (London, 1677), pp. 30–1.

6 Orrery, *Art of War*, pp. 31–2.

7 Henry Hexham, *The First Part of the Principles of the Art Military* (Delft, 1642), pp. 12 and 16.

8 Sir James Turner, *Pallas Armata* (London, 1683), p. 216; Barriffe, *Military Discipline* (1635), p. 184; Richard Elton, *The Compleat Body of the Art Military* (London, 1668), pp. 192–3.

9 Barriffe, *Military Discipline* (1635) p. 27.

10 Elton, *Compleat Body*, pp. 192–3.

11 Robert Ward, *Animadversions of Warre* (London, 1639) pp. 259–76.

12 Anon., *Generall Lessley's Direction and Order for the Exercising of Horse and Foot* (London, 1642).

13 Anon., *A True Description of the Discipline of War both for Horse and Foot* (no place, no date).

14 Barriffe, *Military Discipline* (1635), pp. 190–5; Elton, *Compleat Body*, p. 52.

15 Barriffe, *Military Discipline* (1635), pp. 186–9; Elton, *Compleat Body*, p. 52.

16 Barriffe, *Military Discipline* (1635), p. 21.

17 Barriffe, *Military Discipline* (1635), p. 201.

18 William S. Brockington, Jr. (ed.), *Monro: His Expedition with the Worthy Scots Regiment Called Mac-Keys* (Westport, CT, 1999), pp. 322–3.

19 William Watts, *The Swedish Intelligencer, The Second Part* (London, 1632) p. 124; William Watts, *The Swedish Discipline, Religious, Civile and Military* (London, 1632), pp. 80–2.

20 William Barriffe, *Military Discipline: Or the Young Artillery Man* (London, 1639), p. 373.

21 Brigadier Peter Young, *Edgehill, 1642: The Campaign and the Battle* (Kineton, 1967); C. L. Scott, Alan Turton and Dr Eric Gruber von Arni, *Edgehill: The Battle Reinterpreted* (Barnsley, 2004).

22 Although only nine at the time of the battle, James II had considerable opportunity to talk to other eyewitnesses and as a competent soldier in his adult years he would have understood clearly what he was told. The memoirs were probably commenced after 1660, but writing continued up to 1685. They appear to have been complete by 1696. A. Lytton Sells, *The Memoirs of James II* (Bloomington, 1962), pp. 13–23.

23 Rev. J. S. Clarke (ed.), *The Life of James the Second King of England, etc, Collected out of Memoirs Writ of his Own Hand* (London, 1816), vol. i, p. 12.

24 Young, *Edgehill*, p. 307.

25 Clarke, *James II*, p. 14.

26 Clarke, *James II*, p. 14.

27 Young, *Edgehill*, p. 308.

28 Barriffe, *Military Discipline* (1639), p. 371.

29 Elton, *Compleat Body*, p. 139.

30 Sir Richard Bulstrode, *Memoirs and Reflections upon the Reign and Government of King Charles the Ist and K. Charles the II^d* (London, 1721), p. 84.

31 Scott et al, *Edgehill*, pp. 118–24.

32 John Gwynne, *Military Memoirs of the Great Civil War* (Edinburgh, 1822) p. 24.

33 Gwynne, *Memoirs*, p. 55. The usual length of a pike was sixteen feet.

34 Charles E. H. Chadwyck Healey (ed.), *Bellum Civile: Hopton's Narrative of his Campaign in the West* (London, 1902), p. 102. It should be noted that the phrase 'charging their pikes' means to bring it horizontal to the position for combat, not that an assault was made against someone's pikes. The word charge at this time is also frequently used to mean delivering fire, just as loading can be referred to as charging a firearm and an individual load is referred to as a charge.

35 William Watts, *Swedish Discipline*, p. 24.

36 Rev. John Webb (ed.), *Military Memoir of Colonel John Birch* (London, 1873), p. 8.

37 Henry Foster, *A True and Exact Relation of the Marchings of the Two Regiments of the Trained-Bands of the City of London* (London, 1643), n.p.

38 Foster, *A True and Exact Relation*, n.p.

39 Anon., *An Express Relation of the Passages and Proceedings of His Majesties Armie, under the Command of his Excellence the Earle of Newcastle* (1643), p. 2.

40 Margaret, Duchess of Newcastle, *The Life of . . . William Cavendish . . . Earl of Newcastle* (London, 1667), p. 30.

41 Dave Cooke, *The Forgotten Battle – Adwalton Moor* (Heckmondwike, 1996), pp. 20–1.

42 Joseph Lister, *An Historical Relation of the Life of Mr Joseph Lister* (Bradford, 1821), p. 13.

43 Robert Bell (ed.), *Memorials of the Civil War, Comprising the Correspondence of the Fairfax Family* (London, 1849), vol. i, p. 28.

44 Sir Thomas Fairfax, *Short Memorials of Thomas Lord Fairfax* (London, 1699), pp. 9–10.

45 Fairfax, *Short Memorials*, p. 16.

46 Fairfax, *Short Memorials*, p. 30.

47 Brigadier Peter Young, *Marston Moor, 1644, The Campaign and the Battle* (Kineton, 1970); P. R. Newman and P. R. Roberts, *Marston Moor, 1644, The Battle of the Five Armies* (Pickering, 2003).

48 Lionel Watson, *A More Exact Relation of the Late Battell Neer York* (London, 1644), p. 6.

49 C. H. Firth, 'Marston Moor', in *Transactions of the Royal Historical Society*, New Series, 12 (1898), p. 75.

50 Captain William Stewart, *A Full Relation of the Late Victory* . . . (London, 1644), p. 8.

51 George Wishart, *The History of the Kings Majesties Affairs in Scotland* (The Hague, 1647), p. 39.

52 Patrick Gordon of Ruthven, *A Short Abridgement of Britane's Distemper* (Aberdeen, 1844), p. 101.

53 Sir Edward Walker, 'Brief Memorials', in Peter Young, *Naseby 1645* (London, 1985), p. 318.

54 John Rushworth, 'Letter', in Glenn Foard, *Naseby: The Decisive Campaign* (Whitstable, 1995), pp. 403–5.

55 Martin Marix Evans, *Naseby 1645: The Triumph of the New Model Army* (Oxford, 2007), pp. 58–9.

56 Richard Collings, *The Kingdomes Weekly Intelligencer, 24 June to 1 July* (London, 1645), p. 847.

57 Foard, *Naseby*, p. 263.

58 Thomas Carlyle, *Oliver Cromwell's Letter and Speeches* (London, 1849), p. 347.

59 Elton, *Compleat Body* (1650), pp. 52–4.

60 Elton, *Compleat Body* (1659), n.p.

61 Elton, *Compleat Body* (1659), n.p.

62 Elton, *Compleat Body* (1650), p. 54.

63 Gil: Batt:, *Some Particular Animadversions of Marke, for the Satisfaction of the Contumatious Malignant* . . . (London, 1646), pp. 25–6.

64 Firth, *Clarke Papers*, vol. iii, p. 158.

65 Major General Morgan, *A True and Just Relation of Maj. Gen. Sir Thomas Morgan's Progress in France and Flanders* (London, 1699), p. 9.

66 Lytton Sells, *James II*, p. 265.

67 Lytton Sells, *James II*, p. 266.

68 John Childs, 'The English Brigade in Portugal, 1662-68', *Journal of the Society for Army Historical Research*, 53:215 (1975), p. 136.

69 Historic Manuscripts Commission (HMC), *The Manuscripts of J. M. Heathcote Esq.* (London, 1899), p. 104.

70 James Howell, *Proedria Vasilike a Discourse Concerning the Precedency of Kings* (London, 1664), p. 38. The reference here to musket rests is probably a reference to the musket stocks and using them to club down the enemy rather than to the forked musket rest for taking the weight of the musket and which had gone out of use during the English Civil War.

71 HMC, *Heathcote Manuscripts*, p. 104.

72 Captain John Hodgson and Sir Henry Slingsby, *Memoirs Written during the Great Civil War* (Edinburgh, 1806), p. 116.

73 Morgan, *Relation*, p. 6.

74 Morgan, *Relation*, p. 8; Lytton Sells, *James II*, p. 264.

75 Brent Nosworthy, *The Anatomy of Victory: Battle Tactics 1689–1763* (New York, 1992), pp. 48–50.

76 See below, pp. 46–7.

77 Nosworthy, *Anatomy of Victory*, p. 107.

78 *An Abridgement of the English Military Discipline* (London, 1676).

79 *An Abridgement of the Military Discipline Appointed by His Majesty to be Used by All His Forces in His Ancient Kingdom of Scotland* (Edinburgh, 1680).

80 See below, pp. 44–6.

81 *Abridgement* (1676), p. 76.

82 These were 1678, 1680 (Edinburgh), 1682, 1684, 1685 (two editions, in London and Dublin) and 1686. The 1678 edition had an addition of detailed instructions for each movement in both musket and pike drill, as well as additional sections dealing with grenadiers and dragoons. The solid square was dropped from it. The 1680 Edinburgh edition differed only in the title. The 1682 edition had some useful explanatory diagrams added. The 1684 edition was effectively a reprint of the latter.

83 *An Abridgement of the English Military Discipline* (London, 1685), p. 138.

84 *Abridgement* (1685), pp. 160–1.

85 *Abridgement* (1685), pp. 161–2.

86 *Abridgement* (1685), pp. 128–9.

87 David Chandler, *The Art of Warfare in the Age of Marlborough* (Staplehurst, 1990), p. 116.

88 Turner, *Pallas Armata*, p. 238.

89 J. Demoriet, *Le Major Parfait* (1863), in Harleian Ms 4655, p. 43, as cited in Chandler, *Art of Warfare*, p. 116.

90 Richard Coe, *An Exact Diarie or a Briefe Relation of the Progress of Sir William Wallers Army* (London, 1644), p. 6.

91 Morgan, *Relation*, p. 8.

92 Daniel MacKinnon, *Origin and Services of the Coldstream Guards* (London, 1833), p. 167.

93 Firelock and snaphance were the contemporary terms for the flintlock.

94 MacKinnon, *Coldstream Guards*, p. 189.

95 E. M. G. Routh, 'The English at Tangier', *English Historical Review*, 26:103 (July 1911), pp. 469–81.

96 John Ross, *Tangers Rescue or a Relation of the Late Memorable Passage at Tanger* (London, 1681), p. 10.

97 Ross, *Tangers Rescue*, p. 14.

98 Ross, *Tangers Rescue*, pp. 26–7.

99 Anon., *A True Description of the Discipline of War both for Horse and Foot* (n.d.), p. 2.

100 George Monck, Duke of Albemarle, *Observations upon Military and Political Affairs* (London, 1671) (written in 1646 when a prisoner in the Tower of London), p. 103.

101 John Cruso, *Militarie Instructions for the Cavallrie* (Cambridge, 1631), p. 41; Orrery, *Art of War*, pp. 31–2.

102 See below, p. 41.

Chapter 3

1 David Chandler, *The Art of Warfare in the Age of Marlborough* (Staplehurst, 1990), p. 116; Brent Nosworthy, *The Anatomy of Victory: Battle Tactics 1689–1763* (New York, 1992), p. 55.

2 Chandler, *Art of Warfare*, p. 116.

3 Chandler, *Art of Warfare*, pp. 117–20; Brigadier General Richard Kane, *Campaigns of King William and Queen Anne; From 1689 to 1712. Also, A New System of Military Discipline for a Battalion of Foot on Action* (London, 1745).

4 Guillaume Le Blond, *Elemens de Tactique* (Paris, 1758), pp. 405–6.

5 Chandler, *Art of Warfare*, p. 116.

6 Chandler, *Art of Warfare*, pp. 116–17.

7 William S. Brockington, Jr. (ed.), *Monro: His Expedition with the Worthy Scots Regiment Called Mac-Keys* (Westport CT, 1999), p. 316.

8 Brockington, *Monro*, p. 323.

9 Sir James Turner, *Pallas Armata* (London, 1683), p. 238.

10 William Watts, *The Swedish Intelligencer, The First Part* (London, 1632), p. 124.

11 See above, p. 17.

12 William Watts, *The Swedish Intelligencer, The Second Part* (London, 1632), p. 169.

13 Brockington, *Monro*, p. xvi.

14 Sir James Turner, *Memoirs of His Own Life and Times* (Edinburgh, 1829), pp. 4–5.

15 Turner, *Pallas Armata*, p. 228.

16 Keith Roberts, *Cromwell's War Machine: The New Model Army, 1645–1660* (Barnsley, 2005), p. 152.

17 Turner, *Pallas Armata*, pp. 216–17.

18 Turner, *Pallas Armata*, p. 217.

19 Brockington, *Monro*, p. 323.

20 Brockington, *Monro*, pp. 322–3.

21 Brockington, *Monro*, p. 322; Richard Elton, *The Compleat Body of the Art Military* (London, 1668), pp. 192–3.

22 Brockington, *Monro*, p. 322.

23 Elton, *Compleat Body*, pp. 192–3.

24 Roger, Earl of Orrery, *A Treatise of the Art of War* (London, 1677), p. 38.

25 Orrery, *Art of War*, p. 31.

26 See above, p. 9.

27 Chandler, *Art of Warfare*, pp. 78–9.

28 Turner, *Pallas Armata*, p. 237

29 *An Abridgement of the English Military Discipline* (London, 1676).

30 *Abridgement* (1676), pp. 31–2.

31 *Abridgement* (1676), p. 74.

32 The strength of a company was variable, but in the English army of the 1680s was between forty and sixty: Chandler, *Art of Warfare*, p. 96.

33 Elton, *Compleat Body*, (1659), p. 154.

34 Brockington, *Monro*, p. 319.

35 Brockington, *Monro*, p. 322.

36 Brockington, *Monro*, p. 323.

37 Elton, *Compleat Body*, (1659), p. 54.

38 Ofwersteleut Iulius Richard De Lachapelle, *Een Militarisch Exercitiae Book* (Stockholm, 1669).

39 Louis Paan, *Den korter weg tot de Nederlandsche Militaire Exercitie, Inhoudende verscheide extraordinaire Evolutien ende Bataillons, Mitsgaders de formen der Batailles, Vol. 2* (Leuwarden, 1684).

40 Paan, *Nederlandsche Militaire Exercitie*, p. 40.

41 Turner, *Pallas Armata*, p. 238.

42 BL Additional Manuscript, 21506, f. 98, cited in Chandler, *Art of Warfare*, p. 116.

43 For instance, David Chandler, *The Art of Warfare*, p. 116.

44 George Warter Story, *A True and Impartial History of the Most Material Occurrences in the Kingdom of Ireland during the Two Last Years* (London, 1691), p. 23.

45 Story, *True and Impartial History*, p. 24.

46 Story, *True and Impartial History*, p. 26.

47 Major General Hugh Mackay, *Memoirs of the War Carried on in Scotland and Ireland* (Edinburgh, 1833), p. 55.

48 *The Exercise of the Foot with the Evolutions, According to the Words of Command, As they are Explained. As also, the forming of Battalions, With Directions to be observed by all Colonels, Captains, and other Officers in Their Majesties Armies. Like wise The Exercise of the Dragoons Both on Horse-back and Foot. With the Rules of War in the day of Battel, when Encountering with the Enemy* (Edinburgh, 1693).

49 *The Exercise of the Foot with the Evolutions, According to the Words of Command, As they are Explained. As also, the forming of Battalions, With Directions to be observed by all Colonels, Captains, and other Officers in Their Majesties Armies* (London, 1690).

50 *The Exercise of the Foot with the Evolutions, With the Rules of War in the day of Battel, when Encountering with the Enemy*, n.p.

51 Major General Hugh Mackay, 'Rules of War', in *The Exercise of the Foot with the Evolutions, With the Rules of War in the day of Battel, when Encountering with the Enemy*, n.p. (hereafter Mackay, *Rules of War*), Article VI.

52 Orrery, *Art of War*, p. 38.

53 Mackay, *Rules of War*, Article X

54 J. A. Houlding, *Fit for Service: The Training of the British Army, 1715–1795* (Oxford, 1981), p. 281.

55 Chandler, *Art of Warfare*, p. 119.

56 Cornwall Record Office, DD.RH.388, fol. 7, *Exercise of Firelock and Bayonet appointed by his Excie. Lieut. Genll. Ingoldsby*; British Library, Add Mss 27892, Brig. Gen. James Douglass, *Schola Martis, or the Art of War . . . as Practised in Flanders, in the Wars, from Anno 1688 to An: 1714,*

ff. 209–55; Humphrey Bland, *A Treatise of Military Discipline* (London, 1727), p. 72.

57 Mackay, *Rules of War*, Article IX.

58 Mackay, *Rules of War*, Article X.

59 Mackay, *Rules of War*, Article XVIII.

60 Mackay, *Rules of War*, Article X.

61 Mackay, *Rules of War*, Article XI.

62 Edward D'Auvergne, *A Relation of the Most Remarkable Transactions of the Last Campaign, 1692* (London, 1693), p. 44.

63 D'Auvergne, *A Relation, 1692*, p. 47.

Chapter 4

1 See above, p. 31.

2 *Exercise for the Horse, Dragoon and Foot Forces* (London and Dublin, 1728).

3 Andrew Crichton, *The Life and Diary of Lieutenant-Colonel John Blackader* (Edinburgh, 1824).

4 See above, p. 42.

5 David Chandler, *The Art of Warfare in the Age of Marlborough* (Staplehurst, 1990), p. 78; Brent Nosworthy, *The Anatomy of Victory: Battle Tactics 1689–1763* (New York, 1992), p. 100.

6 Chandler, *Art of Warfare*, pp. 75–81; Howard L. Blackmore, *British Military Firearms, 1650–1850* (London, 1961).

7 Major General Hugh Mackay, *Memoirs of the War Carried on in Scotland and Ireland* (Edinburgh, 1833), p. 55.

8 Mackay, *Memoirs*, p. 52.

9 Mackay, *Memoirs*, p. 59.

10 Mackay, *Memoirs*, p. 52.

11 Mackay, *Rules of War*, Article XVII.

12 British Library, Add Mss 27892, Brig. Gen. James Douglass, *Schola Martis, or the Arte of War . . . as Practised in Flanders, in the Wars, from Anno 1688 to An: 1714*, f. 217v.

13 Douglass, *Schola Martis*, ff. 217v and r.

14 Mackay, *Rules of War*, Article X.

15 Historic Manuscripts Commission, *Leyborne Popham Mss* (London, 1899), p. 273.

16 Anon., *The Field of Mars, Being an Alphabetical Digestion of the Principal Naval and Military Engagements* (London, 1781), vol. ii, n.p.

17 W. Sawle, *An Impartial Relation of all the Transactions between the Army of the Confederates and that of the French King in their Last Summer's Campaign in Flanders with a More Particular Respect to the Battle of Fleury* (London, 1691), p. 8.

18 Chandler, *Art of Warfare*, pp. 67–8.

19 Curt Jany, *Geschichte der Preußischen Armee vom 15. Jahrhundert bis 1914. Eerster Band: Von den Anfängen bis 174.* (Osnabrück, 1967) I., pp. 336–7 as cited in John Stapleton, *Forging A Coalition Army: William III, The Grand Alliance, And The Confederate Army In The Spanish Netherlands, 1688–1697* (unpublished doctoral thesis, Ohio State University, 2003). Jany gives 11 October 1688 as the date when Brandenburg troops officially adopted the 'Holländische Salve'.

20 Nosworthy, *Anatomy of Victory*, p. 107.

21 From the Dutch camp near Walcourt, August 26, *London Gazette*, No. 2482, 22 August to 26 August 1689.

22 David Chandler, *Marlborough as Military Commander* (London, 1973), p. 13.

23 D'Auvergne, *A Relation, 1692*, p. 42. D'Auvergne wrote a series of annual accounts of events in Ireland covering the years 1691 to 1697, each published in either the same or subsequent year as that covered. During this time he served as a chaplain, first to the Earl of Bath's regiment and then the Scots Guards.

24 D'Auvergne, *A Relation, 1692*, p. 44.

25 D'Auvergne, *A Relation, 1692*, pp. 42 and 45.

26 John Childs, *The Nine Years War and the British Army* (Manchester, 1991), p. 76.

27 Chandler, *Art of Warfare*, p. 68.

28 Douglass, *Schola Martis*, ff. 290–6.

29 *The Exercise of the Foot with the Evolutions, According to the Words of Command, As they are Explained. As also, the forming of Battalions, With Directions to be observed by all Colonels, Captains, and other Officers in Their Majesties Armies. Like wise The Exercise of the Dragoons Both on Horse-back and Foot. With the Rules of War in the day of Battel, when Encountering with the Enemy* (Edinburgh, 1693).

30 Douglass, *Schola Martis*, f. 210v.

31 Douglass, *Schola Martis*, f. 229v; and Mackay, *Rules*, Article VI.

32 Charles Dalton, *English Army Lists and Commission Registers, 1661–1714* (London, 1898), vol. iv, p. 193.

33 Douglass, *Schola Martis*, ff. 217v and 232v.

34 Douglass, *Schola Martis*, f. 229v.

35 Mackay, *Rules of War*, Article XI; and Douglass, *Schola Martis*, f. 229v.

36 Mackay, *Rules of War*, Articles XIX and XX.

37 Douglass, *Schola Martis*, ff. 209v and 229v.

38 *The Exercise of the Foot* (1693), p. 62.

39 Douglass, *Schola Martis*, f. 209v; and *The Exercise of the Foot* (1693), p. 62.

40 Douglass, *Schola Martis*, f. 233r.

41 Douglass, *Schola Martis*, f. 229v.

42 In this context to 'keep up' fire means to reserve it rather than the modern meaning of continuing to fire.

43 Douglass, *Schola Martis*, f. 233r.

44 Edward D'Auvergne, *The History of the Last Campagne in the Spanish Netherlands, Anno Dom. 1693* (London, 1693), p. 78.

45 Childs, *Nine Years War*, pp. 72–4.

46 Mackay, *Rules of War*, Article XVIII; and Douglas, *Schola Martis*, f. 233r.

47 Chandler, *Art of Warfare*, p. 111.

48 Douglass, *Schola Martis*, f. 233r.

49 Mackay, *Rules of War*, Article XVIIII.

50 Mackay, *Rules of War*, Article XVII.

51 Douglass, *Schola Martis*, f 253v.

52 Mackay, *Rules of War*, Article XVII.

53 Douglass, *Schola Martis*, ff. 211r and 217v.

54 Douglass, *Schola Martis*, f. 217r.

55 Chandler, *Art of Warfare*, pp. 114–15 and Nosworthy, *Anatomy of Victory*, p. 60.

56 See above, p. 85XXX.

57 George Warter Story, *A True and Impartial History of the Most Material Occurrences in the Kingdom of Ireland during the Two Last Years* (London, 1691), p. 54.

58 D'Auvergne, *A Relation, 1692*, p. 44.

59 Story, *True and Impartial History*, pp. 129–30.

60 Mackay, *Memoirs*, pp. 52, 55 and 59.

61 Comte Maurice de Saxe, *Reveries or Memoirs Concerning the Art of War*, trans. Sir William Fawcett (Edinburgh, 1757), p. 31.

62 Chandler, *Art of Warfare*, p. 113.

63 Chandler, *Art of Warfare*, pp. 131 and 133.

64 Nosworthy, *Anatomy of Victory*, p. 61.

65 D'Auvergne, *Last Campagne 1693*, p. 73.

Chapter 5

1 David Chandler, *Marlborough as Military Commander* (London, 1973), p. 331.

2 Montgomery of Alamein, *A History of Warfare* (London, 1968), p. 291.

3 Richard Holmes, *Marlborough, Britain's Greatest General* (London, 2008); John Keegan and Andrew Wheatcroft, *Who's Who in Military History* (London, 1976); J. W. Fortescue, *A History of the British Army* (London, 1910, 20 vols).

4 John Houlding, *Fit for Service: The Training of the British Army, 1715–1795* (Oxford, 1981), p. 174.

5 Houlding, *Fit for Service*, pp. 172–4.

6 Houlding, *Fit for Service*, p. 174.

7 Houlding, *Fit for Service*, p. 167.

8 Brigadier General Richard Kane, *Campaigns of King William and the Duke of Marlborough, Also a New System of Military Discipline, for a Battalion of Foot on Action* (London, 1745) and Robert Parker, *Memoirs of the Most Remarkable Military Transactions from the Year 1683 to 1718* (Dublin, 1746), pp. 138–9.

9 See above, pp. 64–5.

10 *The New Exercise of Firelocks & Bayonets; Appointed by his Grace the Duke of Marlborough to be Used by all the British Forces* (London, 1708).

11 Walter C. Horsley (trans.), *The Chronicles of an Old Campaigner, M. De La Colonie, 1692–1717* (London, 1904), pp. 184–5.

12 Chandler, *Marlborough as Military Commander*, pp. 141–51; Holmes, *Marlborough*, pp. 282–96; Charles Spencer, *Blenheim: Battle for Europe* (London, 2004), pp. 229–91.

13 BL Add Mss 61408, Josiah Sandby, Journal, f. 159.

14 BL Add Mss 61408, Josiah Sandby, Journal, f. 159.

15 National Army Museum, 6807/392A+B, Journal of Robert Stearne, vol. i, n.p.

16 Parker, *Memoirs*, p. 89.

17 BL Add Mss 61408, Josiah Sandby, Journal, f. 168.

18 David G. Chandler (ed.), *A Journal of Marlborough's Campaigns During the War of the Spanish Succession, 1704–1711, by John Marshall Deane* (JSAHR, Special Publication no. 12, London, 1984), p. 11.

19 David Chandler, *Military Memoirs of Marlborough's Campaigns, 1702–1712* (London, 1998), pp. 171–2.

20 Chandler, *Marlborough*, pp. 172–8; Holmes, *Marlborough*, pp. 332–47.

21 BL Add Mss 61371, f. 119, Marlborough's instructions to Ingoldsby, 4th November 1706.

22 John Millner, *A Compendious Journal of all the Marches, Famous Battles and Sieges* (Uckfield, 2004), p. 194.

23 BL Add Mss 61398, Adam Cardonnel's letters, June 06 to Sept 07, Whitehall, 16 Dec 1706 to Ingoldsby.

24 BL Add Mss 61163, Ingoldsby Correspondence, Ingoldsby to Marlborough, 31 December 1706, ff. 44–6.

25 *The Exercise of the Foot with the Evolutions* (Dublin, 1701).

26 BL Add Mss 61163, f. 45.

27 For the training in general of the British Army during the eighteenth century see Houlding, *Fit for Service.*

28 BL Add Mss 61163, Ingoldsby Correspondence, Ghent, 2 March, 1707, to Marlborough.

29 Humphrey Bland, *A Treatise of Military Discipline* (London, 1727), p. 146.

30 Dutch Nationaal Archief, Familiearchief Van Wassenaer van Duvenvoorde, Inv. Nr. 1223, Stukken van Willem Baron van Wassenaer, colonel-commandant van het eerste bataljon gardes.

31 Mackay, *Rules of War*, Article VI.

32 Millner, *Compendious Journal*, p. 199.

33 Chandler, *Deane*, p. 48.

34 Winston S. Churchill, *Marlborough: His Life and Times* (two volumes, London, 1947), vol. ii, p. 448.

35 C. T. Atkinson, 'Wynendael', *JSAHR*, 34 (1956), p. 30.

36 Cathcart Mss, National Library of Scotland, Acc 12686, as cited in Atkinson, C. T., 'Gleanings from the Cathcart Mss', *JSAHR*, 29 (1951), p. 67.

37 Chandler, *Marlborough*, pp. 213–22; Holmes, *Marlborough*, pp. 382–90.

38 Chandler, *Deane*, p. 60.

39 Millner, *Compendious Journal*, p. 216.

40 Matthew Bishop, *The Life and Adventures of Matthew Bishop* (London, 1744), p. 169.

41 Parker, *Memoirs*, p. 125.

42 Kane, *Campaigns*, p. 1.

43 BL Add Mss 23642, Parker's letter to Lt. Col. Kane, Dublin, 13 Sept 1708.

44 Houlding, *Fit for Service*, p. 177.

45 Parker, *Memoirs*, p. 125.

46 Cornwall Record Office, DD.R.H.839 (formerly DD.R.H.388) *Exercise of Firelock and Bayonet . . . appointed by his Excie. Lieut. Genll. Ingoldsby.*

47 BL Add Mss 29477, The Exercise of the Firelock and Bayonett with ye Doublings and Hollow Square.

48 *The New Exercise of Firelocks & Bayonets.*

49 Chandler, *Marlborough*, pp. 254–67; Holmes, *Marlborough*, pp. 423–32.

50 John Wilson, 'The Journal of John Wilson', in David G. Chandler (ed.), *Military Miscellany II: Manuscripts from Marlborough's Wars, the American War of Independence and the Boer War* (Stroud, 2005) p. 78.

51 Parker, *Memoirs*, pp. 138–9.

52 Parker, *Memoirs*, pp. 138–9.

53 Chandler, *Art of Warfare*, pp. 117–20; Nosworthy, *Anatomy of Victory*, pp. 56–7; Kane, *Campaigns of King William*, p. 112.

54 Mackay, *Rules of War*, Article XVIII.

55 D'Auvergne, *A Relation, 1692*, p. 48.

56 Chandler, *Art of Warfare*, p. 78.

57 BL Add Mss 23642, Parker's letter to Lt. Col. Kane, Dublin, 13 Sept 1708.

58 Bishop, *Life*, p. 213.

59 BL Add Mss 29477, ff. 117v–107r, the folios with the drill on are written from the back of the book.

60 BL Add Mss 29477, f. 107v.

61 BL Stowe Mss, 481, f. 131r.

62 BL Stowe Mss, 481, f. 131v.

63 BL Stowe Mss, 481, f. 134v–135r.

Chapter 6

1 For an extensive discussion of the negative effects of peacetime soldiering on the army's readiness for war see John Houlding, *Fit for Service: The Training of the British Army, 1715–1795* (Oxford, 1981).

2 Roger, Earl of Orrery, *A Treatise of the Art of War* (London, 1677); Sir James Turner, *Pallas Armata* (London, 1683).

3 *Exercise for the Horse, Dragoons and Foot Forces* (London, 1728), hereafter the '1728 regulations'.

4 Humphrey Bland, *A Treatise of Military Discipline* (London, 1727); Brigadier-General Richard Kane, *Campaigns of King William and the Duke of Marlborough, Also A New System of Military Discipline, for a Battalion of Foot on Action* (London, 1745).

5 Royal Collection, Cumberland Papers, Orderly Book Extracts, 2/2 f.4r (M), Lt. Col. John La Fausille's Ms.

6 Houlding, *Fit for Service*, p. 179.

7 Bland, *Military Discipline*, Preface, n.p.

8 It went unrevised until the eighth edition of 1759 and the last, ninth edition was published in 1762.

9 Bland, *Military Discipline*, p. 73

10 Bland, *Military Discipline*, p. 72; Mackay, *Rules*, Article IX; see above, p. 52.

11 British Library Add Mss 29477, ff. 117v–107v, see above, p. 91.

12 Bland, *Military Discipline*, opposite p. 2

13 National Army Museum, NAM6807.205, The Exercise of the Firelock and Bayonett that was ordered to be used by all the Regim^ts in Ireland 1723.

14 *1728 Regulations*, p. 80

15 Bland, *Military Discipline*, p. 60.

16 Bland, *Military Discipline*, p. 69.

17 Bland, *Military Discipline*, p. 68.

18 Bland, *Military Discipline*, p. 81.

19. Bland, *Military Discipline*, p. 68.

20 Bland, *Military Discipline*, p. 66.

21 See above, p. 45.

22 *1728 Regulations*, p. 76.

23 Bland, *Military Discipline*, p. 127.

24 Bland, *Military Discipline*, pp. 67–8.

25 See above, p. 86.

26 Bland, *Military Discipline*, p. 80.

27 Bland, *Military Discipline*, p. 79.

28 Bland, *Military Discipline*, p. 92.

29 Bland, *Military Discipline*, p. 94.

30 Bland, *Military Discipline*, pp. 81–2.

31 Bland, *Military Discipline*, p. 91.

32 Bland, *Military Discipline*, p. 134.

33 Bland, *Military Discipline*, p. 133.

34 Bland, *Military Discipline*, p. 146.

35 Kane, *Campaigns*, p. iv.

36 Kane, *Campaigns*, p. 109.

37 Kane, *Campaigns*, p. 111.

38 Kane, *Campaigns*, p. 112.

39 Kane, *Campaigns*, p. 113.

40 Kane, *Campaigns*, p. 110.

41 Kane, *Campaigns*, p. 117.

42 Kane, *Campaigns*, p. 118.

43 Kane, *Campaigns*, pp. 119–20.

44 Kane, *Campaigns*, pp. 125–6.

45 Lieutenant General Richard, 3rd Viscount Molesworth, *A Short Course of Standing Rules, For the Government and Conduct of an Army* (London, 1744), pp. iv and 12.

46 Houlding, *Fit for Service*, p. 147.

47 In 1726 Henry Hawley, Colonel of the 33rd Foot expressed a preference for wooden ramrods, Rev. P. Sumner (ed.),'General Hawley's "Chaos"', *JSAHR*, 26 (1948), p. 93; however, in 1754 the 3rd Foot were reported as loading 'very slow' in part because they had wooden ramrods, Houlding, *Fit for Service*, p. 147, n. 105.

48 Houlding, *Fit for Service*, p. 194.

49 Cumberland Papers, Orderly Book Extracts, 2/2 ff. 3v–4r (M).

50 Centre for Kentish Studies (CKS), Amherst Papers, U1350/01/2.

51 Cumberland Papers, Orderly Book Extracts, 2/2 f. 3v (M).

52 Cumberland Papers, Orderly Book Extracts, 2/2 f. 4r (M).

53 Cumberland Papers, Orderly Book Extracts, 2/2 f. 5r (M).

54 Bland, *Military Discipline*, pp. 73–4.

55 Cumberland Papers, Orderly Book, 1742, vol. i, 3 February (M).

56 Rex Whitworth, *Field Marshal Lord Ligonier* (Oxford, 1958), pp. 69–88.

57 HMC, *Report on the Manuscripts of Mrs. Frankland-Russell-Astley of Chequers Court, Bucks* (London, 1900), p. 278.

58 HMC, *Chequers Court*, pp. 260–2.

59 In a letter, Stair wrote: 'I was entirely ignorant of all the operations of our army, excepting on the day of battle, when I thought it was my duty to meddle. The consequences of our victory might have been as great as our hearts could desire, but those whose advice the King took have not thought fit to take any advantage of the French.' HMC, *Manuscripts of the Earl Of Buckinghamshire* (London, 1895), p. 90.

60 HMC, *Chequers Court*, p. 252.

61 Beckles Willson, *The Life and Letters of James Wolfe* (London, 1909), pp. 36–8.

62 Lieutenant Colonel E. A. H. Webb, *History of the 12ᵗʰ (The Suffolk) Regiment* (London, 1914), p. 63.

63 Cumberland Papers, Orderly Book Extracts, 2/2 f. 3v (M).

64 Cumberland Papers, Orderly Book Extracts, 2/2 f. 4r (M).

65 *Gentleman's Magazine*, 1743, vol. xiii, p. 386.

66 *Gentleman's Magazine*, 1743, vol. xiii, p. 386.

67 Webb, *Suffolk Regiment*, p. 70.

68 Anon, *British Glory Reviv'd* (London, 1743), p. 10.

69 Anon, *The Journal of the Battle of Fontenoy . . . translated from the French* (London, 1745), p. 6.

70 Whitworth, *Ligonier*, pp. 97–104.

71 Cumberland Papers, Orderly Book, vol. 6/88 (M).

72 William F. Fleming (trans.), *The Works of Voltaire* (New York, 1901), vol. xvi, p. 238.

73 Thomas Carlyle, *History of Friedrich II of Prussia* (New York, 1864), vol. iv, pp. 438–9.

74 Fleming, *Voltaire*, p. 239.

75 *Penny Post* or *The Morning Advertiser* (London), 10–13 May 1745, issue 317.

76 Cumberland Papers, Orderly Books, vol. 6/176 (M).

77 Fleming, *Voltaire*, p. 239.

78 Mackay, *Memoirs*, p. 51.

79 Katherine Tomasson and Francis Buist, *Battles of the '45* (London, 1978), pp. 93–4.

80 CKS, Amherst Papers, Volume 02, Military Orders 9 November 1745 to 13 December 1745, 30 November, 1745, Amherst MSS, Kent County Record Office.

81 See above, pp. 56–7.

82 CKS, Amherst Papers, Volume 02, Military Orders 9 November 1745 to 13 December 1745, 30 November, 1745, Amherst MSS, Kent County Record Office.

83 Anon, *The Report of the Proceedings and Opinion of the Board of General Officers on their Examination into the Conduct, Behaviour, and Proceedings of Lieutenant-General Sir John Cope* (London, 1749), pp. 53–4 and 69.

84 For general accounts of the battles of the '45 Rebellion see Christopher Duffy, *The '45* (London, 2003); Stuart Reid, *1745: A Military History of the Last Jacobite Rising* (Staplehurst, 1996).

85 For a study of the battle of Falkirk see Geoff B. Bailey, *Falkirk or Paradise* (Edinburgh, 1996).

86 *London Evening Post*, 6 February 1746, issue 2849.

87 *London Evening Post*, 30 January 1746, issue 2845.

88 George Faulkener, *The Dublin Journal*, 28 January to 1 February 1746, issue 1971.

89 Anon, *The History of the Rebellion in 1745 and 1746 Extracted from the Scots Magazine* (Aberdeen, 1755), p. 124.

90 Nottingham University, Hallward Library, Galway Collection, Ga 12835.

91 Bland, *Military Discipline*, pp. 145–7.

92 Anon, *The History of the Rebellion, 1745 and 1746* (no place or date), p. 216.

93 John Marchant, *The History of the Present Rebellion* (London, 1746), pp. 398–9.

94 Anon, *The History of the Rebellion*, p. 216.

95 'Essay on Regular and Irregular Forces', *Gentleman's Magazine*, 1746, vol. xvi, p. 31.

96 Cumberland Papers, Box 14/57 (M).

97 Cumberland Papers, Box 14/7 (M).

98 See above, p. 98.

99 Anon, *The History of the Rebellion*, p. 216; Andrew Henderson, *The History of the Rebellion* (London, 1758, 5th edn), p. 327; Michael Hughes, *A Plain Narrative and Authentic Journal of the Late Rebellion Begun in 1745* (London, 1747), pp. 38–9.

100 Cumberland Papers, Box 14/7 (M).

101 Newcastle Journal, 1746, as cited in Stuart Reid, 'The Battle of Culloden: A Narrative Account', in Tony Pollard (ed.), *Culloden: The History and Archaeology of the Last Clan Battle* (Barnsley, 2009), p. 114.

102 Pollard, *Culloden*, p. 119.

103 Pollard, *Culloden*, p. 114.

104 Cumberland Papers, Box 14/57 (M), Cumberland to Lord Loudon, 19 April 1746.

105 Henderson, *History of the Rebellion*, p. 327.

106 Hughes, *A Plain Narrative*, p. 40.

107 Tomasson and Buist, *Battles of the '45*, p. 158.

108 This figure was arrived at using information in two chapters, 'The Jacobite Army at Culloden' and 'The Battle of Culloden: A Narrative Account' by Stuart Reid in Pollard, *Culloden*.

109 Anon, *The History of the Rebellion ... from the Scots Magazine*, p. 197.

110 Nottingham University, Hallward Library, Galway Collection, Ga 12835.

111 Whitworth, *Ligonier*, pp. 134–41.

112 Whitworth, *Ligonier*, pp. 149–60.

113 *Gentleman's Magazine*, 1747, vol. xvii, p. 345.

114 Cumberland Papers, Orderly Book Extracts, 2/2 f. 61v (M); and Anon, *A System of Camp Discipline... Kane's Discipline for a Battalion on Action... General Kane's Campaigns...* (London, 1757), pp. 29–31.

115 Cumberland Papers, Orderly Book, 4/165 (M).

116 Amherst Papers, Volume 02, Military Orders 9 November 1745 to 13 December 1745, 30 November, 1745, Amherst MSS, Kent County Record Office.

117 Cumberland Papers, Orderly Book 5/89 (M); and Houlding, *Fit for Service*, p. 418.

118 Cumberland Papers, Box 14/7 (M).

119 Anon, *The History of the Rebellion ... from the Scots Magazine*, p. 197.

120 Cumberland Papers, vol. 2/2 3v (M).

121 Cumberland Papers, vol. 2/2 4v and 4r (M).

Chapter 7

1 Tom Pocock, *Battle for Empire: The Very First World War, 1756–63* (London, 2002), p. 13; John Mollo, *Uniforms of the Seven Years War, 1756–1763* (New York, 1977), p. 7.

2 Frank McLynn, *1759: The Year Britain Became Master of the World* (London, 2005), p. 276; and Jeremy Black, *Warfare in the Eighteenth Century* (London, 1999), p. 188.

3 David Chandler, *The Art of Warfare in the Age of Marlborough* (Staplehurst, 1990), pp. 130–1.

4 Comte Maurice de Saxe, *Reveries or Memoirs Concerning the Art of War*, trans. Sir William Fawcett (London, 1757).

5 Chandler, *Art of War*, pp. 131–6.

6 Brent Nosworthy, *The Anatomy of Victory: Battle Tactics 1689–1763* (new York, 1992), pp. 60–1.

7 Chandler, *Art of War*, p. 125.

8 Nosworthy, *Anatomy of Victory*, p. 201.

9 Frederic Bere, *L'Armee Francais* (Paris, n.d.), p. 42, as cited in Nosworthy, *Anatomy of Victory*, p. 208.

10 Nosworthy, *Anatomy of Victory*, pp. 209–10.

11 Knoch, 'The insufficiency of fire-arms for attack or defence, demonstrated from facts, &c', *The Edinburgh Magazine*, 3 (November 1759), pp. 583–85.

12 James Wolfe, *General Wolfe's Instructions to Young Officers* (London, 1967), p. 32.

13 Wolfe, *Instructions*, p. 35.

14 For a general treatment of Wolfe as a professional army officer see Stuart Reid, *Wolfe: The Career of General James Wolfe from Culloden to Quebec* (Staplehurst, 2000).

15 William C. Lowe, 'Lennox, Charles, third duke of Richmond, third duke of Lennox, and duke of Aubigny in the French nobility (1735–1806)', *Oxford Dictionary of National Biography*, Oxford University Press, 2004; online

edn, October 2008 (www.oxforddnb.com/view/article/16451, accessed 27 Feb 2012).

16 Major General R. H. Whitworth, 'Some unpublished Wolfe letters', *JSAHR*, 53 (1975), pp. 65–86.

17 See Figure 6.5 above, p. 117.

18 Duke of Cumberland to Lord Barrington, 28 August 1757, in Stanley Pargellis, *Military Affairs in North America, 1748–1765: Selected Documents from the Cumberland Papers in Windsor Castle* (New York and London, 1936), p. 398.

19 *A New Exercise to be observed by His Majesty's Troops on the Establishment of Great Britain and Ireland* (London, April 1756).

20 Wolfe, *Instructions*, p. 55.

21 Wolfe, *Instructions*, p. 34.

22 Anon., *The Complete Militia-Man* (London), 1760, p. xiii.

23 Wolfe, *Instructions*, pp. 34–5.

24 Wolfe, *Instructions*, p. 49.

25 Wolfe, *Instructions*, p. 49.

26 Wolfe, *Instructions*, p. 52.

27 Wolfe, *Instructions*, p. 40.

28 For the full genesis of the 1756/7 regulations see John Houlding, *Fit for Service: The Training of the British Army, 1715–1795* (Oxford, 1981), pp. 198–201.

29 Bland states that for firing the ranks should be two paces apart when firing, that is six feet. Humphrey Bland, *A Treatise of Military Discipline* (London, 1727), p.10; and *1728 Regulations*, p.76.

30 *A New Exercise to be Observed by His Majesty's Troops on the Establishment of Great Britain and Ireland* (London, 1757); and *New Manual Exercise as Performed by His Majesty's Dragoons, Foot Guards, Foot, Artillery, Marines And by the Militia* (London, 1758), pp. 15–16.

31 *Exercise for the Horse, Dragoons and Foot Forces* (London, 1728), hereafter *1728 Regulations*, pp. 22–5.

32 Reverend Percy Sumner (ed.), 'General Hawley's "Chaos"', *JSAHR*, 26 (1948), p. 93.

33 Cumberland Papers, Order Book, 30 April to 18 June 1748 (M).

34 *A New Exercise*, 1757, p. 9.

35 See above, pp. 91–2.

36 See above, p. 98.

37 *A New Exercise*, 1757, p. 5.

38 For an example of such criticism see British Library, Add Mss 27892, Brig. Gen. James Douglass, *Schola Martis, or the Art of War . . . as Practised in Flanders, in the Wars, from Anno 1688 to An: 1714*, , f. 219r.

39 The feather spring is at the muzzle end of the musket lock and acts on the pan cover and frizzen, holding it either open or closed. *A New Exercise*, 1757. pp. 7–8.

40 *New Manual Exercise*, 1758, p. 13.

41 *A New Exercise*, 1757, p. 10.

42 *A New Exercise*, 1757, p. 6.

43 Bland, *Military Discipline*, p. 10.

44 Houlding, *Fit for Service*, p. 199.

45 Douglass, *Schola Martis*, f. 219r.

46 See above, pp. 111–12.

47 'Observations relating to military exercise as now practised in the English Army', *Lloyd's Evening Post and British Chronicle* (London, 1759), 28–30 March 1759, p. 310, the piece was written in 1757.

48 Anon., *The Complete Militia-Man* (London, 1760), p. 38. Square toes is a reference to old-fashioned footwear and thus, here, to the older officers of the army.

49 Anon, *A System of Camp Discipline . . . to which is Added General Kane's Campaigns of King William* (London, 1757), p. 59.

50 See above, p. 112.

51 'An officer's observations on the present methods of firing, from his letter to his friend, lately published', *London Magazine or Gentleman's Monthly Intelligencer*, 29 (December 1760), p. 631.

52 'Observations on the present methods of firing', *London Magazine*, p. 631.

53 'Observations on the present methods of firing', *London Magazine*, pp. 632–3.

54 Wolfe, *Instructions*, p. 35.

55 'Observations on the present methods of firing', *London Magazine*, pp. 631–2.

56 David Blackmore, *British Cavalry of the Mid-18th Century* (Nottingham, 2008), pp. 80–1.

57 'Observations on the present methods of firing', *London Magazine*, p. 631.

58 Anon., 'Observations relating to Military Exercise', p. 310.

59 'A letter from an officer to his friend', *Monthly Review* (November 1760), pp. 375–7.

60 *The Complete Militia-Man*, p. xi.

61 *The Complete Militia-Man*, p. 38.

62 The Duke of Richmond to Lord George Lennox, 9 September 1757, in HMC, *Bathurst Manuscripts*, p. 681.

63 Duke of Cumberland to Lord Barrington, 28 August 1757, in Pargellis, *Military Affairs*, p. 398, quoted above, p. 123.

64 Rex Whitworth, *William Augustus, Duke of Cumberland: A Life* (Barnsley, 1992), pp. 194–9.

65 Wolfe, *Instructions*, p. 45 and the Duke of Richmond to Lord George Lennox, 9 September 1757, *Bathurst Manuscripts*, p. 681.

66 *The Complete Militia-Man*, p. 42.

67 *The Complete Militia-Man*, p. 42.

68 The Duke of Richmond to Lord George Lennox, 9 September 1757, *Bathurst Manuscripts*, p. 681

69 Wolf, *Instructions*, pp. 48–50.

70 Campbell Dalrymple, *A Military Essay* (London, 1761), p. 51, also says that good infantry could fire four times a minute.

71 Knoch, 'The insufficiency of fire-arms for attack or defence, demonstrated from facts, &c', *Edinburgh Magazine*, 3 (November 1759), pp. 583–5.

72 *The Complete Militia-Man*, p. 75.

73 Cumberland Papers, Orderly Book Extracts, 2/2 f. 4r, see above, p. 104.

74 Wolfe, *Instructions*, p. 49, see above, p. 124.

75 *The Complete Militia-Man*, p. 74.

76 Reid, *Wolfe*, p. 115.

77 William Windham, *A Plan of Discipline for the Use of The Norfolk Militia* (London, 1759), n.p. (advertisement) and p. 11.

78 The Duke of Richmond to Lord George Lennox, 9 September 1757, *Bathurst Manuscripts*, p. 681.

79 Mackay, *Rules of War*, Article X , see above, pp. 58–9.

80 *The Complete Militia-Man*, p. 84.

81 Nosworthy, *Anatomy of Victory*, pp. 276–7.

82 Christopher Duffy, *The Military Experience in the Age of Reason* (Ware, 1998), pp. 207–9.

83 George Durant, 'Journal of the expedition to Martinique and Guadeloupe, October 1758 – May 1759', in Alan J. Guy, R. N. W. Thomas and Gerard J. deGroot (eds.), *Military Miscellany I* (Stroud, 1997), p. 51.

84 Andrew Cormack and Alan Jones (eds.), *The Journal of Corporal Todd, 1745–1762* (Stroud, 2001), p. 182.

85 HMC, *Manuscripts of M L Clements* (London, 1913), pp. 560–1.

86 www.kronoskaf.com/syw/index.php?title=1759-08-01_-_Battle_of_ Minden (accessed 3 March 2012); http://vial.jean.free.fr/new_npi/revues_ npi/4_1998/npi_498/4_odbf_010859.htm (accessed 3 March, 2012).

87 NAM 7510/92, A copy of a letter written by an officer of the 12th Foot to his mother on the 9th August 1759.

88 Cormack and Jones, *The Journal of Corporal Todd*, p. 63.

89 NAM 7510/92.

90 NAM 7510/92.

91 NAM 7510/92.

92 'A Letter from Mons. De Contades to Marchal Belleisle, in answer to his published in the London Gazette of the 18th of August', *London Chronicle (Semi Annual)*, 423, 11–13 September 1759.

93 The Hon. J. W. Fortescue, *A History of the Army* (London, 1899–1930), vol. ii, p. 517.

94 Cormack and Jones, *The Journal of Corporal Todd*, p. 141.

95 Cormack and Jones, *The Journal of Corporal Todd*, p. 143.

96 Cormack and Jones, *The Journal of Corporal Todd*, p. 177.

97 Cormack and Jones, *The Journal of Corporal Todd*, p. 165.

98 Fortescue, *History of the Army*, vol. ii, p. 530.

99 Cormack and Jones, *The Journal of Corporal Todd*, pp. 165–6.

100 *A New Manual and Platoon Exercise, with an Explanation* (Dublin, 1764), pp. 5–6.

101 *The Manual Exercise as Ordered by His Majesty in 1764 Together with Plans and Explanations of the Method Generally Practis'd at Reviews and Field Days* (Boston, 1774), pp. 15–16.

102 *A New Manual and Platoon Exercise, with an Explanation* (Dublin, 1764), pp. 15–19.

103 Houlding, *Fit for Service*, p. 418.

104 See above, p. 111.

Chapter 8

1 The nature of the challenges presented to the British Army by the North American environment are discussed in full in Stephen Brumwell, *Redcoats: The British Soldier and War in the Americas, 1755–1763* (Cambridge, 2002).

2 Fred Anderson, *Crucible of War: The Seven Years War and the Fate of Empire in British North America, 1754–1766* (Toronto, London and New York, 2000).

3 Stuart Reid, *Wolfe: The Career of General James Wolfe from Culloden to Quebec* (Staplehurst, 2000), p. 200.

4 Saul David, *All the King's Men: The British Soldier from the Restoration to Waterloo* (London, 2012), p. 188.

5 The Hon. J. W. Fortescue, *A History of the British Army*, vol. ii (London, 1899), p. 381.

6 Colonel J. F. C. Fuller, *British Light Infantry in the Eighteenth Century* (London, 1925).

7 David Gates, *The British Light Infantry Arm, c. 1790–1815* (London, 1987).

8 Ian M. McCulloch and Tim J. Todish, *British Light Infantryman of the Seven Years' War, North America, 1757–63* (Oxford, 2004).

9 Brumwell, *Redcoats*, chapters 6 and 7.

10 Brumwell, *Redcoats*, p. 193.

11 Brumwell, *Redcoats*, p. 6.

12 'Reflections on the War with the Savages of North America', in William Smith, *An Historical Account of the Expedition against the Ohio Indians in the Year MDCCLXIV under the Command of Henry Bouquet Esq.* (London, 1766), pp. 45–6. The author of these reflections is identified as Bouquet by Brumwell, *Redcoats*, p. 198, n. 24.

13 The Journal of Robert Orme, Lieutenant, Orders given at Alexandria 27 March 1755, in Winthrop Sargent (ed.), *The History of an Expedition against Fort DuQuesne in 1755* (Philadelphia, 1856), p. 293; Halkett's Orderly Book, Orders 27 March 1755, in C. Hamilton (ed.), *Braddock's Defeat* (Norman, Oklahoma, 1959).

14 Pierre Pouchot, *Memoirs on the Late War in North America between France and England*, ed. Brian Leigh Dunnigan, trans. Michael Cardy (Youngstown, 1994), p. 82.

15 *The Public Advertiser*, 3 November 1755, in N. Darnell Davis, 'British Newspaper Accounts of Braddock's Defeat', *Pennsylvania Magazine of History and Biography*, October 1899.

16 The Journal of Captain Robert Cholmley's Batman, in C. Hamilton (ed.), *Braddock's Defeat* (Norman, Oklahoma, 1959), p. 28.

17 The Journal of a British Officer, in C. Hamilton (ed.), *Braddock's Defeat* (Norman, Oklahoma, 1959) p. 50.

18 The Journal of Captain Robert Cholmley's Batman, p. 28.

19 The Journal of Robert Orme, p. 356.

20 *London Evening Post*, 26–28 August 1755, in Davis, 'Newspaper Accounts'.

21 Pouchot, *Memoirs*, p. 139; The Journal of Robert Orme, p. 356.

22 Journal of the Operations of the Army from 22nd July to 30th September, 1755, Departement de la Guerre, Paris, in E. B. O'Callaghan and B. Fernow (eds.), *Documents Relative to the Colonial History of the State of New* York (Albany, 1853–7), vol. x, pp. 337–8.

23 The Journal of a British Officer, p. 50.

24 Pouchot, *Memoirs*, p. 83.

25 *Gentleman's Magazine*, August 1755, p. 380.

26 Letter to his father, 21 September 1755, Beckles Willson, *The Life and Letters of James Wolfe* (London, 1909), p. 274.

27 Stanley Pargellis, 'Braddock's Defeat', *American Historical Review*, 41:2 (January 1936), pp. 253–69.

28 Samuel Blodget, A *Prospective Plan of the Battle near Lake George and the Eighth Day of September, 1755* (London, 1756), p. 4.

29 Major Robert Rogers, *Journals of Major Robert Rogers* (London, 1765), pp. 59–65.

30 Captain John Knox, *An Historical Journal of the Campaigns in North America for the Years 1757, 1758, 1759 and 1760* (London, 1769), vol. i, pp. 6 and 54.

31 Smith, *Expedition against the Ohio Indians* p. 49.

32 Huntington Library, LO 6927, George Scott's proposal for light infantry, 13 February 1758.

33 Huntington Library, LO 5065, 5072, 5074, 5075.

34 Knox, *Journal*, vol. i, pp. 159–60.

35 Orders at Halifax, 12 May 1758, Knox, *Journal*, vol. i, p. 161.

36 CSK, Amherst Papers, Orders before Louisbourg, 1758, U1350/ 030/1, Amherst MSS, Kent County Record Office.

37 Knox, *Journal*, vol. i, p. 273.

38 Knox, *Journal*, vol. i, p. 314.

39 Huntington Library, LO 1060, Robert Napier, Exercises for the American Forces, approved by His Royal Highness, 18 April 1756.

40 Wolfe to Lord George Sackville, Halifax, 24 May 1758, in Willson, *Wolfe*, pp. 366–9.

41 Stanley M. Pargellis, *Lord Loudon in North America*, (Yale 1933, reprint 1968), p. 299.

42 National Archives of Scotland, RH 4/86/2, Undated memo in Forbes' hand (early 1757).

43 British Library Add Ms 21640 f. 70, 27 June 1758.

44 Brumwell, *Redcoats*, p. 217; and Pargellis, *Lord Loudon in North America*, p. 300.

45 Forbes to Bouquet, 7 June 1758, in S. K. Stevens, Donald H. Kent and Autumn L. Leonard (eds.), *The Papers of Henry Bouquet* (Harrisburg, 1951), vol. ii, p. 50.

46 William A. Hunter (ed.), 'Thomas Barton and the Forbes Expedition', *Pennsylvania Magazine of History and Biography*, 95:4 (1971), pp. 431–83; p. 449.

47 Hunter, 'Thomas Barton', pp. 431–83; p. 450.

48 7 August 1758, Stevens, *Bouquet*, vol. ii, p. 673.

49 CKS, Amherst Papers, U1350/0100/2, 18 June, 1758, Amherst MSS, Kent County Record Office.

50 CKS, Amherst Papers, U1350/0100/2 10 July 1758, Amherst MSS, Kent County Record Office.

51 Stephens, *Bouquet*, vol. ii, p. 634.

52 Comte Maurice de Saxe, *Reveries or Memoirs Concerning the Art of War*, trans. Sir William Fawcett (London, 1757), p. 72.

53 Knox, *Journal*, vol. i, p. 369.

54 Paul E. Kopperman, 'Braddock, Edward (*bap.* 1695, *d.* 1755)', *Oxford Dictionary of National Biography*, Oxford University Press, 2004; online edn, Jan 2008 (www.oxforddnb.com/view/article/3170, accessed 6 April 2012).

55 William Faucitt (trans.), *Regulations for the Prussian Infantry, Translated from the German Original* (London, 1754).

56 Anderson, *Crucible of War*, p. 72; John Houlding, *Fit for Service: The Training of the British Army, 1715–1795* (Oxford, 1981), p. 421.

57 CKS, Amherst Papers, U1350/030/1, Amherst MSS, Kent County Record Office.

58 William C. Lowe, 'Amherst, Jeffrey, first Baron Amherst (1717–1797)', *Oxford Dictionary of National Biography*, Oxford University Press, 2004; online edn, Sept 2010 (www.oxforddnb.com/view/article/443, accessed 6 April 2012).

59 Orders, 5 May 1759, Knox, *Journal*, vol. i, pp. 360–1.

60 Knox, *Journal*, vol. i, p. 270.

61 Knox, *Journal*, vol. i, p. 239.

62 Knox, *Journal*, vol. i, p. 233.

63 Knox, *Journal*, vol. i, pp. 331–2.

64 Knox, *Journal*, vol. i, p. 332.

65 Knox, *Journal*, vol. i, p.385.

66 J. Clarence Webster (ed.), *The Journal of Jeffrey Amherst, 1758–1763* (Toronto, 1931), p. 224.

67 'A Journal of the Expedition up the River St Lawrence by the Serjeant-Major of Gen. Hopson's Grenadiers', in A. Doughty and G. W. Parmalee, *The Siege of Quebec and the Battle of the Plains of Abraham* (Quebec, 1901), vol. v, p. 5.

68 'Letters and papers relating to the Siege of Quebec in the possession of the Marquess Townshend', in Doughty and Parmalee, *Siege of Quebec*, vol. v., p. 257.

69 'The journal of Major Moncrieff', in Doughty and Parmalee, *Siege of Quebec*, vol. v., p. 47.

70 'Memoirs of the Siege of Quebec and total reduction of Canada in 1759 and 1760 by John Johnson, clerk and quarter mas'r sergeant to the 58th Reg't', in Doughty and Parmalee, *Siege of Quebec*, vol v, pp. 116–17.

71 Louis M. Waddell (ed.), *The Papers of Henry Bouquet* (Harrisburg, 1994), pp. 339–43.

72 Robert Kirk, *The Memoirs of Robert Kirk, Late of the Royal Highland Regiment, Written by Himself* (Limerick, 1791), pp. 77–9.

73 Brigadier R. Alexander (ed.), 'The Capture of Quebec. A Manuscript Journal Relating to the Operations Before Quebec From 8th May, 1759, to 17th May, 1760, Kept by Colonel Malcolm Fraser. Then Lieutenant in the 78th Foot (Fraser's Highlanders)', *JSAHR*, 18 (1939), pp. 135–68; 140–1.

74 'Extract of a letter from an officer in the regulars, dated July 10, 1761', *London Evening Post*, 3–5 September 1761, issue 5284.

75 The National Archives, WO 34/53 f. 6, Massey to Amherst, Oswego, 30 July 1759; The National Archives, PRO 30/8/49 f. 9, Massey to Amherst, Oswego, 30 July 1759; Captain Charles Lee to Sir William Bunbury, 9 August, 1759, in New York Historical Society, *Collections of the New York Historical Society for the Year 1871* (New York, 1872), vol. I, p. 21.

76 Reid, *Wolfe*, pp. 189–94.

77 Knox, *Journal*, vol. i, p. 385.

78 Knox, *Journal*, vol. ii, p. 70.

79 Knox, *Journal*, vol. ii, p. 70.

80 Knox, *Journal*, vol. ii, p.70; 'Letters . . . of the Marquess Townshend', in Doughty and Parmalee, *Siege of Quebec*, vol. v, p. 217; 'Expedition up the River St Lawrence', in Doughty and Parmalee, *Siege of Quebec*, vol. v, p. 10.

81 Knox, *Journal*, vol. ii, p. 71.

82 'Letters . . . of the Marquess Townshend', in Doughty and Parmalee, *Siege of Quebec*, vol. v, p. 271; Alexander, 'Capture of Quebec', *JSAHR*, pp. 135–68; 156.

83 'Memoirs of the Siege of Quebec' in Doughty and Parmalee, *Siege of Quebec*, vol. v, p. 104.

84 British Library Add Mss 45662, Journal of Richard Humphrys, 28th Foot.

85 Knox, *Journal*, vol. ii, p. 71.

86 'Letters . . . of the Marquess Townshend', in Doughty and Parmalee, *Siege of Quebec*, vol. v, pp. 217, 220 and 271; Alexander, 'Capture of Quebec', *JSAHR*, p. 156.

87 Knox, *Journal*, vol. ii, p. 97.

88 'Memoirs of the Siege of Quebec' in Doughty and Parmalee, *Siege of Quebec*, vol. v, p. 121.

89 The National Archives, WO 71/68, General Court Martial, 1 June 1761, Quebec, Lieutenant Eubele Ormsby, 35th Regiment.

90 Knox, *Journal*, vol. ii, p. 57.

91 Knox, *Journal*, vol. ii, p. 327.

Chapter 9

1 David Chandler, *The Art of Warfare in the Age of Marlborough* (Staplehurst, 1990), p. 113.

2 *Exercise for the Horse, Dragoons and Foot Forces* (London, 1728), p. 80.

3 Humphrey Bland, *A Treatise of Military Discipline* (London, 1727), p. 69; Brigadier General Richard Kane, *Campaigns of King William and Queen Anne; From 1689 to 1712. Also, A New System of Military Discipline for a Battalion of Foot on Action* (London, 1745), p. 112.

4 See above, p. 21 for Tippermuir and p. 104 for Laffeldt.

5 Bland, *Military Discipline*, pp. 145–7.

6 Matthew H. Spring, *With Zeal and with Bayonets Only* (University of Oklahoma Press, 2008), pp. 243–4.

7 Richard Holmes, *Dusty Warriors: Modern Soldiers at War* (London, 2007), p. 332.

Bibliography

1: Manuscripts

British Library (BL)
Cumberland Papers (on microfilm)

Add Mss 21506, f. 98, [John Churchill, Earl, afterwards Duke of] Marlborough to William Blathwayt, Secretary at War; Maestricht, Breda, 29 May 1689

Add Mss 21640, Forbes Papers

Add Mss 23642, miscellaneous papers and correspondence of Lord Tyrawley, 1679–1759

Add Mss 27892, Douglass, Brig. Gen. James, *Schola Martis, or the Art of War . . . as Practised in Flanders, in the Wars, from Anno 1688 to An: 1714*

Add Mss 29477, 'The exercise of the Firelock and Bayonett, with ye Doublings and Hollow Square', with copies of orders and regulations by the Duke of Marlborough by Capt. John Foster, of Dulwich

Add Mss 45662, Journal of Richard Humphrys, 28th Foot

Add Mss 61163, Ingoldsby Correspondence

Add Mss 61371, f. 119, Marlborough's instructions to Ingoldsby, 4th November 1706

Add Mss 61398, Adam Cardonnel's letters, June 06 to Sept 07

Add Mss 61408, Josiah Sandby, Journal

Cornwall Record Office
DD.RH.839 (formerly DD.R.H.388), *Exercise of Firelock and Bayonet . . . appointed by his Excie. Lieut. Genll. Ingoldsby*

Dutch Nationaal Archief
Familiearchief Van Wassenaer van Duvenvoorde, Inv. Nr. 1223, Stukken van Willem Baron van Wassenaer, colonel-commandant van het eerste bataljon gardes

Kent County Record Office
U1350 Amherst Family Papers

Historical Manuscripts Commission
J. M. Heathcote Esq. London, 1899
Leybourne Popham. London, 1899
Mrs. Frankland-Russell-Astley of Chequers Court, Bucks. London, 1900
The Earl of Buckinghamshire. London, 1895
The Earl of Bathurst. London, 1923
M L Clements. London, 1913

Huntington Library, California
Loudoun Papers, LO 1060, 5065, 5072, 5074, 5075, 6927

The National Archives
WO 34/53
WO 71/68
PRO 30/8/49

National Archives of Scotland
Register House Series (Microfilms) 4/86/2, Papers of Brigadier General John
   Forbes, 1755–9

National Army Museum
NAM 6807/392A+B, Journal of Robert Stearne, 2 vols.
NAM 7510/92, A copy of a letter written by an officer of the 12th Foot to his
   mother on the 9th August 1759
NAM 6807/205, The Exercise of the Firelock and Bayonett that was ordered to
   be used by all the Regimts in Ireland 1723

Nottingham University
Hallward Library, Galway Collection, Ga 12835

2: Regulations, by date

An Abridgement of the English Military Discipline. London, 1676
An Abridgement of the Military Discipline Appointed by His Majesty to be Used by
   All His Forces in His Ancient Kingdom of Scotland. Edinburgh, 1680
An Abridgement of the English Military Discipline. London, 1685

The Exercise of the Foot with the Evolutions, According to the Words of Command, As they are Explained. As also, the Forming of Battalions, With Directions to be Observed by all Colonels, Captains, and other Officers in Their Majesties Armies. London, 1690

The Exercise of the Foot with the Evolutions, According to the Words of Command, As they are Explained. As also, the Forming of Battalions, With Directions to be Observed by all Colonels, Captains, and other Officers in Their Majesties Armies. Like wise The Exercise of the Dragoons Both on Horse-back and Foot. With the Rules of War in the Day of Battel, When Encountering with the Enemy. Edinburgh, 1693

The Exercise of the Foot with the Evolutions. Dublin: R. Thornton and M. Gunne, 1701

The New Exercise of Firelocks & Bayonets; Appointed by his Grace the Duke of Marlborough to be Used by all the British Forces. London: John Morphew, 1708

Exercise for the Horse, Dragoons and Foot Forces. London, 1728

A New Exercise to be Observed by His Majesty's Troops on the Establishment of Great Britain and Ireland. London: 1756; 2nd edition, London, 1757

New Manual Exercise as Performed by His Majesty's Dragoons, Foot Guards, Foot, Artillery, Marines And by the Militia. London, 1758, 2nd edition

A New Manual and Platoon Exercise, with an Explanation. Dublin, 1764

The Manual Exercise as Ordered by His Majesty in 1764 Together with Plans and Explanations of the Method Generally Practis'd at Reviews and Field Days. Boston, T. & J. Fleet, 1774

Newspapers/Periodicals
Gentleman's Magazine
Lloyd's Evening Post and British Chronicle
London Chronicle (Semi Annual)
London Evening Post
The London Gazette
London Magazine or Gentleman's Monthly Intelligencer
Monthly Review

3: Published Primary Sources
Albemarle, George Monck, Duke of, *Observations upon Military and Political Affairs.* London: Henry Mortlocke, 1671

Alexander, Brigadier R. (ed.), 'The Capture of Quebec. A Manuscript Journal Relating to the Operations Before Quebec From 8th May, 1759, to 17th May, 1760, Kept by Colonel Malcolm Fraser. Then Lieutenant in the 78th Foot

(Fraser's Highlanders)', *Journal of the Society for Army Historical Research*, 18 (1939)

Anon, *A System of Camp Discipline ... to which is Added General Kane's Campaigns of King William*. London: J. Millan, 1757, 2nd edition

Anon., *A True Description of the Discipline of War both for Horse and Foot*. No place or date

Anon., *An Express Relation of the Passages and Proceedings of His Majesties Armie, under the Command of his Excellence the Earle of Newcastle*. No place, 1643

Anon, *British Glory Reviv'd*. London: J. Roberts, 1743

Anon., *The Complete Militia-Man*. London: R Griffiths, 1760

Anon., *The Field of Mars, Being an Alphabetical Digestion of the Principal Naval and Military Engagements*. 2 vols. London: J. MacGowan, 1781

Anon., *Generall Lessley's Direction and Order for the Exercising of Horse and Foot*. London: L. Blaikelock, 1642

Anon, *The History of the Rebellion in 1745 and 1746 Extracted from the Scots Magazine*. Aberdeen: F. Douglas and W. Murray, 1755

Anon, *The Journal of the Battle of Fontenoy ... translated from the French*. London: M. Cooper, 1745

Anon, *The Report of the Proceedings and Opinion of the Board of General Officers on their Examination into the Conduct, Behaviour, and Proceedings of Lieutenant-General Sir John Cope*. London: W. Webb, 1749

Barriffe, William, *Military Discipline: Or the Young Artillery Man*. London: Ralph Mab, 1635; 1639, 2nd edition; 1661, 6th edition

Batt:, Gil:, *Some Particular Animadversions of Marke, for the Satisfaction of the Contumatious Malignant ...* London, 1646

Bell, Robert (ed.), *Memorials of the Civil War: Comprising the Correspondence of the Fairfax Family*. London: Richard Bentley, 1849

Bishop, Matthew, *The Life and Adventures of Matthew Bishop*. London: J. Millan, 1744

Bland, Humphrey, *A Treatise of Military Discipline*. London: Sam. Buckley, 1727, 2nd edition

Blodget, Samuel, *A Prospective Plan of the Battle near Lake George and the Eighth Day of September, 1755*. London, 1756

Brockington, Jr., William S. (ed.), *Monro: His Expedition with the Worthy Scots Regiment Called Mac-Keys*. London, 1637; Westport, CT: Praeger, 1999

Carlyle, Thomas, *Oliver Cromwell's Letter and Speeches*. London: Chapman and Hall, 1849, 2nd edition

Chadwyck Healey, Charles E. H. (ed.), *Bellum Civile: Hopton's Narrative of his Campaign in the West*. London: Somerset Record Society, 1902

Chandler, David, *Military Memoirs of Marlborough's Campaigns, 1702–1712* (London: Greenhill Books, 1998)

Chandler, David G. (ed.), *A Journal of Marlborough's Campaigns During the War of the Spanish Succession, 1704–1711, by John Marshall Deane* (*Journal of the Society for Army Historical Research*, special publication no. 12, London, 1984)

Clarke, Rev. J. S. (ed.), *The Life of James the Second King of England, etc, Collected out of Memoirs Writ of his Own Hand.* London: Longman, Hurst, Rees, Orme and Browne, 1816

Coe, Richard, *An Exact Diarie or a Briefe Relation of the Progress of Sir William Wallers Army.* London: Humphrey Tuckey, 1644

Collings, Richard, *The Kingdomes Weekly Intelligencer, 24 June to 1 July.* London, 1645

Cormack, Andrew, and Alan Jones (eds.), *The Journal of Corporal Todd, 1745–1762.* Stroud: Sutton Publishing, 2001

Crichton, Andrew, *The Life and Diary of Lieutenant-Colonel John Blackader.* Edinburgh: H. S. Baynes, 1824

Cruso, John, *Militarie Instructions for the Cavallrie.* Cambridge: University of Cambridge, 1631

Dalrymple, Campbell, *A Military Essay.* London: D. Wilson, 1761

D'Auvergne, Edward, *A Relation of the Most Remarkable Transactions of the Last Campaign, 1692.* London: Dorman Newman, 1693

D'Auvergne, Edward, *The History of the Last Campagne in the Spanish Netherlands, Anno Dom. 1693.* London: John Newton, 1693

Davis, N. Darnell, 'British Newspaper Accounts of Braddock's Defeat', *Pennsylvania Magazine of History and Biography*, October 1899

Doughty, A. and G. W. Parmalee, *The Siege of Quebec and the Battle of the Plains of Abraham.* 6 vols. Quebec: Dussault & Proulx, 1901

Durant, George, 'Journal of the Expedition to Martinique and Guadeloupe, October 1758 – May 1759', in Alan J. Guy, R. N. W. Thomas and Gerard J. deGroot (eds.), *Military Miscellany I.* Stroud: Sutton Publishing, 1997

Elton, Richard, *The Compleat Body of the Art Military.* London: W.L., 1668, 3rd edition. 1st edition, London: Robert Leybourn, 1650; 2nd edition, London: R & W Leybourn, 1659.

Fairfax, Sir Thomas, *Short Memorials of Thomas Lord Fairfax.* London: Richard Chiswell, 1699

Faucitt, William (trans.), *Regulations for the Prussian Infantry, Translated from the German Original.* London: Paul Vaillant, 1754

Faulkener, George, *The Dublin Journal, 28 January to 1 February 1746*, issue 1971

Firth, C. H., 'Marston Moor', *Transactions of the Royal Historical Society*, new series, 12 (1898)

Firth, C. H. (ed.), *The Clarke Papers*. London: Longmans, Green & Co, 1899, 4 vols.

Fleming, William F. (trans.), *The Works of Voltaire, 21 vols* (New York: E. R. DuMont, 1901)

Foster, Henry, *A True and Exact Relation of the Marchings of the Two Regiments of the Trained-Bands of the City of London*. London: Benjamin Allen, 1643

Gwynne, John, *Military Memoirs of the Great Civil War*. Edinburgh: Hurst, Robinson & Co, 1822

Henderson, Andrew, *The History of the Rebellion*. London: A. Millar, 1758, 5th edition

Hamilton, C. (ed.), *Braddock's Defeat*. Norman: University of Oklahoma Press, 1959

Hexham, Henry, *The First Part of the Principles of the Art Military*. Delft, 1642

Hodgson, Captain John and Sir Henry Slingsby, *Memoirs Written during the Great Civil War*. Edinburgh: Arch. Constable, 1806

Horsley, Walter C. (trans.), *The Chronicles of an Old Campaigner, M. De La Colonie, 1692–1717*. London: John Murray, 1904

Howell, James, *Proedria Vasilike a Discourse Concerning the Precedency of Kings*. London: Sam. Speed and Chr. Ecclestone, 1664

Hughes, Michael, *A Plain Narrative and Authentic Journal of the Late Rebellion Begun in 1745*. London: Henry Whitridge, 1747

Kane, Brigadier General Richard, *Campaigns of King William and the Duke of Marlborough, Also a New System of Military Discipline, for a Battalion of Foot on Action*. London: J. Millan, 1747, 2nd edition. (First edition, 1745 had slightly different title: '...of King William and Queen Anne')

Kirk, Robert, *The Memoirs of Robert Kirk, Late of the Royal Highland Regiment, Written by Himself*. Limerick: J. Ferrar, 1791

Knoch, 'The insufficiency of fire-arms for attack or defence, demonstrated from facts, &c', *Edinburgh Magazine*, 3 (November 1759)

Knox, Captain John, *An Historical Journal of the Campaigns in North America for the Years 1757, 1758, 1759 and 1760*. 3 vols. London, 1769

Lachapelle, Ofwersteleut Iulius Richard De, *Een Militarisch Exercitiae Book*. Stockholm, 1669

Le Blond, Guillaume, *Elemens de Tactique*. Paris, 1758

Lister, Joseph, *An Historical Relation of the Life of Mr Joseph Lister*. Bradford: W. H. Blackburn, 1821

Mackay, Major General Hugh, *Memoirs of the War Carried on in Scotland and Ireland*. Edinburgh, 1833

Mackesy, Piers, *The Coward of Minden: The Affair of Lord George Sackville*. London, 1979

Marchant, John, *The History of the Present Rebellion*. London: R. Walker, 1746

Millner, John, *A Compendious Journal of all the Marches, Famous Battles and Sieges*. Uckfield: Naval and Military Press, 2004

Molesworth, Lieutenant General Richard, 3rd Viscount, *A Short Course of Standing Rules, For the Government and Conduct of an Army*. London: R. Dodsley, 1744

Morgan, Major General, *A True and Just Relation of Maj. Gen. Sir Thomas Morgan's Progress in France and Flanders*. London: J. Nutt, 1699

New York Historical Society, *Collections of the New York Historical Society for the Year 1871*. New York, 1872

Newcastle, Margaret, Duchess of, *The Life of . . . William Cavendish . . . Earl of Newcastle*. London: A. Maxwell, 1667

O'Callaghan, E. B. and B. Fernow (eds.), *Documents Relative to the Colonial History of the State of New York*. 15 vols. Albany: Weed, Parsons, 1853–7

Orrery, Roger, Earl of, *A Treatise of the Art of War*. London: Henry Herringman, 1677

Pargellis, Stanley M., *Lord Loudon in North America*. Yale: Yale University Press, 1933; reprint Hamden, CT: Archon Books, 1968

Pargellis, Stanley, *Military Affairs in North America, 1748–1765: Selected Documents from the Cumberland Papers in Windsor Castle*. New York and London: D. Appleton and Century, 1936

Paan, Louis, *Den korter weg tot de Nederlandsche Militaire Exercitie, Inhoudende verscheide extraordinaire Evolutien ende Bataillons, Mitsgaders de formen der Batailles, Vol. 2*. Leuwarden, 1684

Parker, Robert, *Memoirs of the Most Remarkable Military Transactions from the Year 1683 to 1718*. Dublin, 1746

Pouchot, Pierre, *Memoirs on the Late War in North America between France and England*, ed. Brian Leigh Dunnigan, trans. Michael Cardy. Youngstown: Old Fort Niagara Association, 1994

Rogers, Major Robert, *Journals of Major Robert Rogers*. London: J. Millan, 1765

Ross, John, *Tangers Rescue or a Relation of the Late Memorable Passage at Tanger*. London: Hen. Hills, 1681

Rushworth, John, 'Letter', in Glenn Foard, *Naseby: The Decisive Campaign*. Whitstable: Pryor Publications, 1995

Sargent, Winthrop (ed.), *The History of an Expedition against Fort DuQuesne in 1755*. Philadelphia: Pennsylvania Historical Society, 1856

Sawle, W., *An Impartial Relation of all the Transactions between the Army of the Confederates and that of the French King in their Last Summer's Campaign in Flanders with a More Particular Respect to the Battle of Fleury*. London: James Fraser, 1691

Saxe, Comte Maurice de, *Reveries or Memoirs Concerning the Art of War*, trans. Sir William Fawcett. London: J. Nourse, 1757; reprinted 1759, 1776

Simcoe, J. G., *Simcoe's Military Journal*. New York: Bartlett and Welford, 1844

Smith, William, *An Historical Account of the Expedition against the Ohio Indians in the Year MDCCLXIV under the Command of Henry Bouquet Esq*. London: William Bradford, 1766

Stevens, S. K., Donald H. Kent and Autumn L. Leonard (eds.), *The Papers of Henry Bouquet*. Harrisburg: Pennsylvania Historical and Museum Commission, 1951

Stewart, Captain William, *A Full Relation of the Late Victory* . . . London: L. Blaiklock, 1644

Story, George Warter, *A True and Impartial History of the Most Material Occurrences in the Kingdom of Ireland during the Two Last Years*. London: Richard Chiswell, 1691

Turner, Sir James, *Memoirs of His Own Life and Times*. Edinburgh: n.p., 1829

Turner, Sir James, *Pallas Armata*. London: Richard Chiswell, 1683

Waddell, Louis M. (ed.), *The Papers of Henry Bouquet*. Harrisburg: Pennsylvania Historical and Museum Commission, 1994

Walker, Sir Edward, 'Brief Memorials', in Young, Peter, *Naseby 1645*. London: Century Publishing, 1985

Ward, Robert, *Animadversions of Warre*. London: John Dawson, 1639

Watson, Lionel, *A More Exact Relation of the Late Battell Neer York*. London: H. Overton, 1644

Watts, William, *The Swedish Discipline, Religious, Civile and Military*. London: Nath. Butter and Nicholas Bourne, 1632

Watts, William, *The Swedish Intelligencer, The Second Part*. London: Nath. Butter and Nicholas Bourne, 1632

Webb, Reverend John (ed.), *Military Memoir of Colonel John Birch*. London: Camden Society, 1873

Webster, J. Clarence (ed.), *The Journal of Jeffrey Amherst, 1758–1763*. Toronto: Ryerson Press, 1931

Whitworth, Major General R. H., 'Some unpublished Wolfe letters', *Journal of the Society for Army Historical Research*, 53 (1975), pp. 65–86

Willson, Beckles, *The Life and Letters of James Wolfe*. London: William Heineman, 1909

Wilson, John, 'The Journal of John Wilson', in David G. Chandler (ed.), *Military Miscellany II: Manuscripts from Marlborough's Wars, the American War of Independence and the Boer War*. Stroud: Sutton Publishing, 2005

Windham, William, *A Plan of Discipline for the Use of the Norfolk Militia*. London: J. Shuckburgh, 1759

Wishart, George, *The History of the Kings Majesties Affairs in Scotland*. The Hague: Samuel Browne, 1647

Wolfe, James, *General Wolfe's Instructions to Young Officers*. London: J. Millan, 1780; 2nd edition, reprinted 1967

4: Secondary Sources

Anderson, Fred, *Crucible of War*. Toronto, London and New York: Random House, 2000

Atkinson, C. T., 'Wynendael', *Journal of the Society for Army Historical Research*, 34 (1956), pp. 26–31

Atkinson, C. T., 'Gleanings from the Cathcart Mss', *Journal of the Society for Army Historical Research*, 29 (1951), pp. 20–5, 64–8, 97–103

Bailey, Geoff B., *Falkirk or Paradise*. Edinburgh: John Donald Publishers, 1996

Bennett, Martyn, *The Civil Wars in Britain and Ireland*. Oxford: Blackwell, 1997

Black, Jeremy, *Warfare in the Eighteenth Century*. London: Cassell, 1999

Blackmore, David, *British Cavalry of the Mid-18th Century*. Nottingham: Partizan Press, 2008

Blackmore, Howard L., *British Military Firearms, 1650–1850*. London: Herbert Jenkins, 1961

Brumwell, Stephen, *Redcoats: The British Soldier and War in the Americas, 1755–1763*. Cambridge: Cambridge University Press, 2002

Bulstrode, Sir Richard, *Memoirs and Reflections upon the Reign and Government of King Charles the Ist and K. Charles the IId*. London: Charles Rivington, 1721

Carlton, Charles, *Going to the Wars: The Experience of the British Civil Wars 1638–1651*. London: Routledge, 1992

Carlyle, Thomas, *History of Friedrich II of Prussia*, 21 vols (New York: Hurd and Houghton, 1864)

Chandler, David, *Marlborough as Military Commander*. London: Batsford, 1973

Chandler, David, *The Art of Warfare in the Age of Marlborough*. London: Batsford, 1976; revised edition, Staplehurst, 1990

Childs, John, 'The English Brigade in Portugal, 1662–68', *Journal of the Society for Army Historical Research*, 53 (1975), pp. 135–47

Childs, John, *The Nine Years War and the British Army*. Manchester: Manchester University Press, 1991

Churchill, Winston S., *Marlborough: His Life and Times*, two volumes. London: George G. Harrap, 1947

Cooke, Dave, *The Forgotten Battle: The Battle for Adwalton Moor*. Heckmondwike: Battlefield Press, 1996

Dalton, Charles, *English Army Lists and Commission Registers, 1661–1714*. London: Eyre & Spottiswood, 1898

David, Saul, *All the King's Men: The British Soldier from the Restoration to Waterloo*. London: Viking, 2012

Duffy, Christopher, *The Military Experience in the Age of Reason*. London: Routledge & Keegan Paul, 1987; Ware, 1998, paperback edition

Duffy, Christopher, *The '45*. London: Cassell, 2003

Firth, Sir Charles, *Cromwell's Army*. London: Methuen, 1902

Foard, Glenn, *Naseby: The Decisive Campaign*. Whitstable: Pryor Publications, 1995

Fortescue, The Hon. J. W., *A History of the British Army*. 20 vols. London: MacMillan, 1899–1930

Fraser, Antonia, *The Weaker Vessel*. London: Weidenfeld, 1984

Fuller, Colonel J. F. C., *British Light Infantry in the Eighteenth Century*. London: Hutchinson, 1925

Gates, David, *The British Light Infantry Arm, c. 1790–1815*. London: Batsford, 1987

Gentles, Ian, *The New Model Army in England, Ireland and Scotland, 1645–1653*. Oxford: Blackwell, 1992

Holmes, Richard, *Redcoat: The British Soldier in the Age of Horse and Musket*. London: Harper Collins, 2001, paperback edition

Holmes, Richard, *Dusty Warriors: Modern Soldiers at War*. London: Harper Perennial, 2007

Holmes, Richard, *Marlborough, Britain's Greatest General*. London: Harper Press, 2008

Houlding, John, *Fit for Service: The Training of the British Army, 1715–1795*. Oxford: Clarendon Press, 1981

Hughes, Major General B. P., *Firepower: Weapons Effectiveness on the Battlefield, 1630-1850*. London: Arms & Armour Press, 1974

Hunter, William A. (ed.), 'Thomas Barton and the Forbes Expedition', *Pennsylvania Magazine of History and Biography*, 95:4 (1971), pp. 431–83

Keegan, John and Andrew Wheatcroft, *Who's Who in Military History*. London: Weidenfeld & Nicholson, 1976

Kishlansky, Mark A., *The Rise of the New Model Army*. Cambridge: Cambridge University Press, 1979

Kopperman, Paul E., 'Braddock, Edward (*bap.* 1695, *d.* 1755)', *Oxford Dictionary of National Biography*, Oxford University Press, 2004; online edn, Jan 2008, www.oxforddnb.com/view/article/3170, accessed 6 April 2012

Lowe, William C., 'Amherst, Jeffrey, first Baron Amherst (1717–1797)', *Oxford Dictionary of National Biography*, Oxford University Press, 2004; online edn, Sept 2010, www.oxforddnb.com/view/article/443, accessed 6 April 2012

Lowe, William C., 'Lennox, Charles, third duke of Richmond, third duke of Lennox, and duke of Aubigny in the French nobility (1735–1806)', *Oxford Dictionary of National Biography*, Oxford University Press, 2004; online edn, October 2008 (www.oxforddnb.com/view/article/16451, accessed 27 Feb 2012).

Lytton Sells, A. (ed.), *The Memoirs of James II*. Bloomington: Indiana University Press, 1962

Mackesy, Piers, *The Coward of Minden: The Affair of Lord George Sackville*. London: Allen Lane, 1979

MacKinnon, Daniel, *Origin and Services of the Coldstream Guards*. London: Richard Bentley, 1833

Marix Evans, Martin, *Naseby 1645: The Triumph of the New Model Army*. Oxford: Osprey, 2007

McLynn, Frank, *1759: The Year Britain Became Master of the World*. London: Pimlico Jonathan Cape, 2004; reprinted 2005.

Mollo, J., *Uniforms of the Seven Years War, 1756–1763*. New York: Hippocrene, 1977

Montgomery of Alamein, *A History of Warfare*. London: Collins, 1968

Morrill, John, *The Nature of the English Revolution*. Harlow: Longman, 1993

McCulloch, Ian M. and Tim J. Todish, *British Light Infantryman of the Seven Years' War, North America, 1757–63*. Oxford: Osprey, 2004

Newman, P. R. and P. R. Roberts, *Marston Moor, 1644, The Battle of the Five Armies* (Pickering: Blackthorn Press, 2003)

Nosworthy, Brent, *The Anatomy of Victory: Battle Tactics 1689–1763*. New York: Hippocrene, 1992

Nosworthy, Brent, *Battle Tactics of Napoleon and his Enemies*. London: Constable, 1995

Pargellis, Stanley, 'Braddock's Defeat', *American Historical Review*, 41:2 (1936), pp. 253–69

Pocock, Tom, *Battle for Empire: The Very First World War, 1756–63*. London: Michael O'Mara, 1998, Caxton Editions, 2002

Pollard, Tony (ed.), *Culloden: The History and Archaeology of the Last Clan Battle*. Barnsley: Pen & Sword Books, 2009

Reid, Stuart, *1745: A Military History of the Last Jacobite Rising*. Staplehurst: Spellmount, 1996

Reid, Stuart, *Wolfe: The Career of General James Wolfe from Culloden to Quebec*. Staplehurst: Spellmount, 2000

Roberts, Keith, *Cromwell's War Machine: The New Model Army, 1645–1660*. Barnsley: Pen & Sword Books, 2005

Routh, E. M. G., 'The English at Tangier', *English Historical Review*, 26:103 (1911), pp. 469–81

Ruthven, Patrick Gordon of, *A Short Abridgement of Britane's Distemper*. Aberdeen: Spalding Club, 1844

Scott, C. L., Alan Turton and Dr Eric Gruber von Arni, *Edgehill: The Battle Reinterpreted*. Barnsley: Pen & Sword Books, 2004

Spencer, Charles, *Blenheim: Battle for Europe*. London: Weidenfeld & Nicolson, 2004

Spring, Matthew H., *With Zeal and with Bayonets Only*. Oklahoma: University of Oklahoma Press, 2008

Stapleton, John, *Forging a Coalition Army: William III, the Grand Alliance, and the Confederate Army in the Spanish Netherlands, 1688–1697* (unpublished doctoral thesis, Ohio State University, 2003)

Stern, Walter M., 'Gunmaking in Seventeenth Century London', *Journal of the Arms and Armour Society*, 1:5 (1953–6), pp. 55–100

Sumner, Reverend Percy (ed.), 'General Hawley's "Chaos"', *Journal of the Society for Army Historical Research*, 26 (1948), pp. 91–94

Tomasson, Katherine and Francis Buist, *Battles of the '45*. London: Batsford, 1962; London: Book Club Associates, 1978, 2nd edition

Turner, Pierre, *Soldiers' Accoutrements of the British Army 1750–1900*. Marlborough: Crowood Press, 2006

Webb, Lieutenant Colonel E. A. H., *History of the 12th (The Suffolk) Regiment*. London: Spottiswoode & Co., 1914

Whitworth, Rex, *Field Marshal Lord Ligonier*. Oxford: Oxford University Press, 1958

Whitworth, Rex, *William Augustus, Duke of Cumberland: A Life*. Barnsley: Leo Cooper, 1992

Young, Brigadier Peter, *Edgehill, 1642: The Campaign and the Battle*. Kineton: Roundwood, 1967

Young, Brigadier Peter, *Marston Moor, 1644, The Campaign and the Battle* (Kineton: Roundwood Press, 1970)

Index